Adolphus Washington Greely

Explorers and Ttravellers

Adolphus Washington Greely

Explorers and Ttravellers

ISBN/EAN: 9783337205850

Printed in Europe, USA, Canada, Australia, Japan

Cover: Foto ©ninafisch / pixelio.de

More available books at **www.hansebooks.com**

MEN OF ACHIEVEMENT

EXPLORERS AND TRAVELLERS

BY

GENERAL A. W. GREELY, U.S.A.

GOLD MEDALLIST OF ROYAL GEOGRAPHICAL SOCIETY AND SOCIÉTÉ DE GÉOGRAPHIE, PARIS

NEW YORK
CHARLES SCRIBNER'S SONS
1894

PREFACE

The compiler of a series of sketches of American Explorers and Travellers experiences at the very outset a serious embarrassment from the superabundant wealth of original material at his command. The history of America for two hundred years after the voyage of Joliet has been the history of courageous, persistent, and successful exploration, wherein the track of the explorer, instantly serving as a trail for the pioneer, has speedily broadened into the wagon-road of invading immigrants.

Explorations and journeys of such an extent as in other and older lands would have excited praise and merited reward have been so frequent in this continent as to pass almost unnoticed. Hence the scope of this modest volume is necessarily confined to explorations of great importance or peculiar interest, and when made by men of American birth who are no longer living.

In deference to the author's advisers, two exceptions have been made—Du Chaillu and Stanley, Americans by adoption—otherwise African exploration, so wondrously successful in this generation and so fruitful in its results, would have been unrepresented. Again, the unparalleled growth and progress of our American republic owes no small debt to the wealth of physical vigor and strong intellectuality contributed by its sturdy emigrants. These men, American in idea, purpose, and action, whose manhood outgrew the slow evolution of freedom in their natal country, merit recognition. What thousands of other naturalized citizens have industrially wrought of the wonderful and great in this country, these selected representatives have equalled in African exploration.

A chronological arrangement appeared best suited to these sketches, which from Joliet to Fremont exhibit the initiation, growth, and development of geographic discovery in the interior and western portions of the United States. Since the sketches rest very largely on original narratives some current errors at least have been avoided.

Generalization and criticism have been made always with reference to later exploration, which necessarily enhances or diminishes the importance of any original work.

CONTENTS

	PAGE
I. LOUIS JOLIET, Re-discoverer of the Mississippi,	9
II. PETER LE MOYNE, SIEUR D'IBERVILLE, Founder of Louisiana,	41
III. JONATHAN CARVER, the Explorer of Minnesota,	71
IV. CAPTAIN ROBERT GRAY, the Discoverer of the Columbia River,	88
V. CAPTAIN MERIWETHER LEWIS AND LIEUT. WILLIAM CLARK, First Trans-Continental Explorers of the United States,	105
VI. ZEBULON MONTGOMERY PIKE, Explorer of the Sources of the Mississippi and Arkansas Rivers,	163
VII. CHARLES WILKES, the Discoverer of the Antarctic Continent,	194
VIII. JOHN CHARLES FRÉMONT, the Pathfinder,	212
IX. ELISHA KENT KANE, Arctic Explorer,	240
X. ISAAC ISRAEL HAYES, and the Open Polar Sea,	272
XI. CHARLES FRANCIS HALL, and the North Pole,	293
XII. GEORGE WASHINGTON DE LONG, and the Siberian Arctic Ocean,	312
XIII. PAUL BELLONI DU CHAILLU, Discoverer of the Dwarfs and Gorillas,	330
XIV. STANLEY AFRICANUS AND THE CONGO FREE STATE,	349

LIST OF ILLUSTRATIONS

FULL-PAGE

	FACING PAGE
GENERAL A. W. GREELY, U. S. A., . . (*Frontispiece.*)	
ON THE SHORES OF THE PACIFIC, ...	96
A BLACKFOOT TEPEE, ...	112
CASTLE ROCK, ON THE COLUMBIA RIVER, . . .	140
CHARLES WILKES, ...	194
PAUL BELLONI DU CHAILLU, ...	330
HENRY M. STANLEY, ...	349

ILLUSTRATIONS IN THE TEXT

	PAGE
SIGNATURE OF JOLLIET (OLD SPELLING), . . .	10
"MARQUETTE'S MAP,"	15
THE RECEPTION OF JOLIET AND MARQUETTE BY THE ILLINOIS, ...	25
DE SOTO, ...	34
SIGNATURE OF LE MOYNE, ...	42
BIENVILLE, ...	57
BIENVILLE'S ARMY ON THE RIVER, . . .	63
NEW ORLEANS IN 1719, ...	70
INDIAN TOMAHAWK, ...	74
THE FALLS OF ST. ANTHONY IN THE RIVER MISSISSIPPI,	77
A CALUMET, ...	80
NAUDOWESSIE INDIANS, ...	85
INDIAN MAUL, ...	93
CAPTAIN MERIWETHER LEWIS, ...	119
BUFFALO HEAD, ...	125
LIEUTENANT WILLIAM CLARK, ...	132

LIST OF ILLUSTRATIONS

	PAGE
BUFFALO SKULL,	162
GENERAL Z. M. PIKE,	165
INDIAN SNOW-SHOES,	172
THE ICE-BARRIER,	199
THE VINCENNES IN A STORM,	202
VIEW OF THE ANTARCTIC CONTINENT,	205
IN AN ICE-FIELD,	208
JOHN CHARLES FRÉMONT,	214
JESSIE BENTON FRÉMONT,	215
ASCENDING FRÉMONT'S PEAK,	218
KIT CARSON,	226
LAKE KLAMATH,	231
ELISHA KENT KANE,	242
THE ARCTIC HIGHWAY,	246
A SLEEPING-BAG FOR THREE MEN,	251
THE COMING ARCTIC NIGHT,	256
ESQUIMAU BOYS FISHING,	260
AN ARCTIC STREAM,	264
ISAAC ISRAEL HAYES,	273
UPERNIVIK,	276
HAYES'S WINTER-QUARTERS,	280
ADRIFT ON A BERG,	285
CHARLES FRANCIS HALL,	294
IGLOOS, OR ESQUIMAU HUTS,	299
IN WINTER-QUARTERS,	302
AN ARCTIC FIORD,	305
A WOMAN OF THE ARCTIC HIGHLANDERS. SKETCHED FROM LIFE,	308
ESQUIMAU WOMAN. SKETCHED FROM LIFE,	310
GEORGE WASHINGTON DE LONG,	313
HERALD ISLAND,	317
IN THE PACK,	321
WHERE THE BODIES WERE FOUND,	323

LIST OF ILLUSTRATIONS

	PAGE
NOROS AND NINDEMANN,	326
FINDING THE BODIES,	328
THE GORILLA (TROGLODYTES GORILLA),	334
A VILLAGE OF DWARFS,	339
A PIGMY WARRIOR,	342
A DWARF PRISONER,	345
ARROWS OF THE AFRICAN PIGMIES,	348
THE HUT WHERE LIVINGSTONE DIED,	352
MAP SHOWING POSITION AND BOUNDARIES OF THE CONGO STATE,	355
TIPPU TIB,	359
EMIN PASHA,	363
FINDING NELSON IN DISTRESS AT STARVATION CAMP,	366
A STOCKADED CAMP,	370
RUWENZORI (THE SNOWY MOUNTAIN), IDENTIFIED BY STANLEY WITH "THE MOUNTAINS OF THE MOON,"	372

EXPLORERS AND TRAVELLERS

I.

LOUIS JOLIET,

Re-discoverer of the Mississippi.

If one should ask which is the most important river basin in the world, there is no doubt that the Mississippi would be named, with its million and a quarter square miles of area and its twenty-five or more billions of aggregated wealth. Favored in climate, soil, and navigable streams, and endowed with practically inexhaustible veins of coal, copper, iron, and silver, feeding the world with its hundreds of millions of bushels of corn and wheat, and clothing it by other millions of bales of cotton, it is hardly so astonishing that within 217 years from its discovery by Joliet this greatest of river basins should be the abiding-place of twenty-seven and a half millions of people.

Speaking of Joliet, Bancroft wrote that his short voyage brought him immortality; but in the irony of fate his explorations have not even given his name a place in the last edition of the Encyclopædia Britannica. In writing on American explorers, it seems most fitting that this series of sketches should be headed by this Canadian, whose name is scarcely known by one in a thousand. That aught is obtainable concerning the details of his life is due to the investigations of Shea, which later were admirably summed up by Parkman.

Signature of Jolliet (Old Spelling).

Louis Joliet, the son of John Joliet and Mary d'Abancour, was born at Quebec, September 21, 1645. His father was a wagon-maker, in the service of the Company of One Hundred Associates, then owners of Canada.

The son in youth was imbued with devout feelings, which, possibly fostered by the elder Joliet as certain to bring station and influence in manhood, led to his being educated in the Jesuit College for the priesthood, in which indeed he received the minor orders in 1662. Four years later, in the debates on philosophy, which were participated in by the Intendant and listened to by the colonial dignitaries, Joliet showed such skill as to elicit especial commendation from the Fathers.

His future career shows that his studies with the Fathers were not lost on him, and doubtless they contributed largely to make Joliet that intelligent, well-poised leader who filled with credit all duties and positions incident to his varied and adventurous life.

It is probable, however, that during all these

years he was at heart a true voyageur, and that his thoughts turned continually from the cloister and books to the forest and its attractive life. Be this as it may, he practically abandoned all ideas of the priesthood at the age of twenty-two, and turned to the most certain, and indeed, in Canada, the only path to wealth, that of a trader in furs with the Indians. In this trade only the hardy, shrewd, intelligent, and tireless subordinate could hope to thrive and rise. Success meant long and hazardous journeys into the very heart of the Indian country, where were needed great physical courage and strength, perfect skill with gun, paddle, axe, sledge, or snow-shoe, a thorough knowledge of wood-craft, indomitable will or casuistry and tact according to the occasion. To paddle a canoe from sunrise to sunset of a summer day, to follow the sledge or break a snow-shoe path before it as far as a dog can travel in a march, to track a moose or deer for leagues without rest, to carry canoes and heavy packs over long portages through an untravelled country, were the ordinary experiences of a voyageur, which were accomplished for the great part on a diet of smoked meat and boiled Indian corn, with no shelter in fair weather and the cover of an upturned canoe or bark hut in stress of storm.

Joliet did not long remain in private adventure, for in 1669 Talon, then Intendant of Canada, sent him to discover and explore the copper-mines of Lake Superior, in which quest he failed. It was on his return trip that Joliet met with La Salle and the priests Dolier and Galinée, on September 24, 1669, near the present town of Hamilton, in which direction Joliet's Indian guide had misled him when returning from Lake Erie, through fear of meeting enemies at the Niagara portage.

Joliet's facility for map-making in the field is evident from the fact that at this time he showed to the priests with La Salle a copy of the map that he had made of such parts of the upper lakes as he had visited, and gave them a copy of it. He moreover evidenced continued interest in religious matters by telling them that the Pottowattamies and other Indian tribes of that region were in serious need of spiritual succor. La Salle later, in November, 1680, repaid this frank tender of information of the little-known west by intimating his belief that Joliet never went but little south of the mouth of the Illinois, and is also stated to have declared that Joliet was an impostor.

In his account of La Salle's last journey, Father Douay, referring to Joliet's discoveries as related by Marquette, says: "I have brought with me the printed book of this pretended discovery, and I remarked all along my route that there was not a word of truth in it."

The efforts to deprive Joliet of the credit of the original discovery of the Mississippi falls before the despatch of Count Frontenac to Colbert, then Minister, dated Quebec, November 14, 1674: " VI. Sieur Joliet, whom Monsieur Talon advised me, on my arrival from France, to despatch for the discovery of the South Sea, has returned three months ago, and discovered some very fine country, and a navigation so easy through the beautiful rivers he has found, that a person can go from Lake Ontario and Fort Frontenac in a bark to the Gulf of Mexico, there being only one carrying-place, half a league in length, where Lake Ontario communicates with Lake Erie. . . . He has been within ten days of the Gulf of Mexico. . . . I send you by my secretary the map he has made of it. . . . He has lost all his minutes and journals in the shipwreck he suffered in sight of Montreal. . . . He left with the Fathers at Sault St. Marie copies of his journal."

But to return to the circumstances under which Joliet made the voyage. Among other orders of Louis XIV. regarding Canada was a charge to discover the South Sea and Mississippi, and Jean Talon, Intendant of Canada, lost no chance of furthering this object. La Salle's journey of 1670 had failed to reach the great river, though he descended the Ohio to the falls at Louisville, and at his recall in 1672 Talon had the subject of further exploration in hand. Joliet had lately returned from his unsuccessful efforts to discover copper mines on Lake Superior, during which he had probably been the first white man to pass through the Straits of Detroit. Despite his late failure he had impressed Talon as the man best fitted to lead such an expedition, and so before sailing for France the Intendant recommended Joliet for the work to Count Frontenac, the new Governor.

In those days the Church and Government went hand in hand, and but few French expeditions went westward from Montreal without a priest to carry the faith to such Indian tribes as were allies of France or liable to be won over. As Joliet's priest-associate, James Marquette, a young Jesuit, then a missionary at St. Esprit, La Pointe, Lake Superior, was chosen.

No better man could have been sent. Marquette was in the prime of life, an expert linguist —as he had learned in six years to speak fluently six Indian languages—gentle, patient, and tactful with the natives, devout in faith, singularly holy in life, fearless, imaginative, nature-loving and observant, as shown by his journal, which, owing to Joliet's shipwreck, is the only original story of the voyage. His enthusiasm is shown by the opening sentences of his journal: "I have obtained from God the favor of being enabled to visit the nations on the Mississippi River, . . . and find myself in the happy necessity of exposing my life for the salvation of all these tribes, especially the Illinois."

Joliet followed the St. Lawrence to Fort Frontenac, at the entrance of Lake Ontario, and with the exception of the portage at the Falls of Niagara, skirted in his canoe the shores of the Great Lakes until he reached the Straits of Mackinaw, on the north side of which, at Point St. Ignace, he found the enthusiastic Marquette devotedly laboring for the spiritual welfare of the Hurons and Ottawas there gathered.

The contemplated line of travel was that of

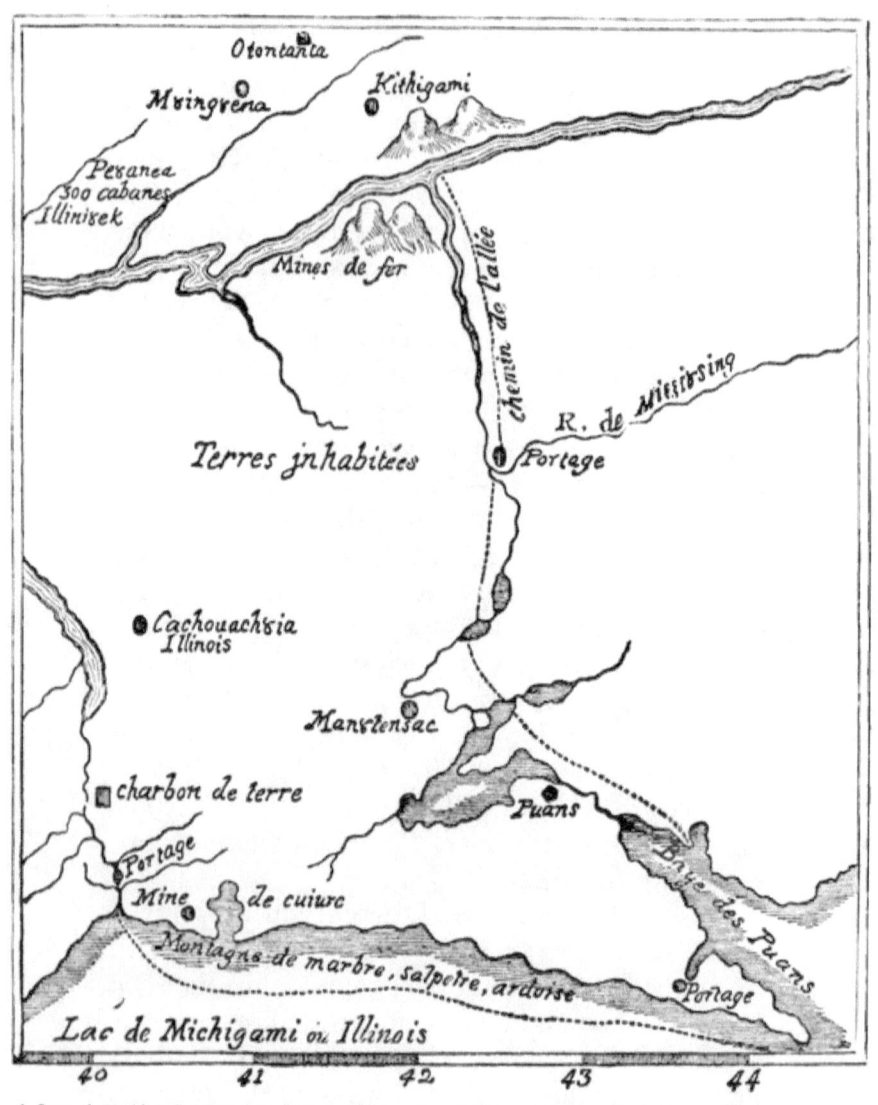

A Part of the Map Published in Paris by Thevenot as "Marquette's Map." It shows the route taken by Joliet across Wisconsin from the Baie des Puans (now Green Bay) to the Mississippi River, also part of the return journey, that is, from the present site of Chicago, northward along Lake Michigan.

Jean Nicollet, an interpreter who had spent many years with the Indian tribes, who was sent in 1638 to bring about a peace between the Hurons and Winnebagoes who lived near Green Bay. After his negotiations he ascended the Fox River, and making a portage to the Wisconsin, descended that stream some distance, so that, as he thought, from the designation of "the great water" by the Indian guide to the Mississippi, he was within three days of the South Sea.

Joliet, however, was too practical to trust entirely to tradition or oral description. He had already carefully charted all that was definitely known of the western lake regions, and now at St. Ignace, with Marquette's invaluable assistance, gathered all possible information from such Indians at the mission as had frequented the unknown country. This information being duly weighed and considered, Joliet extended his map to cover all the new country, marking thereon the navigable rivers, the names of nations and villages along their proposed route, the course of the great river, and other useful information.

Their means of subsistence and travel were the simplest imaginable, two canoes and as large quantities of smoked meat and Indian corn as could be conveniently carried. Their canoes were of the usual Canadian pattern, of birch-bark covering, stayed with spruce-root ribs and cedar-splint, with white-pine pitch smeared over the birch-bark joints so as to render them watertight. Such canoes were of astonishing strength and carrying capacity, and of such lightness that four men could carry the largest across portages.

On a bright spring morning, May 17th, Joliet and Marquette, with five other men, left behind them the palisaded post and chapel of St. Ignace. Plying briskly their paddles from sunrise to sunset, they made rapid progress, coasting the lake shore until they turned aside to visit the Menominees, or Wild-rice Indians, whose village was on the river of that same name. Here inquiries for information of the "great river" brought from the savage allies strenuous efforts to dissuade them from visiting this Mississippi, where, they said, the unsparing ferocity of the tribes brought unfailing death by the tomahawk to even inoffensive strangers, and that war now raged among the intervening nations. They further recited the dangers of navigating the rapids of the Great River, the presence of frightful water monsters who swallowed up men and canoes, the roaring demon who engulfed all travellers, and lastly the existence of such excessive heat as to ensure certain death. After religious instruction and service the explorers embarked in their canoes and soon reached the southern extremity of Green Bay, where, says Marquette, "our fathers labor successfully in the conversion of these tribes, having baptized more than 2,000."

Joliet from Green Bay entered Fox River, finding it a gentle, beautiful stream, promising easy and pleasant passage and abounding in wildfowl. Soon, however, these agreeable aspects gave way to the sterner phases of exploration, for sharp rapids were fallen in with where the strong and uncertain cross-currents often threatened the total destruction of their frail canoes, which would have proved fatal to their plans, by dashing them against the sharp bowlders.

A serious but lesser evil to these enduring voyagers was the injury to their mocassin-shod feet, which were cut and bruised by the sharp edges of the rocky bed of the river over which they slowly and painfully dragged their canoes for long distances.

The many rapids were safely passed, and on the 7th of June, 1673, our explorers reached an Indian town which marked the extreme western limits of French discoveries, being the farthest point reached by Nicollet in his adventurous journey.

In this town dwelt bands from three different tribes, the Miamis, Maskoutens, or Fire Nation, and Kickapoos. The latter two were inferior in manners and appearance to the Miamis, who, more civil, liberal, and well-made, wore two long earlocks that Marquette thought becoming; besides they were reputed warriors, who rarely failed in their forays. They proved docile, attentive, and interested in religious matters, as was shown not only by their talk with Father Allouez, but also by a cross standing in the centre of the town, which was adorned with votive offerings of skins, belts, bows and arrows to the Great Manitou for an abundance of game during the dreaded famine time of winter.

The Indians used for their beds mats, probably made of rushes, which in default of bark also served as material for the walls and roofs of their unsubstantial shelters. Since Marquette refers to the advantage of such building material as capable of being rolled up and easily moved during hunts, it is probable that this town was of a temporary character. It appears to have been well located, being on an eminence, whence the approach of an enemy or the presence of game could be readily observed in the open country. Marquette says of it: "The view is beautiful and very picturesque, for from the eminence on which it is perched are seen stretching out on every side, as far as eye can reach, prairies broken by thickets or groves of lofty trees." The Indians grew much corn, and gathered wild plums and "grapes, from which," his thoughts turning to home, he says, "good wine could be made if they chose."

Joliet lost no time, but immediately on arrival assembled the sachems and told them that he was sent by his Governor to discover new countries. He made them a present and asked that two guides be sent to show him the way, which resulted in the gift to Joliet of a mat to serve as a bed, and the sending of two Miamis as guides.

The next day, June 10th, they proceeded, two Miamis and seven Frenchmen in two canoes, up the river to the portage, through a net-work of marshes, little lakes, and meandering channels so hidden by the wild rice that their guides were very useful. Conducting Joliet to a portage of 2,700 paces, and assisting in the transportation of the canoes across it, the Miamis then returned.

leaving the explorers "alone in an unknown country, in the hands of Providence."

Before launching their canoes into strange waters, which were to bear them into unknown lands, they knelt on the bank and offered up devout aspirations to God for continued success. The new river was the Weskousing (Wisconsin), whose broad shallows and sandy bottom, while rendering navigation slow and very laborious, yet contrasted delightfully with the rocky rapids of the Fox.

Father Marquette sets forth delightfully the ideal voyage down this stream, past vine-clad islets, along sloping banks, now bordered by the lovely prairie, with its sweet odors of fresh grasses and blooming flowers, and anon fringed by the primeval forest, beautiful with its tangle of shrubbery and in its June foliage. The gnarled oak, the straight walnut, the elegant whitewood, and other stately trees of unknown species met their vision at times, while again their eyes scarcely separated from the heavens the distant horizon of the green level plains, whose luxuriant vegetation afforded the richest pasturage for numerous herds of deer and moose, and in spots showed the fertility of its alluvial soil by the fields of Indian corn.

Each morning, before they relaunched their canoes, they attuned their voices to the praise of God, and, in their unique joy of successful discovery, must have felt on those delightful June days that their devotions had not been uplifted in vain. From sunrise to sunset they labored unceasingly, now paddling briskly along the deep reaches, and then struggling stoutly through mazes of shallows and sand-bars, where tedious and frequent portages were patiently made.

Each evening their hearts rejoiced and their tired limbs found delightful repose at some spot where Joliet's judgment directed the canoes to be drawn out, inspected, and upturned by some, while others started the camp-fire and prepared the evening meal. This camp was always so placed that the approach of an enemy could be seen from afar, and where fuel for fire and branches for bedding were at hand. The best hunter was told off for game, and rarely did the meal lack fresh meat or fruit and berries in season. After supper the soothing pipe, prayers and songs of praise, and then under the overarching trees such sound slumber as only comes to men sleeping under the open sky.

As they advanced it was often possible to use sail and relieve the men to some extent from the fatigue of the paddle, and such rapid progress was made that, on June 17th, they safely entered the long-desired Mississippi, " with a joy," writes Marquette, " which I cannot express." They were then in latitude 43° 03′ N., opposite the site of the present city of Prairie du Chien.

Turning eagerly southward, their progress facilitated by the gentle current of the Mississippi, they journeyed more than a hundred leagues without seeing on the land aught save birds and beasts. The solitude of the great river appalled them: a vast torrent of rolling water, bordered by forest and plain, so well fitted for the happiness of man, and yet no human being in all this land! What could it mean, and what would be the outcome? Joliet, of long experience with savage tribes, and astute in forest craft, distrusted the silence and solitude, and kept as keen guard as though on the war-path. A tiny camp-fire was built only for meals, and the nights were passed in the crowded canoes as far from shore as it was possible to anchor them in the deep river. Even then strict watch was kept, and every strange or unusual noise excited feelings of trepidation lest a hidden foe be the cause.

Their journey by day was not entirely devoid of incident and excitement, says Marquette. "From time to time we met monstrous fishes, one of which struck the canoe so violently I took it for a large tree. Another time we perceived on the water a monster [probably an American tiger-cat] with a head like a tiger and a pointed snout like the wild-cat, with beard and ears erect, a grayish head, and entirely black neck." They cast their nets successfully, and once caught a spade-fish, whose appearance caused much astonishment. In 41° 28′ N. latitude (near Rock Island), wild turkeys took the place of wild fowl; while as to animals, only buffalo were seen, being so numerous and fearless as to be easily killed, and thus offering a welcome change of food. These new beasts presented themselves to our explorers as hideous, especially those with thick, long manes falling over their eyes in such tangles as to prevent their seeing clearly. Marquette records that the Indians tan buffalo-skins into beautiful robes, which they paint into various colors; and further recites the ferocity of the buffalo as yearly causing the death of some Indian. When near the present city of Keokuk, at the mouth of the Des Moines River, on June 25th, they perceived the first signs of man in all this solitude: foot-prints by the riverside, and then a beaten path, which, entering a beautiful prairie, impressed them as leading to some Indian village.

They had journeyed seventeen days without seeing the face of man, and so, after deliberation, they resolved to visit the village: this decision doubtless being urged by Marquette, who for years had sought by prayer "to obtain of God the grace to be able to visit the nations on the river Mississippi," and who now would allow no danger to deter him. Joliet was fully aware of the great risk, and took most careful precautions to ensure the safety of their canoes and people by charging them strictly to beware of surprise, while he and Marquette ventured to put themselves at the discretion of an unknown savage people. Cautiously following the little path in silence across the beautiful prairie and through the thickets for a distance of two leagues, they suddenly came in view of an Indian village, picturesquely placed on a river bank, and overlooked by two others on a neighboring hill; they pressed on with successful caution and silence, but with much doubt and fear.

Having, as Marquette says, "recommended ourselves to God with all our hearts," and "having implored his help, we passed on undiscovered, and came so near we even heard the Indians talking." Stepping into the open, they halted and announced themselves by a loud cry; at which the Indians rushed out of their cabins, and recognizing them as French, and seeing a "Black-gown" (the well-known Indian name for a Jesuit), sent four of their chief warriors forward. Two chiefs, carrying calumets, or tobacco-pipes, elaborately trimmed with various feathers, advanced very slowly and in silence, lifting their calumets as if offering them for the sun to smoke. Marquette, encouraged by their friendly attitude, and still more on seeing that they wore French cloth, broke the silence; to which the Indians answered that they were Illinois, who, in token of peace, presented their pipes to smoke and invited the strangers to their village.

Joliet and Marquette were received at the door of a wigwam, as was usual for strangers, by an old chief, who stood perfectly naked, with outstretched hands raised toward the sun, as if to screen himself from its rays, which nevertheless passed through the open fingers to his face. As they came near him, he said: "How beautiful is the sun, O Frenchmen, when thou comest to visit us. All our town awaits thee, and thou shalt enter all our cabins in peace." After smoking the calumet, they went by invitation to visit the Great Sachem of all Illinois, at a near village. With good nature and childish curiosity, a throng of

The Reception of Joliet and Marquette by the Illinois.

Indians went along, and says Marquette, "could not tire looking at us; they threw themselves on the grass by the wayside; they ran ahead, then turned and walked back to see us again, all in silence, with marks of great respect." They were received by the Great Sachem and two old chiefs, all naked and with their calumet turned to the sun. After smoking the calumet, Marquette, speaking in Algonquin, said that they marched in peace to visit the nations on the river to the sea; that God their Creator had pity, and had sent his messenger to make him known as their Creator, whom they should acknowledge and obey; that Frontenac had spread peace everywhere; and last asked for all the information they had of the sea and the nations between them and it.

The Sachem answered in a beautiful speech worthy of the occasion:

"I thank thee, Blackgown, and thee, Frenchman," addressing M. Joliet, "for taking so much pains to come and visit us; never has the earth been so beautiful, nor the sun so bright, as to-day; never has our river been so calm, nor so free from rocks, which your canoes have removed as they passed; never has our tobacco had so fine a flavor, nor our corn appeared so beautiful as we behold it to day. Here is my son, that I give thee, that thou mayst know my heart. I pray thee to take pity on me and all my nation. Thou knowest the Great Spirit, who has made us all; thou speakest to him and hearest his words: ask him to give me life and health, and come and dwell with us, that we may know him."

It is interesting to note the condition of the Illinois when first visited. Their chiefs wore over the left shoulder a belt, ingeniously made of the hair of bear and buffalo, which passed around the waist and ended in a long fringe; arm, knee, and wrist bands of deer or buffalo-skin, and the rattles of deer hoofs were also worn, and the face was painted with red ochre. In addition to abundant game, they raised beans, melons, squashes, and Indian corn. Their dishes were of wood, their spoons of the bones of buffalo, their knives stone, their arms, bows and arrows with an occasional gun bought from other tribes.

The word calumet is due to Father Marquette, and his description of this interesting Indian pipe and its uses among the Indians over two hundred years ago is best given in his own words:

"It now remains for me to speak of the calumet, than which there is nothing among them more mysterious or more esteemed. Men do not pay to the crowns and sceptres of kings the honor they pay to it. It seems to be the god of peace and war, the arbiter of life and death. Carry it about you and show it, and you can march fearlessly amid enemies, who even in the heat of battle lay down their arms when it is shown. Hence the Illinois gave me one, to serve as my safeguard amid all the nations that I had to pass on my voyage. There is a calumet for peace and one for war, distinguished only by the color of the feathers with which they are adorned, red being the sign of war. They use them also for settling disputes, strengthening alliances, and speaking to strangers. It is made of a polished red stone, like marble, so pierced that one end serves to hold the tobacco, while the other is fastened on the stem, which is a stick two feet long, as thick as a common cane, and pierced in the middle; it is ornamented with the head and neck of different birds of beautiful plumage; they also add large feathers of red and green and other colors, with which it is all covered. They esteem it peculiarly, because they regard it as the calumet, or pipe, of the sun; and, in fact, they present it to him to smoke when they wish to obtain calm, or rain, or fair weather."

Leaving the Illinois one afternoon, about the end of June, they embarked in sight of the whole admiring tribe, and, following the river, reached the mouth of the muddy Missouri. They were the first white men who had ever gazed on the turbulent waters of this mighty stream. Impressed by the size and majesty of the Missouri Marquette believed and hoped that later, by making a prairie portage of twenty or thirty leagues, he could reach a deep westerly running river that would carry him to the Red Sea (the Gulf of California).

The Missouri, or Pekitanoui, as Marquette called it, was evidently at the flood stage, for he says: "A mass of large trees, entire with branches, real floating islands, came rushing from the mouth of the river so impetuously that we could not pass across without exposing ourselves to great danger. The agitation was so great that the water was all muddy."

Immediately above the site of Alton, Ill., they came in sight of the famous Piasa pictograph, which was totally destroyed about fifty years ago. Of it Marquette wrote: "As we coasted along rocks, frightful for their height and length, we saw painted thereon two monsters, which startled us at first, and on which the boldest Indian dare not gaze long. They have a fearful look, are as large as a calf, have red eyes, the horns of a deer, the beard of a tiger, and the face of a man, while around the scale-covered body was a fish's tail twice encircling it. The two monsters were very well painted in green, red, and black colors, and so high upon the rocks that they were apparently inaccessible to man."

Later they discovered a very rich iron-mine of many veins, one a foot thick, and large masses of metal combined with pebbles; also purple, violet, and red clay, which colored the water a blood red. They now passed the dreaded home of the Manitou, or demon, who devours all who pass; which proved to be a frightful rapid where large detached rocks and a narrow channel caused a furious commotion of the waters tumbling over each other, and a tremendous roaring, which struck terror to the Indian's heart. Passing this, they reached the mouth of the Ohio, which Marquette calls "Ouaboukidou," on which there were no less than thirty-eight villages of the Chaouanons (Shawnees). A little beyond, Marquette's eye was delighted by the appearance of breaks, wherein the canes were of an exquisite green, with knots crowned by long, narrow-pointed leaves. At every landing the keen eyes of the Canadian explorers searched out everything that was new or that seemed suitable for food; so we find the persimmon and the chicopin and other fruits and nuts described in detail.

By this time, in early July, they found themselves suffering from the double annoyance of mosquitoes and the excessive and insupportable heat of the sun, from which they sheltered themselves as best they could by making a kind of cabin with their sails, while their canoes were borne on by the current.

Finally they perceived on the river-bank Indians armed with guns, who awaited their approach. Joliet, ready either for peace or war, put Marquette forward with his feathered peace calumet upraised, while the rest stood to arms, ready to fire on the first volley of the savages. Marquette hailed them in Huron, and the party was not only peacefully received, but invited to their village and presented with food of various kinds. Joliet found among them guns, axes, hoes, powder, etc., and was assured that they bought cloth and other articles from Europeans to the east, doubtless the Spaniards of Florida. Marquette was troubled to find they had received no instruction in the faith, which, as far as he could, he gave them.

Being assured that the sea was not more than ten days' journey distant, they were greatly encouraged, and instead of drifting with the current, took up their paddles with renewed ardor.

Passing beyond the prairie land, they found both sides of the river lined with dense woods, wherein the cotton-wood, elm, and white-wood were of such height and size as to excite their admiration. That the forests were not dense seemed evident from the bellowing of cattle behind the fringe of trees, which were enlivened for our travellers by flocks of quail along the water's edge and an occasional parrot with its brilliant coloring of red, yellow, and green.

Nearing the mouth of the Arkansas, they saw on the river-bank an Indian village called Mithiganea, near which Joliet and his party had an exciting and fearful experience, which Marquette thus describes:

"We heard from afar the Indians exciting one another to the combat by continual yells. They were armed with bows, arrows, axes, war-clubs, and bucklers, and prepared to attack us by land and water. Some embarked in large wooden canoes, a part to ascend, the rest to descend, the river, so as to cut our way and surround us completely. Those on shore kept going and coming, as if about to begin the attack. In fact, some young men sprang into the water to come and seize my canoe, but the current having compelled them to return to the shore, one of them threw his war club at us, but it passed over our heads without doing us any harm. In vain I showed the calumet, and made gestures to explain that we had not come as enemies. The alarm continued, and they were about to pierce us from all sides with their arrows, when God suddenly touched the hearts of the old men on the water side, doubtless at the sight of our calumet, which at the distance they had not distinguished; but as I showed it continually, they were touched, restrained the ardor of their youth, and two of the chiefs, having thrown their bows and quivers into our canoe, and as it were at our feet, entered and brought us to the shore, where we disembarked, not without fear on our part."

An old chief was at last found who spoke a little Illinois, and through him they were told that they could get full information regarding the sea at another great village called Akamsea, about ten leagues down the river. Presents were exchanged and the night passed among them with some uneasiness. The loving missionary spirit of Marquette is shown here for, he says: "I know not whether they understood what I told them of God and the things which concerned their salvation. It is a seed cast in the earth which will bear its fruit in season."

At Akamsea (Arkansas) they were received by the sachem holding up a peace calumet, after which they had the customary smoke and a repast of different dishes made of Indian corn. Presents were interchanged and speeches made through a young Indian who understood Illinois. The whole day was spent in feasting, and the dishes of Indian corn were continuously supplemented by pieces of dog flesh

Joliet and Marquette learned from them that the sea was only ten days' journey distant for the Indians, which meant five days for our explorers in their birch canoes. They further set forth the very great danger of passing on, owing to the continual war parties moving along the river. A secret council of the sachems with a view to killing the party for plunder was only broken up through the influence of the chief, who, sending for the explorers, danced a calumet dance as a mark of perfect assurance, and then to remove all fears, presented his peace calumet to Marquette as a guarantee of safety.

The famous calumet dance is performed only on important occasions—to strengthen peace, for a war assembly, at public rejoicings, and in honor of important personages or invited strangers. The principal features are, first, a dance; second, a mock combat; third, a self-laudatory speech, during all of which the pipe plays an important part, being smoked and handled to the measured cadence of voices and drums.

Joliet and Marquette now took counsel together as to whether they should continue their voyage in face of such adverse conditions or turn back. Finally, after long and careful consideration it was decided to return.

They realized that in their present latitude, 33° 40′ N., they could not be more than two or three days from the sea, and that the Mississippi, by its general course, undoubtedly flowed into the Gulf of Mexico, and not into the South Sea through California.

Neglecting the dangers from warlike Indians along the lower river, they considered, moreover, that they risked losing the fruit of this voyage if they should throw themselves into the hands of the Spaniards, who would at least imprison them.

Joliet's farthest was on the east bank, opposite a river, probably the Arkansas, and could not have been far from the point where De Soto more than a hundred years before, in April, 1541, reached the Mississippi. What a contrast be-

De Soto.

tween the means and experiences of these two explorers! De Soto, a noble Spaniard, with an armament of ten vessels equipped with all the paraphernalia of war, having, with three hundred and fifty horsemen, a thousand picked men in mail who had been chosen from the flower of the Spanish and Portuguese nobility. His followers were animated by ambition, eager seekers for wealth and power, their track marked by fire and sword, their action often treacherous and always characterized by the savageness of their age. They reaped the natural harvest, and although they reached the Mississippi, yet constant warfare, continued privations, toil, and disasters had sadly wasted their strength and numbers, and finally not one man in four ever reached again a Spanish settlement. Joliet, an American of humble birth, with two frail canoes equipped only with an ordinary hunting outfit, had six followers who, inspired by neither hope of gold nor desire of conquest other than that of a spiritual kind, came with peace and confidence, were received by all tribes with hospitality, and returned to their own without harm or contumely.

The result of De Soto's work was an unprofitable, soon-forgotten discovery, utterly barren of results. Joliet reduced the fables of the Indians to facts, discovered the muddy Missouri, and what is more, gave definite knowledge to the world of the fertile valleys of the Mississippi basin, wherein he planted the first germs of civilization, which speedily took the practical form of missions and settlements.

After a day's rest, Joliet and his party left Akamsea July 17th, and tediously retraced their course against the strong currents of the Mississippi. Through the advice of the Indians they quitted the great river at the mouth of the Illinois, which greatly shortened their way and brought them with little trouble to the present site of Chicago, they passing on the way through an Illinois town, Kaskaskia, of seventy-four cabins, from which an escort of braves guided them to Lake Michigan.

Marquette appears to have had a prophetic eye for the great future of the present State of Illinois, for he says, "We have seen nothing like this river for the fertility of the land, its prairies, woods, wild cattle, deer, wild-cats, bustards, swans, ducks, parrots, and even beaver; its many little lakes and rivers."

Coasting the shores of Lake Michigan, the end of September, 1673, brought them to Green Bay, where the rude comforts of a frontier mission and the solace of friendly intercourse were once more theirs. They had been absent four months, and in that time had paddled their frail canoes more than twenty-five hundred miles. Here Marquette remained to recruit his health, impaired by physical hardships, continued exposure, and lack of suitable food. The hardy Joliet lost no time, however, but pressed on, too eager to report his grand discoveries to Frontenac.

As mentioned in Frontenac's dispatch, the misfortunes of Joliet began when his long and perilous voyage was practically ended. In the rapids of La Chine, near Montreal, his canoe overset; three of his party were drowned, all his papers lost, and he himself narrowly escaped. In a letter to Frontenac he says: "I had escaped every peril from the Indians; I had passed forty-two rapids, and was on the point of disembarking, full of joy at the success of so long and difficult an enterprise, when my canoe capsized after all danger seemed past. I lost two men, an Indian boy and my box of papers within sight of the first French settlements, which I had left almost two years before. Nothing now remains to me but my life and the ardent desire to employ it on any service which you may be pleased to direct."

We have to rest content with the graphic account written by Marquette, as it was impossible for Joliet to reproduce his lost journal. As regards the map, his natural and acquired skill in cartography was such that Joliet reproduced his discoveries in the shape of a small map, which he presented to Frontenac, by whom it was sent to Colbert, with a despatch dated November 14, 1674, and now is in the famous Chart Office at Paris. It is entitled, "Map of the Discovery of Sieur Joliet," etc., and has a brief explanatory letter thereon, from which I have quoted above.

Joliet's discoveries were most joyfully received in France, Colbert especially appreciating their value and importance both as regards the extent and fertility of the countries traversed and also as to the easy water communication therewith. It afforded an opportunity of extending the limits of French possessions in America, which was not neglected. It did not fall, however, to Joliet to play any part in this great work, which was the lot of his great rival, the energetic, persistent, and far-seeing La Salle, who received in 1678 a royal patent with seignorial rights over all lands which he might discover and colonize within twenty years, and who gave Louisiana to the French crown.

The natural despondency of Joliet over the

loss of his maps and journals soon gave way to happier experiences; for the following year, October 7, 1675, he married Clare Frances Bissot. His father-in-law, a Canadian, was a wealthy Indian trader, so Joliet naturally resumed his former occupation, and in 1679 made a journey to Hudson Bay by way of the Saguenay. He found the English strongly intrenched in their successful efforts to monopolize the Indian trade of that quarter. The usual attempts to draw Canadians into their service were made in Joliet's case. He not only declined service, but on his return to Quebec made such representations of the inevitable effect of English rivalry, if unopposed, on the trade of Canada, that a competing company was organized by French merchants.

Joliet in the meantime had only received fair words, but after strenuous efforts he succeeded in 1679 in obtaining a grant of the Islands of Mignan, and in the following year the French Government granted him the Island of Anticosti, in the Gulf of St. Lawrence. Here he established himself with his family, and with six servants engaged in fisheries.

In the course of time he added to his buildings and extended his interests, but his peaceful pursuits were destined to interruption and devastation. In 1690 an English fleet, under command of Sir William Phipps, sailed to attack Quebec, and in course of time anchored at Anticosti. In those days war was waged with utter disregard of the rights of private property. Joliet was then absent. A detachment from the English fleet landed on the island, devastated Joliet's establishment, destroyed his buildings by fire, and even carried away as prisoners his wife and mother-in-law, who fortunately were soon exchanged.

Deprived in a day of the accumulation of years, his future actions showed that age and adversity made but small inroads on his manly spirit. Obliged to exertion for the support of his family, he turned again in his fiftieth year to a voyage of exploration and adventure. A Canadian company contemplated the extension of its seal and whale fisheries to the rugged and dangerous coast of Labrador, then little known, and in 1694 Joliet explored the greater part of this ice-covered and rock-bound coast under the auspices and in the interest of this company.

Some years earlier Joliet had shown his merits as a skilful surveyor and navigator by charting the waters of the St. Lawrence, and when, on his return from Labrador, occupation failed, Frontenac recognized his deserving abilities by naming him for the post of royal pilot of the St. Lawrence, still later appointing him hydrographer at Quebec.

The emoluments of his royal offices were a mere pittance, and in 1695 he is found on Mignan Islands, where, with his wife, he contracted with his brother-in-law Bissot and other parties with a view of developing his interests both on land and at sea. In 1697 he was granted by the Crown the Seignory of Joliet. This honor he did not long enjoy, for he died, apparently a poor man, in 1699 or 1700. He was fortunate in his burial place, one of the Mignan Islands, which is forever associated with his fame, having been granted him by the French Crown for that great and dangerous voyage which gave to the world its first definite knowledge of the location, extent, and fertility of the great valley of the Mississippi.

While Joliet followed the rugged and peaceful pursuits of his island-home, ill fared it with his vigorous Norman successor. The great La Salle fell under the hand of a mutinous follower, while his fated Texan colony perished totally by desertion, betrayal, and massacre. So relapsed the lower Mississippi into its primal savagery and grandeur, until the domineering energy of the great Canadian, Iberville, awakened it into a vast dominion, to the glory, if not to the profit, of France.

II.

PETER LE MOYNE, SIEUR D'IBERVILLE.

Founder of Louisiana.

Among the very earliest settlers of Hochelega, now Montreal, was the son of a Norman innkeeper, a young French lad of fifteen, Charles le Moyne, who came to this Indian village in 1641. Apt, strong, daring, and zealous, he soon became one of the most efficient aids to French power. The language, the woodcraft, the arts of the savage soon became his, and added to these such suavity of manner, clearness of perception, and native kindness as made him loved equally by French and savage. As interpreter, soldier, negotiator, and captain of the guard, he rendered such great service to the young and exposed colony as caused him to be made captain of Montreal, and later, in 1668, to be ennobled by Louis XIV. under the title of Sieur of Longueuil. For four years service in the country of the Hurons he received for his entire pay the sum of twenty crowns and his clothing, but he gained also such a knowledge of the possibilities of the country, such an insight into Indian character, and such a wealth of vigorous manhood as enabled him to acquire during his life an estate that was princely. He did better than this, he married a woman worthy of him, whose family is scarcely known, Catherine Tierry, an adopted daughter of Antoine Primot.

In all the history of American families there is none that has as distinguished and brilliant a history as the twelve sons and two daughters born of this French peasant and the son of a Norman innkeeper in the forests of Canada. The two daughters married nobles, and of the twelve sons nine live distinguished in history, three of them were killed in the service of France, ten of them were ennobled, and four, Iberville, Serigny, Chateauguay, and Bienville the younger, played important parts in the founding of Louisiana.

There were many brilliant and picturesque figures among the actors in the founding of a New France in the wilds of North America, but among them all there was scarcely one whose personality and deeds excited more admiration among his contemporaries, or whose services and career are more deserving of recognition by posterity, than Peter le Moyne, Sieur d'Iberville, third son

Signature of le Moyne.

of Longueuil, who was born on the extreme frontier, at the outpost of Montreal, July 16, 1661. As a soldier he rose to be the leader and idol of his fellow-Canadians; as a sailor he became an extremely skilful navigator, who was acknowledged as one of the greatest of French naval commanders; and as an explorer and administrator he so successfully accomplished his plans as to merit and receive the title of the Founder of Louisiana.

The freedom, vigor, and wildness of Canadian life developed men early, and Iberville entered the French Navy as midshipman at the age of fourteen. His first service of note, however, was as a soldier in the wilds of his native land, in the Canadian overland campaign to recover possession of an Indian trading post on Hudson Bay, which it was claimed the English had illegally seized. Iberville volunteered for this campaign under De Troye, and exhibited such judgment and vigor as caused him to be put in command of a small party of nine, some say twelve, men with two canoes, wherewith he did not hesitate to attack and compel the unconditional surrender of an English ship manned by fourteen, including the commander of Hudson Bay. St. Helene, his brother, meantime captured another vessel, and with the two as means of transport, the two brothers pushed on to Fort Quitchitchouen, which surrendered after withstanding a sharp cannonade.

These victories not only insured to the French the command of the entire southern part of Hudson Bay, but put them in possession of a vast amount of stores. Indeed, so destructive to English interests were the campaigns of Iberville in 1687–88, that the Hudson Bay Company declared that their actual losses amounted to 108,520 pounds sterling, an enormous sum in the young colonies of that day. The consequential losses must have been very great, for we are told that the value of furs obtained in the trade of one year amounted to 400,000 livres (francs).

Iberville remained in charge of the country which his valor had recaptured, and in 1688, while the Iroquois were ravaging Canada, waged successful war in Hudson Bay. One of his lieutenants, capturing an English official, found on him an order from the London Company to proclaim English sovereignty over the whole bay. Later two ships, with twenty-eight cannon and eight swivels, appeared before St. Anne in order to expel the French. Eventually Iberville compelled the surrender of the English ships, and releasing the smaller vessel for the safe transport of such prisoners as he paroled, himself navigated the larger ship, with eleven Hudson Bay pilots held prisoners, to Quebec through Hudson Strait.

In 1690 Iberville volunteered, under his brother St. Helene, for the retaliatory expedition in midwinter against Schenectady, wherein a large number of the inhabitants of that unhappy town were ruthlessly massacred by the French and their Indian allies. Iberville seems to have exerted his influence to restrain the savagery of the Indians, and saved the life of at least one Englishman.

It seems that the successes of the young Canadian had attracted attention in France, and when in 1691, through the efforts of the Northern Company, Louis XIV. had decided to recover Port Nelson, Hudson Bay, from the English, Du Tast came to Quebec with fourteen sail, it was with express orders that Iberville should be entrusted with a share of the work and glory. Du Tast objected to such division of honor, and by plausible objections as to the lateness of the season, although it was only the 16th of July, succeeded in delaying the departure of the expedition for that year.

Iberville seemed determined to show the speciousness of the reasons, for he made a trip to the bay and brought back in 1691 two ships loaded with furs, much to the consolation of Frontenac. He immediately went to France to advance the expedition against Port Nelson, which he knew was much favored at court. Iberville found favor with the king, who gave him two ships for the reduction of Port Nelson, and orders to guard it after reduction.

Delays in France and contrary winds on the Atlantic brought Iberville to Quebec only in October, far too late for the safe navigation of Hudson Bay. To fill in his time he set forth to take Pemaquid, but did not make an attack, this being the only instance in his long career where he failed to show extreme daring, even against desperate odds. The delay of the vessels was unfortunate for France as far as Hudson Bay was concerned, for in 1693 three English vessels attacked and captured St. Anne, with fifty thousand peltries, and again the control of the bay passed from France.

In September, 1694, Iberville, with two ships, la Poli and la Charante, the former commanded by his brother, de Serigny, appeared before Port

Nelson, which he was six weeks in approaching owing to the heavy moving ice, which nearly destroyed his vessel. The fort had a double palisade, thirty-two cannon and swivels in the main body, and fourteen cannon in outer works, the whole manned by fifty-three men. Iberville landed without hesitation, invested the fort with forty Canadians, worked with his usual energy and skill, and in fourteen days he had his outworks established, his batteries placed and mortars in position. His final summons for surrender resulted in the capitulation of the fort, on condition that personal property should be spared and safe transport be given the garrison to England the coming year. His success was saddened for Iberville by the death of the elder Chateauguay, the third of his brothers to fall in the service of his king, who perished while gallantly repelling a sortie of the beleaguered garrison. The name of Port Nelson was changed to Fort Bourbon, and the river was re-christened St. Therese, because, says Jeremie, in his *Relation de la Baie de Hudson*, the capitulation was made on October 14th, the day of that holy saint.

The victory did not prove to be cheap, for scurvy, then the dreaded scourge of the sailor, broke out during the long, dark, excessively cold winter, and caused the death of twenty men. Late the next summer, after waiting to the last moment for the English ships he counted on capturing, and leaving a garrison of sixty-seven at Fort Bourbon, Iberville sailed for Quebec; but the winds were so contrary and his crew so debilitated by scurvy, that he turned his prows to France and fortunately arrived at Rochelle, October 9, 1693.

His victories in Hudson Bay so commended him to the king that Iberville was charged with the reduction and destruction of the strong fort which James II. of England had erected at Pemaquid, Maine. While on this cruise our Canadian fell in with three English ships near the mouth of the St. John. He unhesitatingly attacked them, dismasted, fired, and captured the flag-ship of the squadron, the Newport, a ship of eighty men and twenty-four guns.

Reinforced by several hundred Indians, as a land and besieging force, Iberville arrived at Pemaquid, August 13, 1696, and invested the fort the next day. He summoned the commander, Colonel Chubb, to capitulate, but that officer replied that, " if the sea was covered with French vessels and the land with Indians, he would not surrender until compelled to do so." Iberville promptly landed, and used such expedition that within the short space of thirteen hours he established his batteries in position and opened fire, when the garrison surrendered on honorable terms. Iberville, doubtless mindful of his experiences at Schenectady, took the wise and humane precaution of quartering his prisoners under the guns of the royal ships, so as to secure them from the fury of his bloodthirsty allies, the Indians, who desired to supplement the entire destruction of the fort by the slaughter of the garrison.

In withdrawing from the demolished post, while doubling the island at the mouth of the Penobscot, he had an opportunity of justifying his reputation as the most skilful officer in the French service; for, falling in with an English squadron of seven sail, he successfully evaded them by bold seamanship along the very coast line of that dangerous and rock-bound shore.

His capacity as a military commander was now to be tested. Charged by the king to co-operate in the reduction of Newfoundland to French power, Iberville found himself viewed with jealousy by his colleague, Brouillian, governor of Placentia, who assumed entire command, interfered with Iberville's contemplated movements, and declared that his own troops, the Canadians, should not accompany him on the opening campaign.

Iberville realizing the necessity of zealous and concerted action in an enterprise of such importance, decided to leave the field free to Brouillan, and so announced his intention of returning to France. Immediately the Canadians declared to a man that they were bound to him alone, that Frontenac's orders recognized Iberville as commander, and finally, that they would return to Quebec sooner than accept another. Brouillan recognizing that Iberville was the idol of his Canadian countrymen, and unable to deny that the king had confided all the enterprises to be undertaken during the winter to Iberville, made such concessions as brought about reconciliation; nevertheless the campaign undertaken against

St. John's was marked by dissension. Iberville displayed his usual energy and gallantry in the advance and subsequent skirmishes which ultimately resulted in the surrender of St. John's, which was abandoned and destroyed by fire. The campaign was pursued with such energy and success that at the end of two months the English had nothing left in Newfoundland except Bona Vista and Carbonniere Island. During these operations Iberville displayed marked ability in handling troops, both in the field and during siege operations. His eagerness to share every danger, and willingness to undergo every hardship in common with his troops, endeared him to all and contributed much to the enthusiasm with which his men followed him or obeyed his orders.

In May, 1697, his brother Serigny arrived at Placentia with four vessels, destined for the command of Iberville in a proposed attempt to again reduce Hudson Bay. With these ships—le Pelican, fifty guns; le Palmier, forty guns; le Profond, le Vespe, and a brigantine—Iberville entered the mouth of Hudson Strait on August 3d, and was immediately beset with heavy ice. The floes were driven hither and thither with such violence by the currents that Iberville directed, as the best means of safety, that each vessel should moor itself to the largest attainable iceberg. This expedient saved four of the ships, but an unexpected movement of two large bergs crushed so completely the brigantine that she sank instantly, the crew barely escaping with their lives.

After a besetment of twenty-four days, Iberville succeeded in extricating his vessel from the ice and passed into the bay. He was alone and in utter ignorance of the fate of his consorts, which had been hidden from view by the ice for the past seventeen days. Iberville was not the man to turn back, nor indeed to delay in an expedition which demanded haste, so he pushed on alone and reached Port Nelson on September 4th.

The next morning he discovered three ships several leagues to the leeward, tacking to enter the harbor. He hoped that they were his consorts, and he at once made signals, which being unanswered showed that the ships were English. It was indeed an English squadron, consisting of the Hampshire, fifty-two guns and two hundred and thirty men; the Hudson Bay, thirty-two guns, and the Deringue, also of thirty-two guns, against which force Iberville had but one ship of fifty guns. It was with reason that, as Jeremie says, "they flattered themselves with the idea of capturing Iberville, seeing that they were three to one, and they were amazed at the boldness with which he attacked them."

Indeed, almost any other officer in the French navy would have considered an attack as simply madness, but such desperate odds only served to stimulate to the highest degree the known courage and skill of Iberville. He cleared his decks for action, and instantly quitting the shelter and supposed advantage of the harbor, attacked the English squadron in the open sea, where Iberville doubtless counted that his skill in handling ship would inure to his benefit.

Charlevoix thus describes this desperate fight:

"The cannonade opened about half-past nine in the morning and was kept up incessantly till one with great vigor on both sides. Meanwhile the Pelican had only one man killed and seventeen wounded. Then Iberville, who had kept the weather-gauge, bore down straight on the two frigates, pouring in several broadsides at close quarters in order to disable them. At that moment he perceived the third, the Hampshire, coming on with twenty-six guns in battery on each side, with a crew of two hundred and thirty men.

"He at once proceeded to meet her, all his guns pointed to sink her, ran under her lee, yard-arm to yard-arm, and having brought his ship to, poured in his broadside. This was done so effectively that the Hampshire, after keeping on about her own length, went down. Iberville at once wore and turned on the Hudson Bay, the ship of the remaining two that could most easily enter St. Teresa River; but as he was on the point of boarding her, the commandant struck his flag and surrendered.

"Iberville then gave chase to the Deringue, the third, which was escaping to the northeast, and which was only a good cannon-shot off; but as that vessel was as good a sailor as his own ship he soon gave up the chase, not daring to crowd sail, having had much of his rigging cut, two pumps burst, his shrouds considerably injured, hull cut up by seven cannon-balls and pierced at

the water's edge, with no way of stopping the
leak. He accordingly veered and sent the Sieur
de la Sale in his boat with twenty-five men to
man the prize. He then proceeded to repair
damage, and having done so with great expedition, he renewed the chase of the enemy, who
was now three leagues off.

"He began to gain on him when, in the evening,
the wind changed to the north, and a thick fog
suddenly rising, he lost sight of the Deringue.
This accident compelled him to rejoin the Hudson Bay, and he anchored near the Hampshire,
now almost out of sight, and from which not a
soul had been saved."

In this fight with an enemy more than twice
his superior in guns and men Iberville had sunk
one ship, captured another, and put the third to
flight; but this was followed by other experiences, which at the outset presented conditions
apparently not less desperate and discouraging.
Two days later, pending his siege operations
against Port Nelson, a violent gale arose, in
which, says Charlevoix, "In spite of all d'Iberville's efforts to ride it out—and there was not,
perhaps, in the French navy one more skilful in
handling a ship—he was driven ashore with his
vessel, the Pelican, and his prize, the Hudson Bay.
The misfortune happened at night, the darkness
increasing the horrors of the storm and prevent-
ing them from beaching the vessels at a favorable place and so saving them, and before the
break of day they broke up and filled."

Both vessels were crowded with wounded

men and prisoners, who endeavored as best they could to reach the shore in the storm and darkness. Twenty-three perished in the attempt, but fortunately the receding tide left such shallows that the rest reached shore, and most of the prisoners successfully sought the friendly shelter of Fort Nelson.

Iberville now found himself in most desperate plight—shipwrecked on a barren coast, with a hostile garrison on land, the return of the English ship at sea possible, and destitute of provisions. He turned to the wrecked vessels and found that it was possible to obtain from them cannon and other munitions of war, and, undismayed, he set his cold, wet, and hungry crew at this task, resolved to obtain food by carrying the English fort by assault. At this juncture his missing vessels, having extricated themselves from the ice of Hudson Strait, appeared, and the fort surrendered without putting Iberville to the last proof of his courage.

As might be expected, Iberville became the hero of the day on his return to France in 1697; but true to himself and his career, he sought the influence of friends at court only to obtain other difficult and dangerous service that might add to the glory of France. He was now to enter on a new career as an explorer, colonizer, and administrator, where, if he was to perform less brilliant deeds than in earlier life, he was destined to open up to settlement by his countrymen the fertile lands of Louisiana, and thus lay the foundations of its future greatness.

It was now twelve years since the tragic fate of La Salle's colony on the coast of Texas had spread dismay and terror among all who had been especially interested in the scheme of French colonization on the Mississippi River. The sentiment seemed to be that the mouth of the great river could never be found and that further effort would only result in useless sacrifice of life and vessels. With the march of time, however, these impressions of doubt and disaster had faded out of mind, and as now the attention of the ministry was especially turned to that part of Louisiana which could be reached from the St. Lawrence, it appeared to Iberville to be a suitable season to revive the project of discovering the mouth of the Mississippi and of planting a colony.

A plan for the colonization of Louisiana was formally submitted to the French Government by M. de Remonville, while Iberville for his part pledged his reputation as a navigator both to find the mouth of the Mississippi and to successfully plant there a colony. The ministry were easily persuaded that the scheme was practicable and advantageous, their decision being doubtless affected by the knowledge that both Spain and England contemplated the early settlement of the northern coasts of the Gulf of Mexico. It was even reported, as afterward transpired to be the truth, that colonizing expeditions were already en route, and in order to insure protection should Iberville first reach the ground, Count Pontchartrain projected and arranged for the construction of a fort at the mouth of the Mississippi.

As was always the case, schemes of trade were interwoven with the policy of colonization and extension of the royal domain. The principal objects of the trade proved fanciful or chimerical, being, first, the idea of making bison wool an article of trade, a scheme fostered in France by La Salle, and, second, in the hope that valuable pearl fisheries might be found. In Iberville's instructions we find that "one of the great objects proposed to the king, when he was urged to discover the mouth of the Mississippi, was to obtain wool from the cattle (buffalo) of that country, and for this purpose these animals must be tamed and parked and the calves sent to France."

Iberville worked with his usual energy, and the expedition, consisting of two small frigates, the Badine, the Marin, and two Norman fishing-boats, sailed from Brest, October 4, 1698. It was Friday, but Iberville no more than Columbus minded the day, and in the reluctance of the other vessels, himself led in the Badine.

A storm off Madeira caused the disappearance of one of the fishing-boats, but after a short search Iberville tarried no more than he did in the Hudson Straits for his missing consort, but pushed on and reached San Domingo early in December. Here the governor, Ducasse, was so impressed with Iberville's elucidation of his projects that he expressed to the home government his opinion that the views and genius of Iberville seemed to equal his valor in war.

English vessels had been cruising in the neighborhood of San Domingo, which led Iberville to believe that it was a colonizing expedition, so he worked day and night in completing his preparations, and on January 1, 1699, sailed for the Gulf of Mexico. On the afternoon of the twenty-third day, Iberville as usual leading, land was sighted in the northeast. It proved to be the harbor of Pensacola, where Iberville was chagrined to find himself preceded by a Spanish colony under command of Don Andres de la Riola. There were two frigates yet in the harbor, which four months before had brought up three hundred colonists from Vera Cruz. The half-finished fort, the dissatisfied garrison, and the uncertainty of the future explorations to the westward were so many inducements for Iberville to drive out the Spaniards and secure the harbor. Iberville made arrangements to enter the harbor, but was notified by the Spanish governor that he had formal orders from Spain to permit no foreign ships to enter the harbor. Under pretence that he feared heavy weather the French fleet sounded the entrance to the harbor and prepared to enter. The Spanish commander, however, begged that they would retire, and fortunately having been given information by the Spanish pilot, Iberville decided to sail to the west. Iberville, exploring the coast, anchored at the eastern point of the entrance to Mobile Bay, where violent gales nearly destroyed the squadron.

Reconnoitring boats giving such unsatisfactory reports of the depth of the channel, Iberville determined, with his usual energy, to survey it himself. Taking his younger brother Bienville and a crew of his faithful Canadians he started, despite approaching darkness, so as to begin work at day-light; the storm breaking with great violence, Iberville's efforts to make head-

way over the billows were in vain. Finally, his rowers exhausted, the boat was turned to the nearest land, but the sea was so high and the wind so violent that unceasing efforts were needful to prevent the boat from swamping. It was due to Iberville's great skill that the boat was finally beached in a favorable spot on the sandy beach, which the crew reached with difficulty, so exhausted were they with their struggles. Here they were weather-bound three days, and so had an opportunity to explore the island. It was with horror that they discovered in one place ghastly piles of human bones and skulls, mute witnesses of a scene of slaughter, which terrified many of the crew until they found the island to be uninhabited. The island, now known as Dauphin, was called Massacre by Iberville, who, undisturbed by the sight, visited the mainland with a few of his men and made every effort to discover the inhabitants, of whom he found recent traces.

Finally came good weather, and with it the continued voyage to the west brought the fleet to safe anchorage on a bright February morn off Ship Island. The live-stock landed, Iberville gave his freight consorts permission to return to France, while he explored the mainland that now lay fair and bright before him. The Indians were communicated with, after many failures, but, beyond the discovery of the Pascagoula and reports of a larger river to the west, which the Bayagoula Indians called Malbouchia, no valuable information was obtained. Iberville planned to reach the great river by one of its reported outlets, and, following the main channel down, thus learn the way for his vessel; but, the Indians giving him the slip, it only remained to search every foot of the coast until the river was gained. He was thus thrown on his own resources, which had never failed and were not to do so now. Iberville, with his brother Bienville and fifty picked men, largely Canadians, and twenty days' provisions, started February 27th, on two Biscayennes or barges, for his difficult task, the discovery of the mouth of the Mississippi.

It is useless to detail this journey of Iberville through an apparently endless maze of islets, mud-banks, sand-banks, reefs, and marshy shoals, which go to make up the great level delta of the Mississippi. It would, even to-day, be a difficult search for most mariners without a chart, but then well-nigh impossible. Iberville's skill and patience were tasked to the utmost, and, when he did find the mouth of the great river, it almost seemed to be by the intervention of Providence. On the eve of March 3, 1699, while struggling along the mainland, to which they persistently clung, the violence of an increasing gale threatened to swamp their barges, despite every effort, if they kept off shore, while every approach to watch the shore-line, and thus make certain of the river-mouth, incurred danger of beaching and destruction. Darkness came on and the gale increased, making certain, as it seemed to them, that they must choose death at sea or death on land. Suddenly Iberville put his barge before the wind, and into the face of death as his followers thought, but it shot between huge piles of interlaced drift-wood into a turbid stream of whitish water. Iberville put out his hand and tasted. The water was fresh, and the Mississippi was rediscovered.

The Spaniards had spoken of the river as La Palisada, which Iberville thought most appropriate when he saw the bristling barricades of huge jagged trees with outstretched limbs and contorted roots borne incessantly onward by the strong current.

Iberville camped that night at the edge of the dense rank sedge-growth, saying: "Stretched on the sedges and sheltered from the gale, our pleasure is so much the greater that we feel our escape from a great peril. It is a very lively business, this exploring the unknown shores of a sea in shallops too small to carry sail in the open sea, too tiny to anchor, and yet so large that they strand and ground half a league from land."

The next morn was that of Mardi-Gras, when our devout explorers celebrated mass, sang joyfully the Te Deum and raised a commemorative cross before voyaging further.

Never in their wildest dreams could the hardy Canadian explorers from their marshy camp in the delta of the Mississippi ever have presaged, that in the coming time, from the many millions of future inhabitants in the Valley of the Mississippi should be gathered tens of thousands to celebrate the merry day of carnival in the metropolitan city that was to spring up from their memorable voyage.

The Mississippi was near its high stage, so that travel was tediously slow, mostly by oar. The land rose somewhat, the sedge gave way first to cane and willows, and later to richly foliaged trees with graceful festoons pleasing to the eye

and fruitful of promise in the coming autumn.
The country, largely flooded, would have seemed
uninhabited save for the Indian ferry-boats, bundles of cane pointed at both ends and fastened
together by crossbars of wood, and an occasional
column of smoke rising in the distant blue. The
rapid current obliged the oarsmen to hug the
bank closely, while diminishing food and increasing piles of drift-wood discouraged them; but the
indomitable Iberville cheered on his Canadians,
and on the fifth day, some thirty-five leagues from
the river's mouth, six pirogues, or canoes, full
of Indians were seen. The savages fled, but one
was captured, and through him communication
and friendly overtures were established with the
Annochys. Through these Indians Iberville was
taken to the present site of New Orleans and was
shown the portage over which the Indians travelled to Lake Pontchartrain, and thence to the
bay where the ship was at anchor. Farther up
the stream Iberville visited the village of the
Bayougoulas, which consisted of about two hundred souls. The men, well made, with short hair
and painted faces, stalked around most unconcernedly in a naked state. The women blackened
their teeth, tied up their hair in a top-knot, tattooed their faces and breasts, and wore girdles
woven of bark fibre, dyed red or bleached white,
with pendulous fringes reaching to the knee.
The ornaments of the women were metal bracelets and bangles and fancy articles made of
feathers, while the young braves wore sashes of
feathers, which, weighted with bits of metal,

made merry sound as they danced. In short, they were an inoffensive folk, content with the simple fruits of the earth, which largely served as their sustenance.

Iberville visited one of their temples, a structure some thirty feet in diameter, which Charlevoix describes as follows: " In the centre were slowly burning logs (keeping up a perpetual fire), and at the end a platform on which lay skins of deer, buffalo, and bear, offerings to the Chouchouacha (the opossum), the god of the Bayougoulas, which animal was painted in red and black at various points in the temple. The roof was decorated with the figures of various animals, among which a red fox was conspicuous. On either side of the entrance were other animal figures, such as bears and wolves and also various birds, but above all the Chouchouacha (the opossum), an animal about the size and having the head of the sucking pig, the white and gray fur of the badger, the tail of the rat, the paws of an ape, and a sack under its stomach."

The great discrepancies between the topography of the river and the descriptions given in the accounts of the journeys of La Salle and Tonti so impressed Iberville that he was really doubtful if he was on the Mississippi, and so his journey was pursued up the river to the Oumas, a short distance below the mouth of the Red River. Fortunately his brother, Bienville, obtained from an Indian chief a letter, which the savage had carried for thirteen years, given him by Tonti, who descended the river from Illinois in 1686 and left this letter addressed to La Salle, whose active and loyal assistant Tonti was.

Iberville was now over seven hundred miles distant from his ship, and his original stock of

Bierville's Army on the River.

provisions was exhausted, so that the men were obliged to live on the corn of the Indians and such meat or game as could be bought or killed. Sending his men back by the delta with the barges, Iberville decided to try himself the route of portages to the Gulf. With an Indian guide he entered the Ascantia, a narrow, winding bayou, where with his four Canadians and two pirogues fifty portages over fallen trees and drift were made the first day in a distance of seven leagues. It is not surprising that the Indian guide, unaccustomed to such tremendous labor and fatigue, deserted the second day. Iberville none the less pushed on undauntedly, confident that he could reach his ship through this unknown country, guide or no guide. Next, one of his hardy Canadians fell sick, and Iberville took his place and oar, and in the portages carried his end of a pirogue. After eighty portages they passed into Lake Maurepas and next into Lake Pontchartrain, whence the way was easy to the ship, which was reached eight hours in advance of the barges from the delta.

In his absence of six weeks Iberville had found again the Mississippi, explored its shores almost to the Red River, made friends with all its native tribes, discovered the short route to the sea, travelled about fifteen hundred miles, and had returned to his ship with every man of his party. What volumes these few facts speak for the energy, tact, skill, and foresight of this wonderful Canadian!

Casting about for a convenient spot Iberville decided to build his fort at the head of Biloxi Bay, and in this unfortunate location, under the spurring supervision of the chief, Fort Biloxi soon rose, and there on Easter Sunday mass was celebrated, vespers sung, and a sermon preached. On May 2, 1700, Iberville sailed for France, leaving his lieutenant, Sauvole, as the first governor of the province of Louisiana and Bienville second in command.

The action of France and the desperate haste of Iberville in occupying the mouth of the Mississippi were most timely. The very month in which our Canadian sailed from Brest an expedition left England under the auspices of Mr. Cox, who sent out three vessels loaded with emigrants. They wintered in the Carolinas, where many settled, but in 1700 two ships continued their voyage to the Mississippi. One of these vessels was commanded by a Captain Banks, who once captured by Iberville in Hudson Bay now found himself worsted by his rival in the peaceful work of colonization. One of the English ships appeared in the lower Mississippi, into which Banks had found entrance, in September, 1700. Bienville, with five men and two pirogues, met the English vessel, and setting forth to the captain that France was in possession of all the surrounding country, succeeded either by argument or cajolery in persuading the captain to withdraw from the Mississippi.

Iberville was not long delayed by the delights and pleasures of the French court, but speedily returned to Biloxi, where he arrived on the eve of Twelfth Night with supplies, and more important of all, with sixty hardy and energetic Canadians, with whom he established a fort a short distance below the present site of New Orleans. The winter proved a very cold one, the drinking-water freezing in the cups, but it did not delay the rapid progress of the new fort. In the midst of this work Chevalier de Tonti arrived with twenty Canadians from their former settlement in Illinois.

Thus for the first time, with intercommunication established between the permanent settlement in Illinois, Tonti's fort on the Arkansas, and the new colony at the mouth of the Mississippi, Iberville felt that France had indeed entered into actual possession of its great province of Louisiana. He realized, however, the necessity of permanently connecting these settlements, many hundred miles apart, and of facilitating intercommunication through the establishment of intermediate posts.

Iberville contemplated an exploration of the Red River, thinking it might afford access to the gold and silver mines of New Spain, but abandoned the project owing to the representations of the Indians that the river was unnavigable from the interlaced drift-wood, later known as rafts. He turned his attention to the main river, the Mississippi, and visited the Natchez, a brave and powerful tribe of Indians, whose country delighted his heart as resembling France, and where he planned a city to be called Rosalie (now Natchez), which, however, it was not his fate to ever see take definite form, as it was only built long after his death, in 1714, by his brother Bienville. It was at this time that Le Sueur, sent up the Mississippi by Iberville, discovered the St. Peter River, in Minnesota, and attempting mining operations, later brought back a worthless cargo of green earth. To Iberville's credit, it may be said, he viewed this and many other similar schemes of development with a sceptical and practical eye.

Later he sent his brother Bienville across country to explore the Red River, which was done with good success. His priest Montigny was also active in extending the faith, both among the Natchez Indians and in the basin of the Tensas River. Indeed, every effort was made under Iberville's sagacious direction to obtain a knowledge of the possibilities of the country, so that its resources might be properly developed.

Iberville returned to France ill with fever, but despite his disease, he displayed extraordinary energy in personally advancing the practical affairs of his new colony. Moreover, he prepared a memoir urging the cession of Pensacola by Spain to France, which nation was to establish forts and arm the Indians along the Mississippi River, whereby the interior of America from the Gulf of Mexico to Canada would be under French domination, save the narrow strip along the Atlantic coast already occupied by England. It was a sagacious scheme which if it had been properly supported by France would have entirely changed the future of America. It received, however, but a perfunctory support, and only resulted in exciting the jealousy of Spain.

Iberville's last voyage to Louisiana was made in 1701, when his health, undermined by the climate, was impaired by the formation of an abscess which confined him to his bed for two months. His mind worked incessantly, and his activity through other hands was wonderful. He planned the royal magazines on Dauphine

Island, located the new post on Mobile River, told off the relief of workmen for the various enterprises, planned flat-boats for lighters, extended relief to the Spaniards at Vera Cruz, and sent Tonti as an agent to make peace with the Choctaws and Chickasaws and secure them as allies. His sailor's eye was particularly pleased with the magnificent forests of Mobile Bay, where the oaks and pines presented the finest timber for ship-building he had ever seen.

With Mobile commenced, the royal storehouses erected, and the alliance of the Choctaws and Chickasaws secured, Iberville felt that the colony of Louisiana was on a secure foundation, and on March 31st he sailed from Dauphine Island, then the headquarters of that colony for which he had done so much, and which he was destined never again to see.

The domain of Louisiana, obtained by so much heroic endeavor and individual suffering on the part of Joliet, Marquette, La Salle, Tonti, Iberville, and their associates, passed at once, by an edict of Louis XIV., into a monopoly and under the control of a courtier, Anton Crozat, for trading purposes, by the decree of September 14, 1712. In this decree the limits of Louisiana were for the first time defined, including "all the territories by us (France) possessed, and bounded by New Mexico and by those of the English in Carolina. . . . The river St. Louis, formerly called the Mississippi, from the sea-shore to the Illinois, together with the rivers St. Phillipe, formerly called the Missouries, and the St. Jerome, formerly called the Wabash (the Ohio), with all the countries, territories, lakes in the land, and the rivers emptying directly or indirectly into that part of the river St. Louis. All the said territories, countries, rivers, streams, and islands we will to be and remain comprised under the name of the government of Louisiana."

There was another and blacker page to the decree, whereby Crozat was further authorized to introduce African slavery: "If the aforesaid Sieur Crozat considers it advisable to have negroes in the said country of Louisiana, for agriculture or other use on plantations, he can send a ship each year to trade directly with the Guinea coast, . . . and is further authorized to sell negroes to the settlers of Louisiana."

But prior to this condition of affairs the great Canadian naval commander had passed to his final reward, having died of yellow fever at Havana, July 9, 1706. The last leaf in his history was, however, an effort, through his personal bravery and skill, to secure French domination in America by driving out of the Antilles the determined English seamen whose successful raids so often militated against the interests of France. Despite his health, undermined by fevers, Iberville left France with a fleet with which he hoped to carry out this great plan. Intending to make a descent upon Barbadoes, he learned that the English, warned of his plans, were prepared for him. He therefore seized on the islands of Nevis and St. Christopher, where his fleet captured an enormous amount of booty

of all kinds. He decided next to ravage the
English colonies in the Carolinas, but stopping
at Havana for reinforcements he lost his own
life by the epidemic which destroyed eight hundred others of his fleet.

Among the qualities of this great Canadian all
must admire his intrepidity in war, his skill as a
navigator, and his capacity as an explorer; but
beyond these were the astonishing administra-
tive ability and political sagacity which he displayed in such an eminent degree in the planning,
founding, and fostering of the great province of
Louisiana.

New Orleans in 1719.

III.

JONATHAN CARVER,

THE EXPLORER OF MINNESOTA.

THROUGHOUT the bloody series of French and Indian wars which ravaged the frontier settlements of America during the first half of the eighteenth century, France maintained secure possession of the regions of the great lakes and the basin of the upper Mississippi. The successful campaign of the gallant Wolfe against the no less gallant Montcalm ultimately resulted in the termination of French supremacy in these sections, and under the treaty of Paris, in 1763, Canada with all other dominions of France east of the Mississippi passed under the control of Great Britain.

To this time the English colonists had confined their operations almost entirely to the region of the Atlantic Coast, so when Great Britain acquired her immense war-inheritance the country to the west of the Appalachian Mountain range was practically an unknown region to its new masters. The extension of English settlements toward the interior of the continent was determined on by the English Government, and the more accessible of the French trading-posts in the northwest were immediately occupied. Maps were few and inaccurate, information as to the Indians vague and exaggerated, while nothing was known as to the resources of the country except that furs were obtainable in large numbers.

Scarcely were the terms of the treaty promulgated than the enterprising pioneers moved westward and gradually pressed back the Indians nearest the English settlements. A few other men, however, undertook to penetrate the valley of the Mississippi to the very frontier of Louisiana, which remained a French possession.

Among these hardy and adventurous Americans the most enterprising was Captain Jonathan Carver, who was born in Stillwater, N. Y., in 1732. He was the grandson of William Joseph Carver, one of the earliest of the royal appointments in Connecticut, and his first public service was at the age of eighteen, when he secured an ensigncy in a Connecticut regiment. In 1757, when Colonel Oliver Partridge raised a battalion of infantry in Massachusetts to serve against Canada, Carver was made a lieutenant therein. Later he served as captain under Colonel Whitcomb, in 1760, and under Colonel Saltonstall, in 1762, and participated in the taking of Crown Point and other operations in northern New York.

Doubtless his association with scouts and camp-followers, largely consisting of fur-traders and frontiersmen, induced a lively interest in their accounts of the western country held by their enemies, the Indian and the Frenchman.

Certain it is that Carver acquired such ideas of the extent, fertility, natural wealth, and possibilities of the great and unknown West as fired his adventurous spirit with a firm determination to solve the important geographical problems connected therewith.

His objects, he states, were to gain knowledge concerning the Indian tribes to the west of the Mississippi, to ascertain the natural resources of the country, and to cross the American continent between the forty-third and forty-sixth degrees of north latitude. Ultimately he contemplated the establishment of a trading-post at some suitable point on the Pacific Coast.

Carver was not ignorant of the great danger involved in such an undertaking, where he was obliged to intrust his life to the mercy of unknown Indians for a prolonged time. Indeed, considering his experiences at the massacre of Englishmen and provincials at Fort Henry, it seems surprising that he would ever trust a savage or a Frenchman. In the campaign of 1757, Carver volunteered to accompany the detachment of fifteen hundred men which General Webb sent forward to reinforce the garrison at Fort Henry, then anticipating an attack from Montcalm. The garrison, commanded by the gallant Monro, who resisted until his guns burst and his ammunition was nearly exhausted, surrendered to the combined force of Indians and French under Montcalm, who promised safe conduct and private property. As the English force moved out the next morning the Indians, inflamed by liquor, song, and dance, butchered the sick and wounded and then fell upon the helpless captives, of whom there were, according to French accounts, about sixty killed and four hundred robbed and maltreated. Montcalm and Levi, to their credit, though too late, made heroic personal efforts which mitigated the horrors of the situation.

Among the unfortunates was Carver, who, robbed and stripped by the savages, appealed to a French sentry for protection only to be repelled with abuse. Realizing finally that to re-

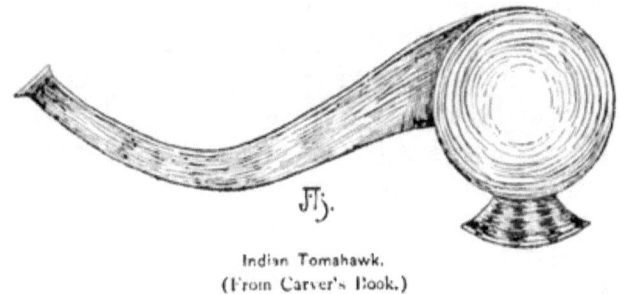

Indian Tomahawk.
(From Carver's Book.)

main quiet was to meet certain death, Carver and a few others attempted to escape by breaking unarmed through the surrounding lines of Indian fiends. In this desperate effort for life Carver was twice wounded, badly beaten, seized by two Indians, and led away to death, which he escaped by the appearance of a British officer in full uniform, who was such a prize that his captors left Carver to secure a more valuable victim. Profiting by the respite Carver fled to the nearest woods, where, exhausted and nearly naked, he concealed himself in a thicket until night. For three days he wandered through the

densest part of the forest, suffering tortures from
travel under such conditions, often in danger of
recapture, and without food until he reached, in
a nearly exhausted condition, the English settlements.

An attempt at transcontinental exploration
was then looked on as foolhardy and visionary
in the extreme, even to those friends of Carver
who never deserted him. One of these, Dr.
Lettsom, wrote in the third edition of Carver's
travels, fifteen years after the journey, as follows:
"He suggested an attempt by land across the
northwest parts of America, and actually drew a
chart of his proposed route for effecting his project, which, however visionary it may now be
deemed, affords at least a proof of the enterprising spirit of Carver."

Unmoved by the sneers of his critics, and undeterred by recollections of Indian cruelty and
perfidy, Carver arranged the details of his journey at his private expense, and in June, 1766,
he quitted Boston, and travelling by the way
of Albany and Niagara reached his headquarters, Michillimackinac, now known as Mackinac.
Here he made definite arrangements for his serious work of exploration. At this time English
traders extended their journeys to Prairie-du-
Chien for the purpose of purchasing furs from
Indians rendezvousing there, and with one of
these parties Carver was to travel, relying on the
Governor of Mackinaw to forward supplies to
St. Anthony. Leaving the Fort, September 3d,
and travelling by canoe, he reached the islands

of the Grand Traverse, and there spent one night. One of the chiefs, to whom a present was given, made, on Carver's departure, the following prayer, which is worthy of reproduction as a specimen of Indian eloquence: "May the Great Spirit favor you with a prosperous voyage; may He give you an unclouded sky and smooth waters by day, and may you lay down by night on a beaver blanket to uninterrupted sleep and pleasant dreams, and may you find continual protection under the calumet of peace."

Carver followed the route of Joliet and Marquette through Green Bay and up Fox River to the great town of the Winnebagoes, where he found the Indians presided over by a queen instead of a sachem. Carver speaks of the extreme richness of soil and abundance of cultivated products and wild game, mentioning grapes, plums, Indian corn, beans, pumpkins, squashes, watermelons, and tobacco from cultivation; fish from the lake; wild fowl so abundant that frequently the sun would be obscured by them for some minutes together, while deer, bears, and beavers were very numerous. The usual portage was made by him from the Fox to the Wisconsin River, into which his canoes were launched on the 8th of October. Seven days carried him to Prairie-du-Chien, at the junction of the Wisconsin and Mississippi, which was at that time a town of some three hundred families and had become a great trading mart for the adjacent tribes, who assembled in great numbers annually in the latter part of May.

The Falls of St. Anthony, on the River Mississippi, near 2400 Miles from its entrance into the Gulf of Mexico.

(From Carver's Book.)

At Prairie-du-Chien Carver parted with the traders, who were to winter at that point, and obtaining a Canadian as interpreter and a Mohawk Indian as a servant, he purchased a canoe, and on October 19th, proceeding up the Mississippi, he fell in with a straggling band of Indians which barely failed of plundering him. November 1st brought him to Lake Pepin, near which he discovered what appeared to be the remains of extended intrenchments, centuries old, as he thought, but which are now known to be Indian mounds, probably erected as sites for their wigwams, so as to keep them above the annual overflow and inundation.

The coming of winter and the forming of river ice obliged him to quit his canoe opposite the mouth of the St. Peter, or Minnesota River, whence by land he reached the Falls of St. Anthony on November 17, 1766, probably the first white American to visit them.

The noise and appearance of the Falls of St. Anthony impressed Carver very strongly, and his account of them is worthy of reproduction in view of the changes that have taken place within the past one hundred and thirty years:

"This amazing body of waters, which are above 250 yards over, form a most pleasing cataract; they fall perpendicularly about thirty feet, and the rapids below, in the space of 300 yards more, render the descent considerably greater; so that when viewed at a distance, they appear to be much higher than they really are.

"In the middle of the Falls stands a small island

about forty feet broad and somewhat longer, on which grow a few cragged hemlock and spruce trees; and about half way between this island and the eastern shore is a rock lying at the very edge of the Fall, in an oblique position, that appears to be about five or six feet broad and thirty or forty long."

Leaving the falls, Carver proceeded up the Mississippi to the mouth of the St. Francis, the farthest of Hennepin in 1680, discovering on the way Rum and Goose Rivers. Warned by the severity of the cold that winter was fast coming on, Carver returned to his canoe at the mouth of the Minnesota River and decided to explore that stream, of which only the lower portion had ever been visited—by Le Sueur in 1700.

Following the Minnesota about two hundred miles he reached, on December 7th, the winter camp of a large tribe of Indians, about one thousand in number, who were designated by Carver as the Naudowessie (Santees). Advancing boldly, with his calumet of peace fastened to the prow of his canoe, he was received in a friendly manner. After the usual smoking of the pipe of peace, during which he says the tent was nearly broken down by the crowd of savages, who, as a rule, had never seen a white man, he was treated with great respect.

Among these Indians Carver passed the winter, filling in his five months' stay by hunting and other Indian amusements. From the Indians he learned that the St. Lawrence, the Mississippi, and the Bourbon (the Red River of the North) had their sources within thirty miles of each other. This led to the natural but erroneous opinion that Carver had reached the highest land of North America, when in reality he was at an elevation of only twelve hundred feet.

Carver also spoke of "the Oregon, or the River of the West," as having its sources somewhat farther to the west. This is the first time that

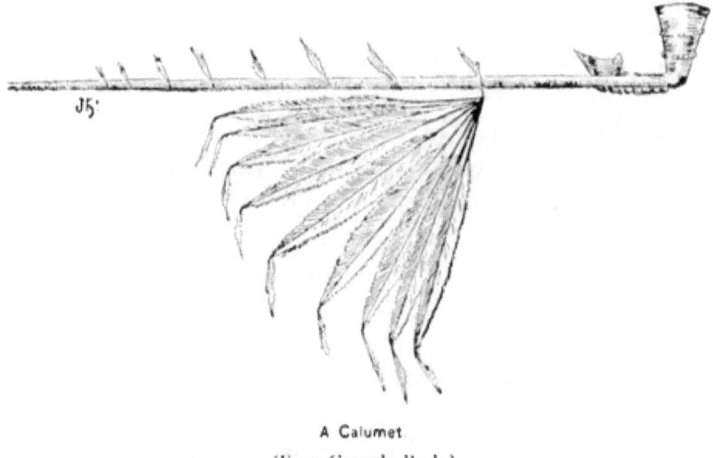

A Calumet
(From Carver's Book.)

the word Oregon appears in literature, and Carver gives no account of its meaning.

The Indians had traditions as to the extreme plentifulness of gold to the west of the "Shining Mountains," of which our explorer says, on the strength of Indian reports :

"The mountains that lie to the west of St. Peter are called the Shining Mountains, from an infinite number of crystal stones of an amazing size with which they are covered and which, when the sun shines full upon them, sparkle so as to be seen at a very great distance."

Carver's enthusiasm and interest in the West led him to make the following striking prediction, which time has fully justified. He says:

"This extraordinary range of mountains is calculated to be more than three thousand miles in length, without any very considerable intervals, which, I believe, surpasses anything of the kind in the other quarters of the globe. Probably, in future ages, they may be found to contain more riches in their bowels than those of Hindostan and Malabar, or than are produced on the golden coast of Guinea, nor will I except even the Peruvian mines. To the west of these mountains, when explored by future Columbuses or Raleighs, may be found other lakes, rivers, and countries, full fraught with all the necessaries or luxuries of life, and where future generations may find an asylum, whether driven from their country by the ravages of lawless tyrants, or by religious persecutions, or reluctantly leaving it to remedy the inconveniences arising from a superabundant increase of inhabitants; whether, I say, impelled by these or allured by hopes of commercial advantages, there is little doubt but their expectations will be fully gratified in these rich and unexhausted climes."

Carver described the valley of the Minnesota as a most delightful country, abounding with all the necessities of life, which grow spontaneously. Fruit, vegetables, and nuts were represented as being particularly abundant, and the sugar-maple grew in amazing numbers.

In April, 1767, the Santees descended the Minnesota in order, among other things, to bury their dead near a remarkable cave on Lake Pepin, known to the Indians as the "dwelling of the Great Spirit."

Finding that supplies had not been sent to the Falls of St. Anthony, Carver returned to Prairie-du-Chien in order to get sufficient stores to enable him to reach Lake Superior, whence he hoped to be able to cross the continent from Grand Portage. Obtaining such supplies, he proceeded up the Mississippi to the Chippeway River, and, after ascending to its head, made portages to the St. Croix, and reached Lake Superior, possibly by the river now known as the Bois Brule.

From this point Carver, in his canoe, skirted the coast of Lake Superior to the Grand Portage, where he awaited the arrival of the Hudson Bay or northern traders, from whom he anxiously hoped to obtain supplies that would enable him to journey west; but he was destined to disappointment, as nothing could be obtained from them. Carver coasted around the north and east borders of Lake Superior, and arrived at the Falls of Ste. Marie the beginning of October, having skirted nearly twelve hundred miles of the shores of Lake Superior in a birch canoe.

The Sault Ste. Marie was then the resort of the Algonquin Indians, who frequented the falls on account of the great numbers of whitefish that

filled the waters, particularly in the autumn,
when that fish leaves the lakes in order to spawn
in shallow running waters.

In November, 1767, Carver arrived at Mackinac, having, as he says, "been sixteen months
on this extensive tour, travelled nearly four
thousand miles, and visited twelve nations of
Indians living to the west and north. His picture of Detroit on his return, in 1768, is of retrospective interest.

"The town of Detroit contains upward of one
hundred houses. The streets are somewhat
regular, and have a range of very convenient
and handsome barracks with a spacious parade
at the south end. On the west side lies the
King's Garden, belonging to the Governor,
which is very well laid out, and kept in good
order. The fortifications of the town consist of
a strong stockade, made of round piles, fixed
firmly in the ground, and lined with palisades.
These are defended by some small bastions, on
which are mounted a few indifferent cannon of an
inconsiderable size, just sufficient for its defence
against the Indians or an enemy not provided
with artillery. The garrison in time of peace
consists of two hundred men, commanded by
a field-officer, who acts as chief magistrate under
the Governor of Canada.

"In the year 1762, in the month of July, it
rained on this town and the parts adjacent a
sulphurous water of the color and consistency of
ink, some of which being collected in bottles,
and wrote with, appeared perfectly intelligible

on the paper, and answered every purpose for that useful liquid. Soon after, the Indian wars already spoken of broke out in these parts. I mean not to say that this incident was ominous of them, notwithstanding it is well known that innumerable well-attested instances of extraordinary phenomena, happening before extraordinary events, have been recorded in almost every age by historians of veracity; I only relate the circumstance as a fact, of which I was informed by many persons of undoubted probity, and leave my readers, as I have heretofore done, to draw their own conclusions from it."

It is beyond question that certain chapters of Carver's work, supplementary to his account of his personal explorations, and especially devoted to Indians and to the natural history of the Northwest, are practically translations of the accounts of Charlevoix, Hennepin, and particularly of Lahontan. It does not appear from the first part of the work that Carver was a man endowed with those powers of observation and assimilation which are essential traits for the successful traveller and author.

When the brief recital of his personal travels is examined, it seems difficult to determine on what grounds his truthfulness has been questioned by a few hostile critics. His story is simple and straightforward, devoid of boastfulness, free from any exaggeration as to his personal prowess, and the statement that he passed a winter of five months in the valley of the Upper Minnesota is, in my opinion, worthy of entire credence.

Fortunately, however, evidence of the most convincing character exists as to Carver's residence among the Naudowessies or Santees. The exhaustive bibliography of the Siouan languages, by Mr. James C. Pilling, indicates that Carver is the first author who ever published a vocabulary of the Santee tongue, and its length, eight pages, renders it evident that it was an original

Naudowessie Indians.

Carver's drawing of "A man and woman of the Naudowessie," herewith reproduced, if somewhat fanciful in its details, must be considered of historical value as indicating in the main the costumes of the Santees when first visited by the whites.

compilation which must have required considerable time and patience.

The importance of Carver's charts and journals at that time was evident to the Lords Commissioners of Trade and Plantations in England to whom Carver was referred when praying for reimbursement of his expenses. Carver appeared before the Board and, after an examination, was granted authority to publish his papers.

Later, after Carver had, as he says, disposed of them and they were nearly ready for the press, an order was issued from the Council Board requiring him to immediately turn in all the originals of his charts, journals, and other papers relative to his discoveries.

Meanwhile interest in the extension of English influence into the interior of North America was waning steadily with the growing conviction that the colonies would establish their independence, and the Government had no mind to reimburse an enterprising American, even though he remained loyal. Carver was reduced gradually to the greatest straits, was compelled to sell his book for a pittance, and finally, his end hastened by lack of proper food and suitable attendance, died in the direst poverty in London, January 13, 1780.

His own generation could best judge as to the timeliness and importance of Carver's exploration, and as to the value of the information set forth in his book of travels. Suffice it to say that no less than twenty-three editions of this book have appeared, in four languages. This, too, at a time when the war of independence naturally destroyed current interest in the extension of English settlements in the interior of North America.

Explorations, however, are wisely esteemed by posterity according to the results which flow therefrom in the shape of definite additions to the knowledge of the world or in the more important direction of disclosing lands suitable for colonization. In this latter manner the exploration of Jonathan Carver and the accounts of his travels had an important influence. They first brought into popular and accessible form information and ideas concerning the interior parts of North America which before had been practically inaccessible to the general public of England and America.

Twenty-five years after this journey toward the "Shining Mountains" and "Oregon, the River of the West," the ultimate scheme of Carver found its justification in the success of Alexander Mackenzie, a young Scotchman, who was the first white man to cross the continent of America to the north of Mexico; and yet ten years later Lewis and Clark were despatched on their famous expedition which explored the valley of the Columbia, where in 1810, under the energetic management of John Jacob Astor, arose the trading-post of Astoria, thus turning into reality the dreams and aspirations of Jonathan Carver, the soldier and explorer.

IV.

CAPTAIN ROBERT GRAY,

THE DISCOVERER OF THE COLUMBIA RIVER.

WITHIN the past century no American explorer has contributed more materially to the welfare of the United States and to its maritime glory than Captain Robert Gray, the discoverer of the Columbia River and the first circumnavigator who carried the flag of the United States around the world.

Robert Gray was born at Tiverton, R. I., in May, 1757, and in early youth, inspired with the spirit of independence which dominated the American Colonies, entered the naval service during the war of the Revolution, wherein he served with credit as an officer.

At the termination of the war it is probable that he continued his natural or acquired vocation as a seaman. At all events, we find him first and foremost among that band of American citizens whose courage, energy, and nautical skill enabled them to attain unsurpassed success as whalers and sealers in the Antarctic Ocean, as traders dealing direct with China, or as explorers and fur dealers on the unsurveyed and dangerous coast of northwest America.

In 1787, J. Barrell, S. Brown, C. Bulfinch, J. Darby, C. Hatch, and J. M. Pintard, merchants of Boston, associated for the purpose of combining the fur traffic of the northwest coast of America with the silk and tea trade of China. For this purpose they sent, under the command of Captain John Kendrick, in 1787, the ship Columbia and the sloop Washington with cargoes of blankets, knives, iron bars, and other articles suitable for the northwest trade. They were provided with sea letters issued according to a resolution of Congress, with passports from the State of Massachusetts, and with commendatory letters from the Spanish minister plenipotentiary to the United States.

Captain Kendrick, who commanded the Columbia, was a man of marked ability and great energy, who withal had most enthusiastic opinions as to the future of the Pacific Coast region, which he believed would in a few years utterly dwarf the growing importance of the Atlantic seaboard. Gray was the master of the Washington, and his professional standing in the eyes of the merchants of Boston was shown by his designation as the most desirable officer to assume command in case of death or injury to Captain Kendrick.

Many aspersions have been cast by English writers on the policy pursued and methods followed by Americans engaged in trading with the Indians of the northwest coast of America. Doubtless such reflections were justified in individual cases of Americans, as of traders of other nationality; but the instructions given by the merchants of Boston to Kendrick and Gray show that fair, honest, and peaceful methods were regarded as the true means of establishing a permanent and profitable trade. Among other injunctions were the following:

"If you make any fort or any improvement of land on the coast, be sure you purchase the soil of the natives. . . . Let the instrument of conveyance bear every authentic mark that circumstances will admit. . . . We cannot forbear to impress on your mind our will and expectation that the most inviolable harmony and friendship may subsist between you and the natives, and that no advantage may be taken of them in trading, but that you endeavor by honest conduct to impress on their minds a friendship for Americans." While enjoining peace, it was not to be a peace on any terms, for thus runs the instructions: "The sea letters from Congress and this State you will show on every proper occasion, and although we expect you will treat all nations with respect and civility, yet we depend you will suffer insult and injury from none without showing that spirit which becomes a free and independent American."

The vessels sailed from Boston September 30, 1787, via the Cape Verde and Faulkland Islands, and in January doubled Cape Horn, when they thought the perils of storm were past. In latitude 59° S., however, a violent gale arose, which not only separated them, but also seriously damaged the Columbia. The storm over, Kendrick found himself in a sad plight, his consort gone, perhaps lost, his ship in an unseaworthy condition, and the nearest spot for repairs a thousand miles distant. This port, that of the island of Juan Fernandez, if now famous and delightful to the adventurous mind through its associations with the fascinating tale of Robinson Crusoe, was then most objectionable from the fact that it was under Spanish rule and so was to be avoided by Kendrick, whose instructions ran as follows:

"You are strictly enjoined not to touch at any port of the Spanish dominion on the western continent of America, unless driven there by unavoidable accident, in which case you are to give no offence to any of the subjects of his Catholic Majesty."

Kendrick, to his surprise, was received with great kindness and aided in repairing his injured vessel by Don Blas Gonzales, the humane commandant of the Spanish garrison of Juan Fernandez.

Spain at this time claimed the right of exclusive jurisdiction over the entire western continent of America by virtue of the papal concession, 1493, and by right of discovery. It had failed to colonize the northwest coast of America, but it prohibited other nations from entering in possession. It now illustrated its narrow and jealous policy in its treatment of a subordinate who had ventured to assist a vessel in distress and provided with letters from the accredited minister of Spain to the United States. Ambrose O'Higgins, then captain-general of Chili, under whom Gonzales was serving, on hearing of this act recalled him and put him in arrest, pending definite orders from his own superior, Teodor Lacroix, viceroy of Peru. After due consideration of the case the unfortunate commandant, Gonzales, was cashiered for his remissness in allowing a strange ship to leave Juan Fernandez instead of seizing her and her crew. The viceroy set forth to the captain-general of Chili the legal opinion that by the royal ordinance of November, 1692, every foreign vessel found in those seas without a license from the court of Spain was to be treated as an enemy, even though belonging to a friend or ally of the king, "seeing that no other nation had, or ought to have, any territories, to reach which its vessels should pass around Cape Horn or through Magellan's Straits." The viceroy therefore sent a ship from Callao to track or intercept the Columbia; the authorities on the coasts of Peru and Chili were especially enjoined to be vigilant, and in case any foreign vessel should appear in the country to seize her.

Under Gray's skilful handling the Washington escaped unharmed from the hurricane, and continuing his course toward King George Sound, the concerted rendezvous, he made the American coast, about 46° N., in August, 1788. Here he barely escaped loss of his vessel in trying to cross the bar of an unknown river, probably the Columbia, when his ship grounded. He, however, visited shore, and found that the sea was perchance the less inhospitable of the two, for he was so savagely and violently attacked by swarms of Indians that he was very glad to escape therefrom with one seaman dead and the mate wounded.

Quitting this unfortunate place he sailed north and entered Nootka Sound, Vancouver Island, September 17, 1788, where he found two English vessels, the Felice and Iphigenia, sailing under the Portuguese flag and commanded by Captains Meares and Douglass. There were no signs of

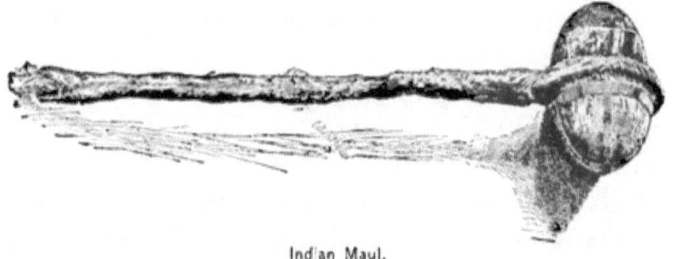

Indian Maul.

the Columbia, but her arrival a few days later relieved Gray from further anxiety in this respect.

Douglass's vessel, the Iphigenia, was in serious need of supplies and assistance, which Gray generously furnished. Later he not only made to the northward a successful trading trip, but in the following year, in June, 1789, explored the whole east coast of Queen Charlotte Islands, to which he gave the name of Washington Islands, in honor of General Washington, then President of the United States. In another trading excursion from Nootka Sound, Vancouver Island, Gray entered the broad opening southeast of the island and sailed to the east-southeast fifty miles, where he found the passage still five leagues wide. This opening was the Straits of Fuca, and the first authentic exploration of the strait is the account of Gray. The credit of first passing through the entire length of the Straits of Fuca is due to Kendrick, who made the passage in the sloop Washington, after the departure of Gray to China on the Columbia.

The account of the passage of the Washington through the Straits of Fuca was especially called to Vancouver's attention by the British Admiralty on the occasion of his surveying voyage of 1791, when he was particularly to "examine the supposed Strait of Juan de Fuca, said to be situated between the forty-eighth and forty-ninth north latitude, and to lead to an opening through which the sloop Washington was reported to have passed in 1789, and to have come out again to the northward of Nootka." Vancouver later denied to Americans the credit of first sailing entirely through the Straits of Fuca, resting his opinion on Gray's statement that he sailed only fifty miles within it, which was true; the credit belonging to Kendrick in his voyage with the Washington after Gray's departure from the coast in 1789.

The efforts of Kendrick and Gray resulted in the obtaining of a full cargo of furs, which in accordance with their instructions were to be sold in China. Kendrick, fascinated with the prospects of fortune and success, and perhaps reluctant to face his owners owing to his lack of caution which resulted in the unfortunate killing of some thirty natives, decided to remain on the northwest coast, his imaginary Eldorado.

Gray consequently transferred to the Columbia and set sail for Canton, then the great fur mart of the world. His voyage across the Pacific was prosperous, his furs were readily sold, and after taking a cargo of tea on board, Gray sailed for the Cape of Good Hope, and on the 10th of August, 1790, the Columbia entered the port of Boston, the first vessel to circumnavigate the world under the flag of the United States.

His success and conduct so impressed the owners of the ship that they immediately decided upon sending Gray back to the northwest coast, and seven weeks later, September 28, 1790, he sailed in the Columbia, which was described as a ship of two hundred and twelve tons, manned by thirty men, and equipped with an armament of ten guns.

Gray was also provided with a sea letter signed by George Washington, then President, which ran as follows:

"To all Emperors, Kings, Sovereign princes, State and Regents and to their respective officers, civil and military and to all others whom it may concern.

"I, George Washington, President of the United States of America do make known that Robert Gray, Captain of a ship called the Columbia of the burden of about 230 tons, is a citizen of the United States and that the said ship which he commands belongs to the citizens of the United States; and as I wish that the said Robert Gray may prosper in his lawful affairs, I do request all the before mentioned, and of each of them separately, when the said Robert Gray shall arrive with his vessel and cargo, that they will be pleased to receive him with kindness and treat him in a becoming manner &c. and thereby I shall consider myself obliged.

"September 16, 1790—New York City
  (Seal U. S.)
              "Geo. Washington,
                          President.
"Thomas Jefferson,
    "*Secy of State.*"

He further was provided with a similar letter from John Hancock, the Governor of Massachusetts.

His letter of instructions from the owners, signed by Joseph Barrell, enjoins, in similar and even stronger terms than those given Kendrick three years before, friendly treatment, strict honesty, honorable conduct, and the avoidance of unjust advantage in trade with the natives, the shunning of Spanish ports, tender treatment of his crew, urgency of despatch in reaching the northwest coast, and the refraining from all unnecessary connections with foreigners or Americans. It further speaks of Gray's rising reputation, and expresses the belief that a regard for his own honor, and a respect for the sea letter with which the President had honored and in-

On the Shores of the Pacific.

dulged him, would cause Gray to doubly exert himself for the success of the voyage.

Gray used such despatch and was so fortunate that he reached Cape Flattery, at the mouth of the Straits of Fuca, June 5, 1791, his voyage of eight months having been devoid of any occurrence worthy of note. Proceeding northward to Queen Charlotte Island for trade, he there fell in with Ingraham, formerly mate of the Columbia, but now, July 23, 1791, in command of the Hope. The autumn was spent in trading and exploring among the islands and along the coast to the east and north of Queen Charlotte Island. During one trip Gray penetrated an inlet near 55° N. latitude, probably the northern extension of Vancouver Strait, to a distance of one hundred miles to the northeastward without reaching the end of the passage, which he supposed to be the Rio de Reyes of Admiral Fonte. Gray's visit was most unfortunate, for a portion of his crew landing at a port on the mainland in 55° N., on August 22d, a large band of savages fell on the party and killed Joshua Caswell, his second mate, and seamen Joseph Barns and Job Folgier. This fatal spot was therefore named Massacre Cove.

The attitude of the Indians was a matter of constant anxiety, so that Gray and his crew were obliged to exercise the greatest caution in all their intercourse with such tribes as they fell in with. In Pintard Sound, 51° 30′ N., near the entrance, an attack was attempted on the Columbia, which obliged Gray to fire on the Indians, whereby two of the chiefs were killed, but it did not excite lasting resentment, as these savages traded with him later as though nothing had happened.

Returning to Clyoquot, Port Cox, Vancouver Island, with the Columbia, Gray went into winter quarters. The owners had sent out the frames for a sloop of about thirty tons, with three carpenters to build the vessel. A fortified habitation, called Fort Defiance, was constructed for occupancy by the working party, which finished and launched the sloop that winter, christening her as the Adventurer.

In the spring of 1792, while the crews of the Columbia and Adventurer were preparing for sea they were visited by many Indians, who, through their chiefs, established such relations with a Sandwich Islander, who was one of the crew of the 'Columbia, as to excite Gray's suspicions. The Islander on being closely questioned by Gray confessed that the Indians had formed a plan to murder the whole party and seize the vessels, the Hawaiian to aid them by wetting the priming of all the guns, and in return be made a chief among the Indians. Gray took immediate steps to keep his crew on their guard during their remaining stay, and thus completely baffled the design of the savages without bloodshed.

In April, 1792, Gray, sending the Adventurer northward under command of Haswell, his first mate, turned himself southward, and on the 29th fell in with Vancouver, who was approaching the northwest coast on a voyage of exploration in the English ship Discovery, with the Rambler under Broughton as a consort.

Vancouver eagerly sought information from Gray as to his knowledge of the coast, which the American gave fully and cheerfully. Gray set forth his voyages in the Straits of Fuca, around Queen Charlotte Island, and further, that in 1788 he had "been off the mouth of a river, in the latitude of 46° 10', where the outset or reflux was so strong as to prevent his entering for nine days." This latter information was most surprising and distasteful to Vancouver, who, fitted out at great expense with two vessels for exploration alone, found the accuracy of his own observations of the coast, as recorded in his journal two days earlier, thrown in doubt by the statements of this American trader.

Vancouver had written before meeting Gray: " The several large rivers and capacious inlets that have been described as discharging their contents into the Pacific, between the fortieth and forty-eighth degrees of north latitude, were reduced to brooks insufficient for our vessels to navigate, or to bays inaccessible as harbors. Under the most fortunate and favorable circumstances of wind and weather, so minutely has this extensive coast been inspected, that the surf has been constantly seen to break on its shores from the mast-head." After hearing Gray's relation Vancouver wrote: " If any inlet should be found, it must be a very intricate one, and inaccessible to vessels of our burden. . . . I was thoroughly convinced, as were also most persons of observation on board, that we could not possibly have passed any safe navigable opening harbor or place of security for shipping on this coast." Later Broughton by Vancouver's orders entered and surveyed a part of the Columbia in the latter part of October, 1792, when very much to his surprise he found himself preceded by another American trader, Captain Baker, master of the brig Jenny, of Bristol, R. I. Vancouver's report of the Columbia is scarcely creditable to that great navigator, for he attempted to prove that the mouth of the Columbia is an inlet separate from the main river, and that Gray is consequently not entitled to the credit of discovering the main river, a misstatement that cannot stand either in light of Gray's journal or the hydrography of the river.

Doubtless Gray was sufficiently irritated by Vancouver's doubts and criticisms as to the existence and navigability of the unknown river, to cause him to again venture the dangers which had so nearly caused the loss of his vessel on his previous visit. Of it Wilkes wrote: "Mere description can give little idea of the terrors of the bar of the Columbia. All who have seen it have spoken of the wildness of the scene, the incessant war of the waters, representing it as one of the most fearful sights that can possibly meet the eye of the sailor."

Gray pursued the even tenor of his way to the southward, and within two weeks justified his previous statements by not only entering and navigating the Columbia, but also discovered a haven (Bulfinch or Gray Harbor) affording safe anchorage and shelter for small vessels.

The following extracts from the log-book of the ship Columbia give the account of Gray's discoveries in his own words:

"1792, May 7. 10 A.M. Being within six miles of the land, saw an entrance in land which had a very good appearance of an harbour. . . . At half-past three bore away and ran in N. E. by E. sounding from 4 to 5 fathoms, sandy bottom, and as we drew nearer in between the bars had from 10 to 12 fathoms. Having a very strong tide of ebb to stem, many canoes came alongside, and at 5 P.M. came to in 5 fathoms of water, sandy bottom, in a safe harbour well sheltered from the sea by long sand-bars and spits. Our latitude observed this day 46° 58′ N." This harbor, called Bulfinch by Gray, now properly bears the name of its discoverer.

"10 (May). Fresh breezes and pleasant weather. Many natives alongside, at noon all the canoes left. At 1 P.M. began to unmoor, took up the best bower anchor and hove short on the small anchor; at half-past four being high water hove up the anchor and came to sail and a beating down the harbour.

"11. At half-past 7 we were out clear of the bar and directed our course to the southward along shore. At 8 P.M. the entrance of Bulfinch harbour bore N, distant 4 miles, the S. one extreme of the land, bore SSE. ½ E.: the N. ditto, NNNW. Sent up the main top-gallant yard and

set all sail. At 4 (?) P.M. saw the entrance of our
desired port, bearing ESE., distance 6 leagues, in
steering sails and hauled our wind in shore. At
8 A. (P.?) M. being a little to the windward of the
entrance to the harbour, bore away and run in
ENE between the breakers having from 5 to 7
fathoms water. When we were over the bar *we
found this to be a large river of fresh water*, up
which we stood. Many canoes came alongside.
At 1 (11?) P.M. came to with the small bower in
10 fathoms, black and white sand; the entrance
between the bars bore WSW, distance 10 miles.
The north side of the river, a half mile distant
from the ship, the south side 2½ miles distance; a
village (Chinook) on the north side of the river,
W. by N., distance ¾ of a mile. Vast numbers
of natives came alongside. People employed in
pumping the salt water out of our water-casks in
order to fill with fresh water which the ship
floated in. So ends.

. . . .

"(May) 14. Sailed upwards of 13 or 15 miles,
when the channel was so very narrow that it was
almost impossible to keep it. . . . Ship took
ground, but she did not lay long before she came
off without any assistance.

. . . .

" The jolly-boat was sent to sound the channel
out but found it not navigable any farther up;
so, of course, we must have taken the wrong
channel.

. . . .

"15 (May). . . . In the afternoon Capt.

Gray and Mr. Hoskins in the jolly-boat went on shore to take a short view of the country. . . .
" 19 (May). . . . Capt. Gray gave this river the name of Columbia's river, and the north side of the entrance Cape Hancock, the south side of the entrance, Adams Point."

The day following (20th) Gray left the river, crossing the bar after several attempts, and sailed northward to rejoin the Adventurer.

Completing his cargo of furs, Gray again visited Canton, and by his former route returned to Boston. He married on the 4th of February, 1794, and died, while in command of a coasting vessel, in the summer of 1806, at Charleston, S. C., leaving a wife and four daughters.

On March 27, 1846, a committee of Congress considered a petition of Martha Gray, his widow, who applied for a pension for his services to the United States in war and as an explorer. The committee in question considered that the most suitable return for Gray's valuable services would be the grant of a township in Oregon, but as surveys had not yet been made it deferred such action as then inexpedient. It recommended, however, that Congress should pass a bill giving Mrs. Gray the sum of five hundred dollars per annum. In its report the committee said that Gray was the first discoverer of the country ; that such discovery conferred on the United States a title to the whole basin drained by the river, known then as Oregon Territory; that the hazard and labor of the journey were great, especially in the unsurveyed bar of the Columbia.

Americans did not confine their title to the valley of the Columbia to the mere right of discovery without occupation and use, but they proceeded to develop its capacities for trade and settlement. From the year 1797 American vessels regularly entered the Columbia and traded with its natives.

When in 1826 the rights of the United States in regard to Oregon were formulated and made the subject of consideration by plenipotentiaries on the parts of Great Britain and the United States, the claims of the latter were urged on three grounds, the most important or first being from their own proper right, which was founded on Gray's discovery of the Columbia River.

If Vancouver had discovered the Columbia prior to Gray, it is impossible to say what complications and results would have arisen in connection with the extension and development of the United States. It is therefore a source of endless gratification that Captain Robert Gray, by his courage, enterprise, and seamanship, in discovering and entering the Columbia, ultimately secured to the United States this fertile territory, almost twice as extensive in area as Great Britian.

With its six hundred and sixty thousand of inhabitants, its great cities, its enormous accumulations of wealth, the young empire added to the United States through Robert Gray is fast shaping into substance the golden visions of the enthusiastic Kendrick.

V.

CAPTAIN MERIWETHER LEWIS AND LIEUT. WILLIAM CLARK.

First Trans-Continental Explorers of the United States.

The burning genius and intense patriotism of Thomas Jefferson found their most brilliant setting in his draft of the most famous paper in the world, the Declaration of Independence. If Jefferson thus struck the keynote of freedom for America, he was not content with a free people restricted in their habitat to the eastern half of the continent, and in his ripest life gave no more conspicuous evidence of his foresight and statesmanship than in the inauguration of a policy which comprehended in its scope the exploration and settlement of the entire trans-Mississippi region. He not only urged and completed the purchase of Louisiana, but sought the extent of its natural resources, appreciated the undeveloped wealth of the great West, and drafted a scheme of land divisions and settlement which foreshadowed the beneficial homestead legislation of later years.

Jefferson was for years interested in the exploration of the western parts of North America, which were absolutely unknown save the coastline of the Pacific. In 1784, while in Paris, he met John Ledyard, who had made an unsuccessful effort to organize a company for the fur trade on the western coast of America. Ledyard, by Jefferson's advice and intercession, attempted to cross by land to Kamschatka, and thence to the west coast of America, and across country to the Missouri River. Ledyard's arrest in Siberia and expulsion from the country by the Russian Government ended this plan. In 1802 Jefferson initiated, through the American Philosophical Society, a subscription for the exploration of the western parts of North America, by ascending the Missouri River, crossing the Rocky Mountains, and descending the nearest river to the Pacific Ocean. Although only two persons were to go, Meriwether Lewis urgently sought the appointment, and with M. André Michaux the voyage was commenced; but his companion being recalled by the French minister at Washington, the journey was abandoned.

On January 18, 1803, Jefferson, then President, recommended in a confidential message to Congress modifications of the act regarding trade with Indians, and with the view of extending its provisions to the Indians on the Missouri, recommended the exploration of the Missouri River to its source, the crossing of the Rocky Mountains, and descent to the Pacific Ocean by the best water communication. Congress approved the plan and voted money for its accomplishment. Captain Meriwether Lewis, of the United States

Army, who had been for nearly two years private secretary to the President, renewed his solicitations for command, which was given him.

Jefferson showed his versatility in the instructions to Captain Lewis, which are a model of fulness and clearness. The route to be followed, natural products and possibilities—animal, vegetable, and mineral—climatic conditions, commercial routes, the soil and face of the country, were all dwelt on. The character, customs, disposition, territory occupied, tribal relations, means of subsistence, language, clothing, disease, moral attributes, laws, traditions, religion, intellectuality, extent and means of trade, war methods, with respect to the Indian tribes visited, were to be studied and reported. The topography of the country was to be accurately determined, astronomically and otherwise, and the maps and notes multiplied to avoid total loss. The goodwill of the chiefs was to be sought, peaceful methods pursued, and the inflexible opposition of any extensive force promising bloodshed was to be met by withdrawal and retreat. The country then being outside the limits of the United States, passports from the ministers of Great Britain, Spain, and France were furnished.

Meriwether Lewis was born August 17, 1774, near Charlottesville, Va., being the son of John Lewis and Miss Meriwether, and grand-nephew of Fielding Lewis, who married a sister of George Washington. Volunteering, at the age of twenty, in the militia called out by Washington to put down the Shay rising, he was made ensign of the Second Sub-Legion May 1, 1795, and appointed in First Infantry November, 1796, where he rose to be paymaster and captain in 1800. He was a considerate and efficient officer, an expert hunter, versed in natural history, familiar with Indian character and customs. Appreciating his deficiencies in certain branches of science important in this expeditionary duty, he at once sought instruction from competent professors.

Jefferson describes Lewis as follows: " Of courage undaunted, possessing a firmness and perseverance of purpose which nothing but impossibilities could divert from its direction, . . . honest, disinterested, liberal, of sound understanding and a fidelity to truth so scrupulous that whatever he should report would be as certain as seen ourselves." The management and success of the expedition, it may here be said, fully justified the selection by and encomiums of Jefferson.

Lewis, given his choice of associate, selected William Clark, who was appointed by Jefferson second lieutenant of artillery. Clark was a brother of George Rogers Clark, by whose valor and sagacity the Illinois or Northwest Territory was secured to the United States, and this connection made his selection for further extension of the country seem most fitting. Moreover young Clark had qualifications and experiences which strongly commended him to Lewis. Born in Virginia, August 1, 1770, William Clark had a thorough knowledge of the privations and conditions of frontier life. Skilful as a hunter, a keen observer, familiar with military life from four years of service as a lieutenant of infantry, and developed from his ill health, which caused him to leave the army in 1796, into a magnificent specimen of manhood, he proved so efficient a coadjutor that his name will ever be inseparably associated with that of Lewis.

Lewis left Washington July 5, 1803, his mission being enhanced in its importance by the formal cession of Louisiana to the United States by the treaty of Paris, April 30, 1803, which news reached him July 1st. The rendezvous was at St. Louis, which was reached via Pittsburgh and the Ohio, recruits being selected at various posts, while Lieutenant Clark joined at Louisville, though he was not commissioned in the army till the following March.

When the party reached St. Louis, in December, 1803, formal notice of the transfer of Louisiana had not reached the Spanish commandant, who would not permit their passage westward. They passed the winter in camp opposite the mouth of the Missouri, where they built a barge with sail-power and two smaller boats, with which they started up the Missouri River on May 14, 1804.

The expedition, commanded by Captain Lewis, with Lieutenant Clark as second, comprised thirty-four selected men, eleven being watermen, a negro servant, and a hunter, who was also an interpreter.

The valley of the lower Missouri was well known to the French Canadians, who, pushed westward by the irruption of English settlers in the Illinois region, sought isolation and freedom from foreign restraint in the country west of the Mississippi. St. Louis was their head-quarters, but the Missouri was their field of fortune. The village of St. Charles, with its single street, had about five hundred souls, who lived by hunting and trade with the Indians, agriculture being quite neglected; and an outpost of seven poverty-stricken families existed at La Charrette, the advance guard of civilization. But the typical French trader and trapper disdained the shelter of a roof and the restraint of communities. His adventurous spirit pushed his frail bark into the quiet waters of the upper Kansas, through the shallows of the Platte, under the overshading trees of the beautiful James, along the precipitous red-clay cliffs of the Big Sioux, and, in search of the beaver, even penetrated the winding narrows of the Cheyenne and Little Missouri. They did not even stop at transient visits, but, fascinated by the roving, aimless life of the savage, took up abode with him, shared his tepee and wanderings, adopted his customs, took his squaw to wife, until longings strange and uncontrollable drew them back in old age to the home and religion of their youth. One of these venturesome wanderers named Durion, who had lived twenty years among the Sioux, was picked up on the river and accompanied Lewis to the mouth of the James, as a much-needed interpreter.

The mouth of the Platte was passed on July 21st, and on the next day Lewis camped on the site of the present city of Council Bluffs, thus named by Lewis on account of his council with the Ottoes and Missouri Indians at this point. Here the first of a continuing series of presents was given to the grand chief: an American flag, a large medal, which was placed around his neck as a mark of consideration, paint, garters, cloth ornaments, a canister of powder, and the indispensable bottle of whiskey. The subordinate chiefs received inferior medals and presents according to their importance. These presents were made with much form and ceremony, wherein an important part were speeches setting forth the transfer of the territory to the United States, the benefits of peace, and the advantages of trade at the new post to be occupied by Americans.

Both Lewis and Clark had been accustomed to Indian life on the Eastern frontiers, but they found much that was strange and striking among the denizens of the great interior plains. Beyond the breech-cloth a loose buffalo robe usually kept the savage from nudity. The necklace of grizzly bear-claws, the ornaments of porcupine and feathers, the scalp-poles, the conical teepes covered with gayly-figured skins, the blue smoke up-curling from the open tent-top, the hoop-tambourine or half-drum, the queer whip-rattle of the hoofs of goats and deer, the bladder-rattle full of pebbles, the shaven heads of the men, the white-dressed buffalo robe with its jingling rows of porcupine quills and uncouth painted figures, emblematic of the brave's war-history, the hawk-feather or eagle-plume head-dress worked with porcupine quills, the polecat skin trailing from the young brave's moccasins, the deer-paunch tobacco-pouch, and a score of other novelties met their observing eyes. Among the Rickarees the octagonal earth-covered lodges, the picketed villages, the cultivated patches of corn, beans, and potatoes, the basket-like boats of interwoven boughs covered with a single buffalo skin, in which squaws paddled unconcernedly over high waves, were unknown phases of savage life.

Even the earth gave up its treasure, and they found the first of the famous petrifactions of the trans-Missouri region in the back-bone of a fish forty-five feet long, in a perfect state.

Game gradually grew plentiful as they ascended the river. Buffalo was not seen till the Big Sioux was reached, but later fifteen herds and three bands of elk were visible at one time, and near Mandan large flocks of goats were seen crossing from their summer grazing grounds to find west of the Missouri winter shelter in the hilly regions. As they passed the Indians drove large flocks of migrating goats into the river, where even boys killed the helpless animals by scores with sticks. Indeed, the Missouri then appears to have been a hunter's paradise, for there are mentioned among the regular game antelope, bear, beaver, buffalo, badger, deer, elk, goats, and porcupine. Three thousand antelope were seen at one time, and of this animal Lewis accurately remarks: "The antelope possesses most wonderful swiftness, the acuteness of their

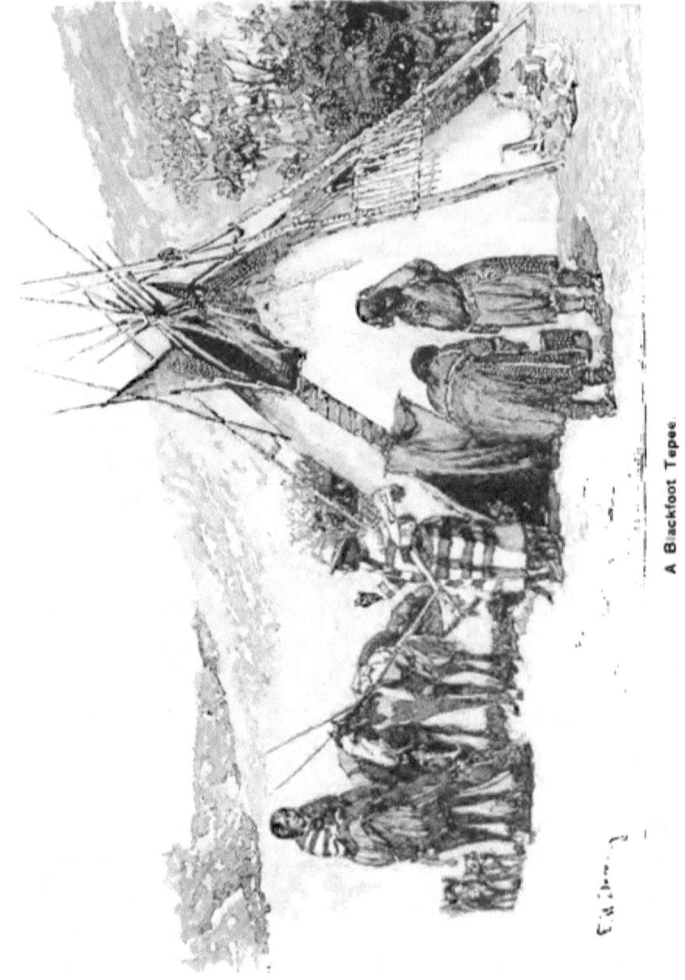

A Blackfoot Tepee.

sight distinguishes the most distant danger, the delicate sensibility of their smell defeats the precautions of concealment, and when alarmed their rapid career seems more like the flight of birds than the movements of an earthly being."

The river furnished abundant supply of cat and buffalo fish, and feathered game, such as plover, grouse, geese, turkeys, ducks, and pelican, also abounded; among the vegetable products are enumerated several kinds of grapes, currants and plums, wild apples, billberries, cherries, gooseberries, mulberries, raspberries, acorns, and hazel-nuts.

As regards the voyage thus far, it was true that the sail could rarely be used, that the labor of propelling the boats by oar or pole was most laborious, and that the shallows gave great trouble; but the Indians, save a single threatening occasion, were most friendly, and the only death, that of Sergeant Floyd, was from acute disease. Indeed, the journey had been most attractive and free from special hazard, and when rapidly advancing winter obliged them to go into permanent quarters, on October 27th, it seemed rather a long hunting excursion than a dangerous voyage of discovery.

Their winter quarters, called Fort Mandan, were on the eastern side of the Missouri, sixteen hundred miles from St. Louis, and in latitude 47° 22′ N., a short distance above the present city of Bismarck. The buildings were wooden huts, which joined and formed two sides of a triangle, while the third side was of pickets. As the huts opened inward, they had a stockaded place easy of defence.

On his arrival at Fort Mandan, Lewis found a Mr. McCracken, of the Hudson Bay Company, engaged in trading for horses and buffalo robes. During the winter ten or twelve different traders of this company visited Mandan, and although one bore a letter from the chief factor, Mr. Charles Chabouilles, offering any service in his power, yet it was evident to Lewis that these traders were cultivating sentiments unfriendly to Americans among the Indians, and Chaboneau, the interpreter was tampered with; but the prompt and judicious action of Lewis resulted in apologies and promises to refrain from such conduct in future. Laroche, one of the Hudson Bay traders, desired to go west with the expedition, but it was thought best to decline the offer. At this time the nearest English trading-post was at the forks of the Assiniboin, about one hundred and fifty miles distant by the way of Mouse River.

The stay at Fort Mandan was marked by two sad experiences for the Indians encamped near the post: an autumnal prairie fire which burned two Indians to death, and an attack of the Sioux, wherein one Mandan was killed and two wounded. A Frenchman, Jesseaume, living with the Indians, served as interpreter, and they learned much of the Mandans, Rickarees, and Minnetarees. The Rickarees appeared in a very sensible light by refusing spirits, with the remark that they did not use it, and were surprised that their father should present to them a liquor which would make them fools. The sensibilities of these Indians in their peculiar way appeared in a chief who cried bitterly at seeing a court-martial sentence of flogging carried out on a soldier. The chief acknowledged the necessity of exemplary punishment, and said that for the same offence he had killed his braves, but that he never whipped any one, not even children.

The Mandans, through intervention, made peace with the Rickarees, and restored traps and furs which they had taken from French hunters. During the entire winter these Indian tribes were most friendly, and their stores of corn, obtained by the expeditionary force by trade or purchase, were of material benefit to the party. The negro was a constant source of wonder to the crowds of Indians who visited them. The one-eyed great chief of the Minnetarees said that some foolish young men had told him there was a person quite black. When York, the negro, appeared, the one-eyed savage, much surprised, examined the negro closely, and spitting on a finger rubbed the skin in order to wash off the paint, and it was not until the negro showed his curly hair that the Indian could be persuaded he was not a painted white man.

Game, though at some distance, was abundant, and seventy head of large animals were obtained in a hunt of ten days. With regard to the Indians Lewis says: "A camp of Mandans caught within two days one hundred goats a short distance below us. Their mode of hunting them is to form a large strong pen or fold, from which a fence is made of bushes gradually widening on each side; the animals are surrounded by the hunters and gently driven toward this pen, in which they imperceptibly find themselves enclosed, and are then at the mercy of the hunters.

"When the Indians engage in killing buffalo, the hunters mount on horseback and, armed with bows and arrows, encircle the herd and gradually drive it into a plain or open place fit for the movement of horse; they then ride in among them, and singling out a buffalo, a female being preferred, go as close as possible and wound her with arrows till they think they have given the mortal stroke; when they pursue another till the quiver is exhausted. If, which rarely happens, the wounded buffalo attacks the hunter, he evades the blow by the agility of his horse, which is trained for the combat with great dexterity."

The winter proved to be of unusual severity, and several times the temperature fell to forty degrees below zero, and proof spirits froze into hard ice. The fortitude with which the hardy savages withstood such extreme cold, half naked as they often were, impressed our explorers.

Spring opened early, and on April 7, 1805, Fort Mandan was abandoned, one party of ten with the barge going down the river with despatches and specimens. Lewis and Clark with their party of thirty started up the Missouri in six canoes and two large open boats, which had been constructed by them. They had three interpreters—Drewyer, Chaboneau, and his wife.

Drewyer was a Canadian half-breed who had always lived in the woods, and while he had inherited from his mother the intuitive sagacity of the Indian in following the faintest trail, he had also acquired to a wonderful degree that knowledge of the shifts and expedients of camp life which is the resource and pride of the frontier huntsman. Chaboneau's life had been largely spent among the Blackfeet, by whom his wife, a Snake Indian, had been taken in war and enslaved when a young girl.

At the mouth of the Little Missouri the three French hunters, who had ventured to follow the party, stopped for trapping, as they found beaver very plentiful. Chaboneau Creek, the farthest point on the Missouri yet visited by white men, was passed, and on April 26th they arrived at the mouth of the Yellowstone. Lewis was here particularly pleased with the wide plains, interspersed with forests of various trees, and expressed his opinion that the situation was most suitable for a trading establishment.

Spring had now fairly opened, the trees were in leaf, a flower was seen, and despite the scanty verdure of the new grass, game was very abundant. In many places, however, the barren banks and sand-bars were covered with a white incrustation of alkali salts, looking like frost or newly fallen snow, which were present in such quantities that all the small tributaries of the Missouri proved to be bitter and unhealthy water. Signs of human life became rarer, but now and then they passed an old Indian camp, and near one saw the burial place of an Indian woman. The body, carefully wrapped in dressed buffalo robes, rested on a high scaffold, with two sleds and harness over it. Nearby lay the remains of a dog sacrificed to the shades of his dead mistress. In a bag were articles fitting for women—moccasins, red and blue paint, beavers' nails, scrapers for dressing hides, dried roots, a little Mandan tobacco, and several plaits of sweet-smelling grass.

The oar was plied unceasingly save when a favoring wind filled their sails and facilitated their progress. In early May they drew up their canoes for the night at the mouth of a bold, beautiful stream, and in the abundant timber found feeding on the young willows so many clumsy porcupines that they called it Porcupine River. Game was present in vast quantities; the elk were tame, and the male buffalo would scarcely quit grazing at the approach of man. As Lewis remarks: "It has become an amusement to supply the party with provisions."

On May 8th they dined at the mouth of a river flowing from a level, well-watered, and beautiful country. As the water had a peculiar whiteness they were induced to call it Milk River. The Missouri now turned to the southwest and south, the country became more open, and timber, of pine mostly, small and scanty.

Although the buffalo were so tame and harmless that the men drove them out of their way with sticks, yet the grizzly bear never failed to be a dangerous and vicious visitor. One day six good hunters attacked a grizzly, and four firing at forty paces, each lodged a ball in the body, two going through the lungs. The animal ran at them furiously, when the other hunters fired

Captain Meriwether Lewis.

two balls into him, breaking a shoulder. The bear yet pursued them, driving two into a canoe and the others into thickets, from which they fired as fast as they could reload. Turning on them, he drove two so closely that they dropped their guns and sprang from a precipice twenty feet high into the river followed by the bear, who finally succumbed to a shot through the head after eight balls had passed completely through his body. Another bear, shot through the heart, ran a quarter of a mile with undiminished speed before he fell dead.

On the 20th, twenty-two hundred and seventy miles from St. Louis, they came to the greenish-yellow waters of the Musselshell, and a short distance beyond Captain Lewis caught his first glimpse of the Rocky Mountains, the object of his hope and ambition. Beyond the Musselshell their experiences were less pleasant: the country became more barren, game and timber scarce, mosquitoes annoying; the high dry winds, full of sand, made their eyes sore; the sun of midday burned, while almost every night ice or frost chilled them.

The clear waters of the Judith River and its woods beautiful with multitudinous mountain roses, the fragrant honeysuckle, and the tiny red willows delighted their eyes; but the sight of a hundred and twenty-six lately abandoned lodge-fires caused some uneasiness, as indicating a late camping-place of a war-party of vicious northern Minnetarees or Blackfeet.

A few miles farther, as they passed a precipice a hundred and twenty feet high, they saw evidence of the cunning and wasteful methods of hunting by Indians, for the remains of over a hundred buffalo were scattered around, though the stream must have washed many away. Lewis adds: " These buffaloes had been chased down the precipice in a way very common on the Missouri, and by which vast herds are destroyed in a moment. The mode of hunting is to select one of the most active and fleet young men, who is disguised in a buffalo skin round his body. The skin of the head, with the ears and horns, are fastened on his own head in such a way as to deceive the buffalo. Thus dressed he fixes himself at a convenient distance between a herd of buffalo and any of the river precipices, which sometimes extend for several miles. His companions, in the meantime, get in the rear and side of the herd, and at a given signal show themselves and advance toward the buffalo. They instantly take the alarm, and finding the hunters beside them they run toward the disguised Indian or decoy, who leads them on at full speed toward the river, when suddenly securing himself in some crevice of the cliff, which he had previously fixed on, the herd is left on the brink of the precipice. It is then in vain for the foremost to retreat or even to stop; they are pressed on by the hindmost ranks, who, seeing no danger but from the hunters, goad on those before them till the whole are precipitated and the shore is strewed with their dead bodies. Sometimes in this perilous seduction the Indian himself is either trodden under foot or, missing his footing in the cliff, is urged down the precipice by the falling herd."

The river now took the form of frequent rapids, which made the work of dragging the heavy canoes very painful, and the narrative runs: " The banks are so slippery in some places, and the mud so adhesive, that the men are unable to wear moccasins. One-fourth of the time they are obliged to be up to their arm-pits in the cold water, and sometimes walk for yards over sharp fragments of rocks."

On June 3d they came to where the river divided into two large streams, and it became of vital importance to the expedition to determine which was the Missouri or Ahmateahza, as the Minnetarees called it, and which they said approached very near to the Columbia. The success of the expedition depended on the right decision, so Captain Lewis concluded to encamp until reconnoitering columns could examine the two forks.

Lewis following up the north branch, two days' march, decided that it was not the Missouri, and named it Maria's River. In returning he narrowly escaped slipping over a precipice some ninety feet high. Lewis had just reached a spot of safety when, says the narrative,

"He heard a voice behind him cry out, 'Good God, Captain, what shall I do?' He turned instantly and found it was Windsor, who had lost his foothold about the middle of the narrow pass and had slipped down to the very verge of the precipice, where he lay on his belly, with his right arm and leg over the precipice, while with the other leg and arm he was with difficulty holding on to keep himself from being dashed to pieces below. His dreadful situation was instantly perceived by Captain Lewis, who, stifling his alarm, calmly told him that he was in no danger, that he should take his knife out of his belt with the right hand and dig a hole in the side of the bluff to receive his foot. With great presence of mind he did this, and then raised himself on his knees. Captain Lewis then told him to take off his moccasins and come forward on his hands and knees, holding the knife in one hand and his rifle in the other. He immediately crawled in this way till he came to a secure spot."

One of Lieutenant Clark's party, on the south fork, at the same time, ran great danger from a grizzly bear which attacked near camp a man whose gun, being wet, would not go off. The man took to a tree, so closely followed by the animal that he struck the hunter's foot as he was climbing. The bear showed his intention of waiting until the man should be forced to descend, but fortunately alarmed by the cries and signal-shots of a searching-party decamped.

While Lewis and Clark concurred in believing the south fork to be the true Missouri, the rest of the party were unanimous in thinking the north the right course. Finally caching their heaviest boat and all the supplies which could well be spared, the entire party followed the south fork.

Lewis, pushing on confidently with four men, confirmed his opinion by reaching, on June 13th, the great falls of the Missouri, which by their sublime majesty and stupendous magnitude fascinated him. The description of these falls at the time of their first view by civilized man is worthy of reproduction. The river, three hundred yards wide, was shut in by precipitous cliffs, and "for ninety yards from the left cliff the water falls in one smooth sheet over a precipice of eighty feet. The rest of the river precipitates itself with a more rapid current, but received as it falls by the irregular and projecting rocks below, forms a splendid prospect of white foam two hundred yards in length. . . . This spray is dissipated in a thousand shapes. . . . As it rises from the fall it beats with fury against a ledge of rocks which extend across the river." On examination Lewis found that "the river for three miles below was one continued succession of rapids and cascades, overhung with perpendicular bluffs from one hundred and fifty to two hundred feet high; in short, it seems to have worn itself a channel through the solid rock." At the main falls, five miles above the first, " the whole Missouri is suddenly stopped by one shelving rock, which without a single niche and with an edge as straight and regular as if formed by art, stretches itself from one side of the river to the other for at least a quarter of a mile. Over this the river precipitates itself in an even, uninterrupted sheet to the perpendicular depth of fifty feet, whence, dashing against the rocky bottom, it rushes rapidly down, leaving behind it a spray of the purest foam across the river. The scene was singularly beautiful, without any of the wild irregular sublimity of the lower falls." In a cottonwood tree, on a small island in the middle of the rapids, an eagle had fixed its nest, a solitary bird which had not escaped the observation of the Indians, who had previously described it to Lewis.

On leaving the falls Lewis saw a herd of a

thousand buffalo, and killed one for supper. In his eagerness he failed to reload his rifle, when he beheld a grizzly bear stealing on him and not over twenty paces distant. "He felt that there was no safety but in flight. It was in the open, level plain, . . . so that there was no possible mode of concealment. . . . As soon as he turned the bear ran, open mouthed and at full speed, upon him. Captain Lewis ran about eighty yards, but finding that the animal gained on him fast . . . he turned short, plunged into the river about waist deep, and facing about presented the point of his spontoon. The bear arrived at the water's edge within twenty feet of him, but as soon as he put himself in this posture of defence, the animal seemed frightened and retreated with as much precipitation as he had pursued."

The means and route for portage presented difficult problems for the exhausted party, as it was clearly evident that the men could not carry the boats on their shoulders such great distances. Fortunately a creek was found at the foot of the falls, where the banks afforded easy access to the highlands. It was first necessary to cross the Missouri, and here the party went into camp while preparations were made for the portage.

Lieut. Clark with a few men carefully surveyed the trail to be followed, others engaged in hunting in order to lay up a store of dried meat, and the handy men of the party set to work on a carriage for the transport of the boats. By good fortune they found a large cottonwood-tree, about twenty-two inches in diameter, large enough to make the carriage-wheels, "perhaps the only tree of that size within twenty miles." As they had decided to cache a part of their stores and leave their largest boat behind, its mast supplied them with two axle-trees.

In the meantime the survey of Clark showed that the series of cataracts had an aggregate descent of three hundred and sixty-three feet in seventeen miles, and that a very difficult portage of thirteen miles was necessary. The country was barely practicable for travel, and was covered with frequent patches of prickly pear, against the tiny penetrating needles of which the moccasins of the dragging men afforded almost no protection. To add to their misfortunes, when about five miles from their destination the axle-trees, made of the old mast, broke, and then the tongues of green cottonwood gave way. After diligent search sweet-willow trees were found with which they managed, by shifts and expedients familiar to frontiersmen, to patch up the carriage so as to go on. It broke down so completely about a half mile from the new camp that it was easier to carry boat and baggage on their shoulders than to build a new conveyance. The condition of the party is evident from the narrative:

"The men are loaded as heavily as their strength will permit; the crossing is really painful; some are limping with the soreness of their feet, others are scarcely able to stand for more than a few minutes from the heat and fatigue; they are all obliged to halt and rest frequently, and at almost every stopping-place they fall, and many of them are asleep in an instant."

Later it was needful to repair the carriage and to travel over and over the portage until, after ten days of weary labor, all the equipage was above the falls.

In the meantime the hunters had accumulated nearly half a ton of dried meat, buffalo being plenty. The grizzly bear, however, was also present, active, aggressive, and dangerous as usual. They infested the camp at night, causing much alarm, and once carried off buffalo-meat from a pole within thirty yards of the men. A hunter sent out to bring in meat was boldly attacked by a bear and narrowly escaped death, being pursued to within forty paces of the camp. Another animal was killed when rushing up to attack men who had to climb a tree, while making sufficient noise to attract their rescuer, Drewyer, the interpreter and hunter, who shot him through the head. He proved to be the largest they had seen, being eight feet seven and a half inches long, while his fore feet measured nine inches and hind feet seven inches across, and eleven and three-quarters long exclusive of the talons. Another hunter was attacked by a grizzly, fortunately near the river, so that he was able to conceal himself under a steep bank; otherwise he would probably have lost his life.

The perils of navigation and the chase were not all, for a cloud-burst and hail-storm contributed to their danger and suffering. The hail was so large and driven so furiously by the high wind that it knocked down several of the men, one three times, bruising another very badly and wounding some so that they bled freely. The fallen hail lay in drifts, which in places completely covered the ground, and some of the stones weighed three ounces and measured seven inches in circumference. Clark, Chaboneau and his wife took shelter under shelving rocks in a deep ravine, congratulating themselves on their protected position. Suddenly, however, the rain fell in a solid mass, and instantly collecting in the ravine, came rolling down in a dreadful torrent, carrying rocks and everything before it.

"But for Lieut. Clark, Chaboneau, his wife and child would have been lost. So instantly was the rise of the water, that as Lieut. Clark had reached his gun and began to ascend the bank, the water was up to his waist, and he could scarce get up faster than it rose, till it reached the height of fifteen feet, with a furious current which, had they waited a moment longer, would have swept them into the river just above the Great Falls, down which they must have inevitably been precipitated."

Though the phases of their daily life brought much that was rough and hard, yet their privations were not unmixed with pleasures, rude though they may seem to the city dweller. Long tramps and exciting rides after game, side marches to commanding hill-tops for grateful views of an unknown country—barren to the eye, perhaps, but grateful to the soul, for were they not the first men of their race who ever looked upon it?—or pleasant journeys through upland forests or the undergrowth of the intervale, to search and gather whatever was beautiful to the eye, novel to the mind, or a welcome addition to their scanty larder; such were their rare pleasures.

Now they waded through waist-high patches of wild rye, recalling with its fine soft beard the waving fields of grain they had left in the far East; again they pushed on in dense copses of the sinuous redwood, whose delicate inner bark furnished pleasant Indian tobacco to the Frenchman and half-breed. Sometimes the trail lay through an open wood with smaller undergrowth, where beds of odorous mint recalled his Virginian home to Lewis; where the delicate mountain-rose, in countless thousands, was born to blush unseen; where, if only one ripened berry to-day invited the hunter, other kinds promised their welcome fruit in due but later season.

Rarely did the dull gray of the sky dim the glory of a whole day, and the short summer showers, freshening the beauty of the landscape and abating the fervid heat of mid-summer, seemed only too infrequent. And above all, the pure, free, upland air, that gives vigor and health to the body, joy and lightness to the heart, almost annihilates distance to the eye; and in breathing which, one drinks into the lungs the very wine of life. Surely more than the heroes of Virgil's song did they feel that sweet in their memory would abide these days forever.

Of the mountains, now always in sight, and a constant source of inspiration to the eager explorers, those to the north and northwest were yet snow-capped, and Lewis says: "They glisten with great beauty when the sun shines on them in a particular direction, and most probably from this glittering appearance have derived the name of the Shining Mountains."

During his explorations of the country around the falls Captain Lewis visited a remarkable and beautiful spring, near the present city of Great Falls, Montana. Of it he writes:

" The fountain, which perhaps is the largest in America, is situated in a pleasant level plain, about twenty-five yards from the river, into which it falls over some steep irregular rocks, with a sudden descent of about six feet in one part of its course. The water boils up from among the rocks with such force near the centre, that the surface seems higher than the earth on the sides of the fountain, which is a handsome turf of fine green grass."

While the main party was making the portage, a detachment was "occupied in fitting up a boat of skins, the iron frame of which, thirty-six feet long, had been prepared for the purpose at Harper's Ferry. The iron frame is to be covered with skins, and requires thin-shaved strips of wood for lining. The skins necessary to cover it have already been prepared—twenty-eight elk and four buffalo skins." This experimental boat proved to be a total failure, and it was not till Lewis's long journey was nearly over that he copied the skin boat of the Indian squaws, which had excited his surprise, and found that the methods of the locality could be followed with advantage in navigation as well as otherwise.

As the six canoes were insufficient to carry

all their men and supplies. Clark was sent ahead
to find suitable wood for two more, there being
no fit trees below the falls. With much difficulty
trees were found, and two canoes, three feet wide

Lieutenant William Clark.

and twenty-five and thirty-three feet long respectively, were fashioned. Near here a deserted Indian lodge or council house was seen.
It was two hundred and sixteen feet in circumference, made of sixteen cottonwood poles, fifty
feet long, converging toward the centre, where

they were united and secured by large withes of sinewy willow.

Although the swivel and some other articles had been cached at the head of the falls, their loads were yet very heavy, and all walked except those engaged in working the canoe. The windings of the river became very tortuous, and frequent rapids made their progress correspondingly slow and laborious.

Game was less plentiful, and, as it was necessary to save the dried and concentrated food for the crossing of the mountains, it became somewhat of a task to provide food for a party of thirty-two which consumed a quantity of meat daily equal to an elk and deer, four deer or one buffalo. Fortunately, the berries were now ripening, and, as they grew in great quantities, proved a not inconsiderable contribution to their food-supply. Of currants there were red, purple, yellow, and black, all pleasant to the taste; the yellow being thought superior to any other known variety. The purple service-berry and pinkish gooseberry were also favorites. Besides, they made use of the very abundant and almost omnipresent sunflower. Of it Lewis says: "The Indians of the Missouri, more especially those who do not cultivate maize, make great use of the seed of this plant for bread or in thickening their soup. They first parch and then pound it between two stones until it is reduced to a fine meal. Sometimes they add a portion of water, and drink it thus diluted; at other times they add a sufficient proportion of marrow grease to reduce it to the consistency of common dough and eat it in that manner. This last composition we preferred to all the rest, and thought it at that time a very palatable dish."

The Missouri now took in general a southerly course, and on July 18th they reached a bold clear stream, which was named Dearborn River for the then Secretary of War. They had intended to send back a small party in canoes with despatches, but as they had not met the Snake Indians, and so were uncertain as to their friendliness, it was thought best not to weaken their already small party for hostilities. Lewis decided, however, to send Clark, with three men, in advance to open up communication with these Indians and, if possible, to negotiate for horses. Clark's journey was a failure, for the Indians, alarmed at the firing of a gun, fled into the mountains.

The mountains now closed in on the explorers and they camped one night at a place named the Gates of the Rocky Mountains. "For five and three-quarter miles these rocks rise perpendicularly from the water's edge to the height of nearly twelve hundred feet. They are composed of black granite near the base, but . . . we suppose the upper part to be flint of a yellowish brown and cream color. Nothing can be imagined more tremendous than the frowning blackness of these rocks, which project over the river and threaten us with destruction . . . For the first three miles there is not a spot, except one of a few yards, in which a man could stand between the water and the towering perpendicular of the mountains."

On July 25th Clark, who was in advance, reached the three forks of the Missouri, where he had to camp, his party worn out, their feet full of prickly pear needles and Chaboneau unable to go farther. The forks were all clear pebbly streams, discharging large amounts of water. The southeast fork was named Gallatin, the middle Madison, and the southwest Jefferson, the latter two, of equal size, being larger branches than the Gallatin.

At the three forks Sacajawea, the wife of Chaboneau, was encamped five years before, when the Minnetarees of Knife River attacked the Snakes, killed about a dozen and made prisoners of her and others of her tribe. Strangely enough Chaboneau nearly lost his life crossing the Madison, where Clark saved him from drowning. Lewis was struck with the seeming indifference of the Snake woman on her return to the spot and her own country.

The party followed Jefferson River, their journey being marked by the killing of a panther seven and a half feet long, and the overturning of a canoe, injuring one of the party, Whitehouse, losing some articles, and wetting others, but the all-important powder was so well packed that it remained dry.

"Persuaded," says the narrative, "of the necessity of securing horses to cross the mountains, it was determined that one of us should proceed . . . till he found the Shoshones, . . . who could

assist us in transporting our baggage." Captain
Lewis with three men preceded, and on August 11,
saw " with the greatest delight a man on horseback, at the distance of two miles, coming down
the plain toward them. On examining him with
the glass, Captain Lewis saw that he was armed
with a bow and a quiver of arrows; mounted on an
elegant horse without a saddle, and a small string
attached to the under jaw answered as a bridle.
Convinced that he was a Shoshonee, and knowing
how much of our success depended on the friendly
offices of that nation, Captain Lewis was full of
anxiety to approach without alarming him, and
endeavor to convince him that he was a white
man. He therefore proceeded on towards the
Indian at his usual pace; when they were within
a mile of each other the Indian suddenly stopped,
Captain Lewis immediately followed his example,
took his blanket from his knapsack, and holding
it with both hands at the four corners, threw it
above his head and unfolded it as he brought
it to the ground, as if in the act of spreading it.
This signal, which originates in the act of spreading a robe or skin as a seat for guests to whom
they wish to show a distinguished kindness, is
the universal sign of friendship among the Indians
on the Missouri and Rocky Mountains." Unfortunately, the brave took alarm at the movement of Lewis's companions and fled. The next
day brought them to the head-waters of the Jefferson. Here, "from the foot of one of the lowest
of these mountains, which rises with a gentle ascent for about half a mile, issues the remotest

water of the Missouri. They had now reached the hidden sources of that river, which had never yet been seen by civilized man; and as they quenched their thirst at the chaste and icy fountain—as they sat down by the brink of that little rivulet, which yielded its distant and modest tribute to the parent ocean, they felt themselves rewarded for all their labors and all their difficulties."

Pushing on they soon saw, to the west, high, snow-topped mountains.

" The ridge on which they stood formed the dividing line between the waters of the Atlantic and Pacific Oceans. They followed a descent much steeper than that on the eastern side, and at the distance of three quarters of a mile reached a handsome, bold creek of cold, clear water running to the westward. They stopped to taste for the first time the waters of the Columbia, and, after a few minutes, followed the road across steep hills and low hollows, till they reached a spring on the side of a mountain. Here they found a sufficient quantity of dry willow brush for fuel, and therefore halted for the night, and, having killed nothing in the course of the day, supped on their last piece of pork, and trusted to fortune for some other food to mix with a little flour and parched meal, which was all that now remained of their provisions."

In the early morn of August 13, Lewis hastened impatiently forward without food, and after a few hours of travel saw three Indians; but they fled. A little later he surprised three women, and succeeded in reaching two, who covered their heads and awaited in silence their expected death. Showing them that he was a white man, and giving them trinkets, they were reassured and recalled their comrade, when he painted their cheeks with vermilion, a Shoshone custom emblematic of peace.

The women pointed out the direction of camp, and Lewis, marching on, soon saw a band of sixty well-mounted Indian warriors riding full speed toward him and his two companions. With perfect composure and undaunted courage Lewis laid down his rifle, and alone marched forward to parley with this horde of unknown savages, relying on the integrity and uprightness of his mission. Received with the greatest cordiality, Lewis at once smoked a pipe of peace with them, and after giving them some blue beads and vermilion went to their camp.

On arrival he was inducted into a council lodge and seated on a robe, when a fire was kindled. " The chief then produced his pipe and tobacco, the warriors pulled off their moccasins, and our party were requested to take off their own. This being done, the chief lighted his pipe at the fire within the magic circle, and then retreating from it, began a speech several minutes long, at the end of which he pointed the stem toward the four cardinal points of the heavens, beginning with the east and concluding with the north."

By this time the day was well spent, and no food of any kind had passed the lips of Lewis and his men since the previous day. On learning this the chief told him that they only had cakes made of sun-dried service- and chokeberries, which served as a hearty meal to the hungry men. Later an Indian gave Lewis a piece of antelope and a bit of salmon, which satisfied him that he was now on the waters of the Columbia.

The next day they had an experience of the Indian mode of hunting, which is thus described: "The chief game of the Shoshonees is the antelope, which, when pursued, retreats to the open plains, where the horses have full room for the chase. But such is its extraordinary fleetness and wind, that a single horse has no chance of outrunning it or tiring it down, and the hunters are therefore obliged to resort to stratagem. About twenty Indians, mounted on fine horses and armed with bows and arrows, left camp. In a short time they descried a herd of antelopes; they immediately separated into little squads of two or three, and formed a scattered circle round the herd for five or six miles, keeping at a wary distance, so as not to alarm them till they were perfectly enclosed, and usually selecting some commanding eminence as a stand. Having gained their positions, a small party rode toward the herd, and with wonderful dexterity the huntsman preserved his seat, and the horse his footing, as he ran at full speed over the hills and down the steep ravines and along the borders of the precipices. They were soon outstripped by the antelopes, which, on gaining the other extremity of the circle, were driven

back and pursued by the fresh hunters. They
turned and flew, rather than ran, in another
direction; but there, too, they found new enemies. In this way they were alternately pursued backward and forward, till at length, notwithstanding the skill of the hunters, they all
escaped; and the party, after running for two
hours, returned without having caught anything,
and their horses foaming with sweat. This chase,
the greater part of which was seen from the camp,
formed a beautiful scene; but to the hunters
is exceedingly laborious, and so unproductive,
even when they are able to worry the animal
down and shoot him, that forty or fifty hunters will sometimes be engaged for half a day
without obtaining more than two or three antelopes."

Captain Lewis succeeded with great difficulty
in persuading the band of Shoshones to pass
over the divide in order to assist in bringing
his impedimenta across. The presence of a
Shoshone woman, the monstrosity of a man entirely black, favorable barter for their horses
were urged; in short he played on their avarice,
curiosity, tribal pride, and by questioning their
courage succeeded in stimulating them to make
the journey.

It transpired that Cameahwait, the Shoshone
chief, was the brother of Sacajawea, and one of
the Shoshone women, now in camp, had been
for some time prisoner with her in the hands of
the Minnetarees. The meeting of these Indians
after long separation disclosed such emotion as

Castle Rock, on the Columbia River.

proved their tender feelings and genuine interest in each other.

A long and tedious council was held, with the usual smoke and speeches. Lewis set forth in lively terms the strength of the government, the advantages of trade, and the importance of hastening the day of fire-arms and supplies by facilitating the journey. Meanwhile they were amused, as the Indian must be, by the queer negro, the sagacious and well-trained dog, the rifles, the air-gun, clothing, canoes, etc. All game brought in was divided; the Indians feasted on hulled corn, and presents were liberally distributed.

The good-will of the Shoshones was finally secured, and four horses purchased by barter; so that Lewis was to send Clark ahead to reconnoitre the route along the Columbia, and build canoes if possible, which the Indians declared to be impracticable, as timber was wanting, and the river and mountains impassable. They said that for seven days the route lay over steep, rocky mountains, with no game and only roots for food; then for ten days an arid sandy desert, where men and horses would perish for want of food and water. On inquiry, Clark learned that Nez Percés came from the west by a very bad road towards the north, where they suffered excessively from hunger and travel. Believing that difficulties surmountable to Indians with women and children could not be formidable, Clark pushed on with a guide, but soon found that the Indian accounts had not been exaggerated, as he fell in with the points of four mountains, which were rocky, and so high that it seemed almost impossible to cross them with horses. The road lay over sharp fragments of broken rock which had fallen from the mountains and were strewed in heaps for miles together.

Occasionally he met small parties of Indians, who, in wretched plight themselves, yet acted most generously, giving him, as he says, willingly what little they possessed, which was usually a few dried berries and a bit of salmon, never enough to entirely appease the hunger of his famished men. Clark says:

"Our men, who are used to hardships, but have been accustomed to have the first wants of nature regularly supplied, feel very sensibly their wretched situation; their strength is wasting away; they begin to express an apprehension of being without food in a country perfectly destitute of any means of supporting life, except a few fish."

Clark's explorations showed that it was impossible to follow the river, to which he gave the name of Lewis, as he was the first white man to visit its waters, either by canoe or along its banks on horses. The mountains were one barren surface of broken masses of rock which crowded into the river, where the stream presented either continuous rapids or series of shoals.

Meanwhile, Lewis moved his necessary baggage to the Shoshone village, previously caching his surplus baggage and sinking his canoes for safety. As a rule the Indians were most friendly, but during a hunting expedition a young brave snatched up his rifle and made off with it. Drewyer pursued him ten miles, and overtaking the women of the party, watched his opportunity, and seeing the Indian off his guard, galloped up to him and seized his rifle. The Indian struggled for some time, but finding Drewyer getting too strong for him, had the presence of mind to open the pan and let the priming fall out; he then let go his hold, and giving his horse the whip, escaped at full speed, leaving the women at the mercy of the conqueror.

Considerable time was spent in making needful preparations for crossing the mountains and in negotiating for horses, of which they obtained twenty-nine—young, vigorous animals, though in poor flesh and with sore backs.

This necessary delay gave Lewis ample opportunity to observe the habits and modes of life of the Shoshones, which are especially interesting as the record of an Indian tribe before it had come in contact with the white men. The Shoshones, or Snakes, who here number four hundred souls, lived a migratory, wretched existence, seeking at one season the salmon of Lewis River, at another the buffalo of the upper Missouri, and again in the mountains barely maintaining life on roots. They were, however, gay, frank, fair-dealing, honest, fond of ornaments, amusements, and games of chance, kind and obliging, and somewhat given to boasting of their warlike exploits. The narrative continues: "The mass of females are condemned, as among all savage nations, to the lowest and most laborious drudgery. When the tribe is stationary they collect the roots and cook; they build the huts, dress the skins, and make clothing, collect the wood, and assist in taking care of the horses on the route; they load the horses, and have charge of all the baggage. The only business of the man is to fight: he therefore takes on himself the care of his horse, the companion of his warfare, but he will descend to no other labor than to hunt and to fish."

Their inferior arms put them at the mercy of the Minnetarees of Knife River, who mercilessly stole their horses and killed their braves. They seemed an adventurous and courageous people, and Cameahwait's vehement declaration that, with guns, they would never fear to meet their enemies, did not seem boastful.

Their common arms are bow and arrow, shield, lance, and a weapon called by the Chippeways, by whom it was formerly used, the poggamoggon.

Their method of producing fire was by an arrow and a dry prepared stick, which, being rubbed together vigorously and dexterously for a few minutes, first creates a fine dust, then bursts speedily into flame.

The great wealth of the tribe consists in large numbers of small, wiry, and hardy horses, capable of great endurance, sure footed and fleet. They were second in value to the women alone, who carried the baggage when horses failed.

The Shoshones were well dressed, with shirts, leggings, and moccasins of dressed deer, antelope, etc., skins. A robe with the hair on served as a cloak or as a bed-covering; the shirts were ornamented with porcupine quills of different colors and sometimes by beads, also the moccasins. Elaborate tippets of elegant pattern were also worn, made of otter and fringed with many ermine skins; also collars of various kinds of sea-shells, of the sweet-scented grass, of tusks of the elk, and of the claws of the grizzly bear.

"The names of the Indians vary in the course of their life. Originally given in childhood from the mere necessity of distinguishing objects, or from some accidental resemblance to external objects, the young warrior is impatient to change it by something of his own achievement. Any important event, the stealing of a horse, the scalping of an enemy, or killing a brown bear, entitles him at once to a new name, which he then selects for himself, and it is confirmed by the nation."

Everything ready, Lewis started on August 27, 1805, with twenty-nine pack-horses, to follow Berry Creek and pass over the mountains to Indian establishments on another branch of the Columbia. In many places a road had to be cut, and even then was barely practicable. Sure footed as is the Indian pony, yet all of the horses were very much injured in passing over the steep rocky ridges. The way was so rough that the horses fell repeatedly down the hillsides, often capsizing with their load, and occasionally one was crippled and disabled. The journey was made yet more disagreeable by a fall of snow and by severe freezing weather, but the spirit of the party is shown by the mention of a "serious misfortune, the last of our thermometers being broken." On September 6th, however, they were safely beyond the mountain in a wide valley at the head of Clark's Fork of the Columbia, where they met about four hundred Ootlashoots, who received them kindly and gave to them of their only food, berries and roots. Following the river they reached Travellers' Rest Creek, where they stopped for hunting, as they were told the country before them had no game for a great distance. Game proved to be so scanty that they moved onward, crossing to the Kooskooskee, where, being without animal food, they killed a colt for supper. Snow fell again, which would not have been so uncomfortable had not their road fallen along steep hillsides, obstructed with dead timber where not covered with living trees, from which the snow fell on them as they passed, keeping them continually wet while the weather was freezing. The road continued difficult. Game was wanting, and as they marched they killed one after another of their colts for food. Their horses were becoming rapidly disabled; the allowance of food scarcely sufficed to check their hunger; while the extreme bodily fatigue of the march, and the dreary prospects before them, began to dispirit the men.

Lewis, appreciating the gravity of the situation, sent Clark ahead, with six hunters, who the next day was fortunate enough to kill a horse, on which his party breakfasted and left the rest for the main expedition. The country continued rugged, and in some places the only road was a narrow rocky path at the edge of very high precipices. One of their horses, slipping, rolled a hundred feet, over and over, down a nearly perpendicular hill strewed with large rocks. All expected he was killed, but he proved to be little injured. Their enforced fasting visibly affected the health of the party; all lost flesh, grew weak, and were troubled with skin eruptions, while several were more seriously ill.

On September 20th, Clark reached a village of the Chopunish or Nez Percés, in a beautiful level valley, where he was kindly received and well fed. Fish, roots, and berries were also obtained, which, sent to Lewis, reached him eight miles out of the village at a time when his party had been without food for more than a day. When the village was reached, the party was in a deplorable condition through long fasting and the exhausting fatigue of the march.

Purchasing from the Indians as much provisions as their weakened horses could carry, they moved on to the forks of the Snake, where the party slowly recruited its health and strength. They killed a horse for the sick, while the party in general lived on dried fish and roots, the latter causing violent pains in the stomach. Five canoes were made, and as the men were weak they adopted the Indian method of burning them out. The twelfth day saw their canoes finished and loaded for the final journey, which was to lead them to the sea. Lewis cached his saddles, the extra powder and ball, and branding his remaining horses, delivered them to three Indians, the principal named Twisted-hair, who agreed to take good care of them till the return of the party, when additional presents were to be given for this service.

Their troubles now seemed to be over and they were congratulating themselves on their safe progress, when they struck a series of fifteen rapids. When passing the last Sergeant Gass's "canoe struck, and a hole being made in her side she immediately filled and sank. Several men who could not swim clung to the boat until one of our canoes could be unloaded, and with the assistance of an Indian boat they were all brought ashore. All the goods were so much wetted that we were obliged to halt for the night and spread them out to dry. While all this was exhibited, it was necessary to place two sentinels over the merchandise, for we found that the Indians, though kind and disposed to give us aid during our distress, could not resist the temptation of pilfering small articles." The Snake River was in general very beautiful, but it was filled with rapids, most of them difficult, and one strewed with rocks, most hazardous.

Food failing, except fish and roots, they concluded, probably at the suggestion of their Frenchmen, to change their diet, and being again reduced to fish and roots, made an experiment to vary their food by purchasing a few dogs, and after having been accustomed to horseflesh, felt no disrelish to this new dish. The Chopunish have great numbers of dogs, which they employ for domestic purposes but never eat, and the practice of using the flesh of that animal soon brought the explorers into ridicule as dog-eaters. "Fortunately, however," says Clark, "the habit of using this animal has completely overcome the repugnance which we felt at first, and the dog, if not a favorite dish, is always an acceptable one." Elsewhere he adds, "having been so long accustomed to live on the flesh of dogs, the greater part of us had acquired a fondness for it, and our original aversion for it is overcome by reflecting that on that food we were stronger and in better health than at any period since leaving the buffalo country."

They were now in Lewis River, a broad greenish-blue stream filled with islands and dangerous rapids, which were passed in canoes, except one near the mouth, where a land portage of a mile was necessary. This brought them to the junction of the Lewis and Columbia Rivers on October 17th, where they parted from the Nez Percés. These Indians lead a painful, laborious life, brightened by but few amusements; are healthy, comely, and generally well dressed; given to ornaments of beads, sea-shells, feathers, and paints. In winter they collect roots and hunt the deer on snow-shoes, toward spring cross the mountains to buy buffalo robes, and in summer and autumn catch salmon, usually by weirs at the rapids, in the following manner: "About the centre of each was placed a basket formed of willows, eighteen or twenty feet in length, of a cylindrical form and terminating in a conic shape at its lower extremity. This was situated with its mouth upward opposite to an aperture in the weir. The main channel of the water was conducted to this weir, and as the fish entered it they were so entangled with each other that they could not move, and were taken out by untying the small end of the willow basket."

Here Lewis began to lay in stores, and, fish being out of season, purchased forty dogs, which for weeks had proved to be the best food available. On October 20th they again launched their canoes in the Columbia, and pushed on through the frequent rapids, looking forward with interest not unmixed with anxiety to the great falls of which the Indians told them. Arrived at the head of the rapids, they made a portage of nearly a mile, availing themselves of the assistance and guidance of the Indians. Owing to the great labor of portages they kept to the river when possible, and " reached a pitch of the river, which, being divided by two large rocks, descended with great rapidity down a fall eight feet in height. As the boats could not be navigated down this steep descent, we were obliged to land and let them down as slowly as possible by strong ropes of elk-skin." They all passed in safety except one, which, being loosed by the breaking of the rope, was driven down, but was recovered by the Indians below.

Finally they came to an extremely dangerous place where a tremendous rock projected into the river, leaving a channel of only forty-five yards, through which the Columbia passed, its waters thrown into whirlpools and great waves of the wildest and most dangerous character. As the portage of boats over this high rock was impossible in their situation, Lewis resolved on a passage in boats, relying on dexterous steering, which carried them through safely, much to the astonishment of the Indians gathered to watch them. Another rapid was so bad that all papers, guns, ammunition, and such men as could not swim made a land portage, while Lewis and Clark took the canoes through safely, two at a time. The 25th brought them to the most dangerous part of the narrows, which they concluded to hazard by canoe after using precautions as to valuable articles and men. The first three canoes escaped very well, the fourth nearly filled, the fifth passed through with only a small quantity of water.

On the 28th Lewis was very much gratified by seeing an Indian with a round hat and sailor's jacket, which had come up the river by traffic; and as he went on similar articles became common. They passed a number of different tribes who behaved in a friendly manner, and among others the Eneeshur, at the great falls, interested them by their cooking utensils, which were baskets so skilfully made of bark and grass as to serve as vessels for boiling their provisions. Some of the party were horrified, however, by " the chief, who directed his wife to hand him his medicine bag, from which he brought out fourteen fore-fingers, which he told us had once belonged to the same number of his enemies whom he had killed in fighting."

On the 31st they came to the lower falls, where the river narrowed to one hundred and fifty yards and fell twenty feet in a distance of four hundred yards, while below was another exceedingly bad rapid. The upper rapid was so filled with rocks that Crusatte, the principal waterman, thought it impracticable, so a portage of four miles was made over the route followed by the Indians. "After their example, we carried our small canoe and all the baggage across the slippery rocks to the foot of the shoot. The four large canoes were then brought down by slipping them along poles placed from one rock to another, and in some places by using partially streams which escaped alongside of the river. We were not, however, able to bring them across without three of them receiving injuries which obliged us to stop at the end of the shoot to repair them."

On November 2d, Lewis was intensely gratified by the first appearance of tide-water, and pushed on with the greatest eagerness until he reached Diamond Island, where "we met fifteen Indians ascending the river in two canoes; but the only information we could procure from them was that they had seen three vessels, which we presumed to be European, at the mouth of the Columbia."

As he went on, small parties of Indians in canoes were seen and many small villages, principally of the Skilloots, who were friendly, well disposed, desirous of traffic, and visited so frequently as to be troublesome. One Indian, speaking a little English, said that he traded with a Mr. Haley. The weather had become foggy and rainy, but on November 7, 1805, while pushing down the river below a village of the Wahkiacums, the "fog cleared off and we enjoyed the delightful prospect of the ocean—that ocean, the object of all our labors, the reward of all our anxieties. This cheering view exhilarated the spirits of all the party, who were still more delighted on hearing the distant roar of the breakers, and went on with great cheerfulness."

Lewis, not content with a sight of the ocean, went on, determined to winter on the coast. A severe storm forced him to land under a high rocky cliff, where the party had scarcely room to lie level or secure their baggage. It "blew almost a gale directly from the sea. The immense waves now broke over the place where we were encamped, and the large trees, some of them five or six feet thick, which had lodged at the point, were drifted over our camp, and the utmost vigilance of every man could scarcely save our canoes from being crushed to pieces. We remained in the water and drenched with rain during the rest of the day, our only food being some dried fish and some rain-water which we caught. Yet, though wet and cold and some of them sick from using salt water, the men are cheerful and full of anxiety to see more of the ocean." Here they were confined six days, and the rain had lasted ten days, wetting their merchandise through, spoiling their store of dried fish, destroying and rotting their robes and leather dresses.

A series of gales and long-continued rain did not prevent Lewis and Clark from exploring the country for a suitable place for winter quarters. Lewis finally discovered a point of high land on the river Neutel, where a permanent encampment was established which was called Fort Clatsop. It was situated in a thick grove of lofty pines several miles from the sea and well above the highest tide.

The fort consisted of seven wooden huts, which were covered in by the 20th of November and later picketed, so as to afford ample security. The party subsisted principally on elk, of which they killed one hundred and thirty-one. Fish and berries were much used in the early spring. Salt was made in considerable quantities on the sea-shore, and some blubber was secured from a stranded whale, 105 feet in length. In general, the winter passed without serious results, except that the health of some of the men was impaired by the almost constant rains, there being but four days without rain in the first two months.

The conduct of the many Indian tribes with whom they had communication was almost always friendly, and in only one or two cases did even strange Indians from a distance show signs of hostility. The northwest coast had been visited so often that little could be added to the knowledge of their customs and mode of life. One comment of Lewis, is, however, worthy of reproduction. " We have not observed any liquor of an intoxicating quality used among these or any Indians west of the Rocky Mountains, the universal beverage being pure water. They sometimes almost intoxicate themselves by smoking tobacco, of which they are excessively fond, and the pleasure of which they prolong as much as possible by retaining vast quantities at a time, till after circulating through the lungs and stomach, it issues in volumes from the mouth and nostrils."

It appears surprising that Lewis was ignorant of the discovery of the Columbia River by Captain Robert Gray, for he says that the name Point Adams was given by Vancouver. Further, he was ignorant of the fact that the trade at the mouth of the Columbia was conducted almost entirely by vessels from New England. From the English phrases of the Indian, he knew that the traders must be " either English or American," and presumed " that they do not belong at any establishment at Nootka Sound."

The original plan contemplated remaining at Fort Clatsop until April, when Lewis expected to renew his stock of merchandise from the traders who yearly visited the Columbia by ship. Constant rains, however, increased sickness among his men, while game failed to such an extent that they only lived from hand to mouth ; and as merchandise lacked wherewith to buy food from the Indians, it became necessary to return. On departing, he left among the Indians a number of notices setting forth briefly the results of his expedition ; one of these, through an American trader, reached Boston via China in February, 1807, about six months after Lewis's own return.

On March 24, 1806, the party commenced to retrace their long and dangerous route of 4,144 miles to St. Louis. Their guns were in good order and the stock of ammunition plentiful, but their entire stock of trading goods could be tied up in a single blanket.

Detained by scarcity of fish, they discovered the Multonah (Willamette) River which, hidden by an island, was not seen on their downward voyage. Lieutenant Clark went up the valley some distance to Nechecole village, where he saw an Indian house, all under one roof, 226 feet long.

Of the valley of the Willamette, Lewis remarks that it was the only desirable place of settlement west of the Rocky Mountains, and it was sufficiently fertile to support 50,000 souls. He mentions its rich prairies, its fish, fowl, and game, its useful plants and shrubs, its abundant and valuable timber.

The conditions of the rapids below The Dalles was such that one boat, fortunately empty, was lost, and the upper rapids being impracticable, they broke up or traded all their boats and canoes but two, which were carried to the upper river. They proceeded with the horses, that had been purchased with the greatest difficulty, Bratton, too ill to walk, being on horseback, and on April 27th reached a village of the Wallawallas, near the mouth of Snake or Lewis River. Here they were so well received that Lewis says: " Of

all the Indians whom we have met since leaving
the United States, the Wallawallas were the
most hospitable, honest, and sincere."

Their horses recruited to twenty-three head,
cheered by information of a new route which
would save eighty miles, and with Wallawalla
guides, they moved in early May up the valley
of Snake or Lewis River, and finding it too early
to cross the mountains, encamped in the fork
of the Kooskoosky, having meanwhile received
back from their savage friend Twisted-hair their
thirty-eight horses intrusted to his care the previous year. Their journey by land was marked
by great scarcity of food, which was roots or
dog, except when the officers, practicing medicine for sick Indians, obtained horses for food.
The use of dog, which was now very palatable,
caused derision among the Indians. On one occasion an Indian threw a half-starved puppy into
Lewis's plate, with laughter, which turned to
chagrin when Lewis flung the animal with great
force into the savage's face and threatened to
brain him with a tomahawk. The Indians lived
almost entirely on fish during the salmon season,
and on roots the rest of the year. Their houses
were collected under one roof, with many apart-
ments, and two were seen each about one hundred and fifty feet long. The difficulties of
communicating with the Chopunnish were very
great, and if errors occurred it was not astonishing. Lewis spoke in English, which was translated by one of the men in French to Chaboneau,
who repeated it in Minnetaree to his wife. She

put it into Shoshonee to a prisoner, who translated it into Chopunnish dialect.

An attempt in early June to cross the mountains failed, the snow being ten feet deep on a level. On June 24th they started again, and with great privations succeeded in following their trail of the previous September across the Bitterroot Mountains to Traveller's-rest Creek, on Clark Fork, which was reached June 30th.

Here the party divided in order to thoroughly explore different portions of the country. Lewis took the most direct route to the great falls of the Missouri, whence he was to explore Maria's River to 50° N. latitude. Clark proceeded to the head of Jefferson River, down which Sergeant Ordway was to go in the canoes cached there. Clark himself was to cross by the shortest route to the Yellowstone, and building canoes, descend to its mouth and rejoin the main party at that point.

Lewis went into the Maria's River country, but was unable to proceed far through lack of game. He there fell in with a band of Minnetarees, who attempted to steal his arms and horses, which resulted in a skirmish wherein two Indians were killed, the only deaths by violence during the expedition. Then turning to the mouth of the Maria's River, they were rejoined by Ordway's party, and on August 7th reached the mouth of the Yellowstone, where a note from Clark informed them of his safe arrival and camping place a few miles below.

Clark had explored portions of the valleys of

the Jefferson, Gallatin, and Madison, and had prescience of the wonders of the Yellowstone in a boiling-hot spring discovered at the head of Wisdom River. His journey to Clark's fork of the Yellowstone was made with comfort and safety, but there an accident to one of his men obliged him to make canoes, during which delay the Indians stole twenty-four of his horses.

As Lewis descended the Missouri he saw that the tide of travel and adventure was already following in his track, and two daring Illinoisans, Dickson and Hancock, were at the mouth of the Yellowstone on a hunting trip. Rapidly descending the river the 23d of September saw the party safe at St. Louis, the initial point of their great and eventful expedition.

The great continental journey to and fro, from ocean to ocean, across barren deserts, through dangerous waterways, over snow-clad mountains, among savage and unknown tribes, had been accomplished with a success unparalleled in the world of modern adventure and exploration.

This expedition was fraught with successful results second to none other ever undertaken in the United States. The extent, fertility, and possibilities of the great trans-Mississippi were made known, the possibility of crossing the American continent was demonstrated, the location of the great rivers and of the Rocky Mountains determined, the general good-will of the interior Indians proved, and the practicability of trade and intercourse established. Furthermore, conjoined with the discovery of the Columbia by

Gray, it laid the foundations of a claim which, confirmed by settlement and acknowledged by Great Britain, gave the United States its first foothold on the Pacific coast, and ultimately secured to the American nation not only the magnificent States of Oregon and Washington, but also the golden vales and mountains of California.

Well might Jefferson declare that " never did a similar event (their successful return) excite more joy through the United States. The humblest of its citizens had taken a lively interest in the issue of this journey."

Clark was an able and faithful assistant to the unfortunate Lewis, who did not live to write the full story of the expedition. It seems, however, that the disposition in some quarters to regard Clark as the man to whom the success of the expedition was in greater part due, finds no justification in a careful perusal of the narratives. So great a work was enough glory for the two men, the commander and the assistant.

Clark's future career must be considered somewhat of a disappointment. During his absence he was promoted to be a first lieutenant of artillery, and on his return was nominated by Jefferson to be lieutenant-colonel of the Second Infantry; but the Senate, by a vote of twenty to nine, declined to confirm him, and he resigned his commission as lieutenant February 27, 1807. Later he was an Indian agent and a brigadier-general of the militia for the territory of upper Louisiana, with station at St. Louis. In 1812 he declined an appointment as brigadier-general, and the opportunity of having Hull's command—a declination which was an injury to his country if he had the military ability attributed to him. Madison appointed him Governor of the Territory of Missouri, which office he filled from 1813 to the admission of Missouri as a State in 1821. Contrary to his wishes, he was nominated for the first governor, but failed of election. Monroe, in May, 1822, appointed him Superintendent of Indian Affairs, with station at St. Louis, which office he filled until his death, September 1, 1838.

Captain Lewis did not live to long enjoy the honors that he had so bravely won. He reached Washington the middle of February, 1807, when Congress, which was in session, made to both leaders and men the donation of lands which they had been encouraged to expect as some reward for their toil and danger.

The President considered the discoveries of sufficient importance to present them to Congress in a special message, on February 19, 1806, and in appreciation of Captain Lewis's valuable services, immediately appointed him to be Governor of Louisiana, which office Lewis accepted, resigning for that purpose from the army on March 4, 1807.

Of the civil services of Governor Lewis, Jefferson says: "He found the Territory distracted by feuds and contentions among the officers, and the people divided into factions. . . . He used every endeavor to conciliate and harmonize. . . . The even-handed justice he administered to all soon established a respect for his person and authority."

While on the way to Washington, in September, 1809, Governor Lewis, in a fit of derangement, killed himself, thus, to quote again from Jefferson, "depriving his country of one of her most valued citizens," who endeared himself to his countrymen by "his sufferings and successes, in endeavoring to extend for them the bounds of science, and to present to their knowledge that vast and fertile country, which their sons are destined to fill with arts, with science, with freedom, and happiness." Surely posterity will declare that Meriwether Lewis lived not in vain.

Buffalo Skull.

VI.

ZEBULON MONTGOMERY PIKE,

Explorer of the Sources of the Mississippi
and Arkansas Rivers.

The trans-continental expedition of Captain Lewis and Lieutenant Clark was only a part of the comprehensive plan of Jefferson, which looked to the acquiring of definite and precise information concerning not only the extreme Northwest Territory, but also of the entire trans-Mississippi regions, whereon might be based intelligent action, so as to insure to the citizens of the United States the greatest benefits of internal trade and commerce. It was surmised that the adventurous and enterprising traders of the Hudson Bay, or Northwest Company, had encroached on the valuable hunting grounds near the sources of the Missouri and Mississippi rivers; while to the southwest the secretive and jealous policy of Spain had so well guarded its limited geographical knowledge, that the United States was in such utter ignorance of its newly acquired territory that it was impossible to even outline a definite proposition for the determination of exact boundary lines between Louisiana and the province of New Spain.

The obtaining of information for the solution of these problems was intrusted, in the order

named, to a young and promising officer of the
regular army, Zebulon Montgomery Pike, then a
first lieutenant and paymaster in the First regiment of Infantry. Pike was of military stock, as
his father, Zebulon Pike, had served as a captain
in the war of the Revolution, and even then a
major of his son's regiment was destined to live
to see that son fall as a general officer. The son,
born at Lamberton, N. J., aspired early to military life, and from a cadet in the ranks rose
through the grades regularly.

1. The Sources of the Mississippi.

In 1805 the governor of Louisiana was James
Wilkinson, a brigadier-general in, and commander-in-chief of, the army of the United States,
who was then stationed at St. Louis. Pike appears to have been considered by Wilkinson as
an officer well suited to obtain definite information about this vast territory, and consequently
Lieutenant Pike, with twenty enlisted men, was
furnished provisions for four months, and, under
orders to visit the sources of the Mississippi, left
St. Louis in a large flat-boat, at about the worst
season of the year, on August 9, 1805.

The first experiences were not encouraging,
for the crew, through inexperience or ill-luck,
developed a faculty of picking up sawyers, or
submerged trees, which on one occasion stove
the boat so badly that, half-sinking, she was
dragged with difficulty on a shoal where the
baggage could be dried and the boat repaired.

Here and there along the river were seen small bands of Indians, and in due time the village of the Sacs was reached at the head of the Des Moines rapids. The Sac chiefs, assembled in

General Z. M Pike.

council, were told that their great and new father had sent one of his young warriors to their nation, in the lately acquired territory of Louisiana, to inquire as to their wants, to give them good advice, to make peace, and to locate, according to their wishes and needs, trading establishments and posts. The Indians answered acceptably, but appeared to appreciate the presents of knives, whiskey, and tobacco more than the speech. Vague rumors obtained as to the value and importance of the lead mine near, below Turkey River, but Mr. Dubuque, the proprietor, was too shrewd for the young officer, and to his inquiries said that information as to the grant, etc., was in St. Louis, that he made from ten to twenty tons of lead yearly, and gave equally indefinite answers to other questions. A journey of four weeks from St. Louis brought Pike to Prairie-du-Chien, then the only place settled by white men in the whole valley of the Mississippi above St. Louis. Originally occupied by three Frenchmen, Giard, Antaya, and Dubuque, in 1783, it was now a scattered settlement of thirty-seven houses, with about three hundred and seventy whites. The Wisconsin River, which here joins the Mississippi, was yet the great line of communication between the great lakes and the entire valley from St. Louis northward, all goods and furs passing to and fro over the route first traced by Joliet in his adventurous voyage of discovery in 1673. At Prairie-du-Chien the Indians assembled each autumn for the annual trade or fair, and every spring the Indian traders here paused in their western journey before plunging into the savage wilderness. Both these occasions, it is needless to say, furnished frequent scenes of violence and dissipation.

Unable to get his large barge above the rapids

at Prairie-du-Chien, Pike hired other boats above the falls and proceeded, his party augmented by an interpreter, Pierre Roseau, and Mr. Fraser, a trader who was going to the Falls of St. Anthony on business.

A short distance above Prairie-du-Chien, Pike had a council with the Sioux, who evidently were recovering from a feast, and here he saw a religious puff dance, "the performance of which was attended with many curious manœuvres. Men and women danced indiscriminately. They were all dressed in the gayest manner; all had in their hands a small skin of some description, and would frequently run up, point their skin, and give a puff with their breath; when the person blown at, whether man or woman, would fall and appear to be almost lifeless, or in great agony; but would recover slowly, rise, and join in the dance. This they called their great medicine."

Tobacco, knives, vermilion, and whiskey cemented the good feeling, the eight gallons of whiskey being more show than reality; for it appears from the context to have been three-fourths water, and probably was of the kind which Pike elsewhere called "made whiskey."

The uncertain weather of Lake Pepin nearly shipwrecked the boats, which reached the Sioux village at the junction of the Mississippi and St. Peters, or Minnesota, on September 11th. Here a council was held with the Sioux, wherein two of the chiefs formally signed away a square league of land at the Falls of St. Anthony. The true value of their signatures may be estimated from Pike's letter to General Wilkinson, wherein he says: "I had to fee privately two (doubtless the signers) of the chiefs, and besides that, to make them presents at the council." In addition to the transfer of land Pike pledged to have a trading post established there, and urged that the Sioux maintain peaceful relations with the Chippeways.

It is somewhat amusing to read Pike's address, where in one breath he states that rum "occasions quarrels, murders, etc., among yourselves. For this reason your father has thought proper to prohibit the traders from selling you any rum;" and then accepting the situation, adds, "before my departure I will give you some liquor to clear your throats." There were two hundred and fifty warriors present, and it appears to have taken sixty gallons of liquor to effect the clearing operation, while peace with the Chippeways assumed an indefinite phase.

The Falls of St. Anthony were passed by land portage. These being the first boats to make the portage, as Pike claims, it was with no small feeling of relief that he saw his boats in the upper river, loaded for the journey, on September 30th. His condition was at the best discouraging, for as he says, "I had not accomplished more than half my route; winter fast approaching; war existing between the most savage nations in the course of my route; my provisions greatly diminished, and but a poor prospect of an additional supply. Many of my men sick, and the others not a little disheartened; our success in this arduous undertaking very doubtful, and about to launch into an unknown wilderness."

Rapids and shoals impeded progress somewhat, but the 10th of October brought them to an island where the interpreter had wintered with another Frenchman in 1797. Pike made every exertion to hasten, for he was very desirous of reaching Crow-wing River, the highest point ever attained by trappers in birch canoes. The bad weather, snow, injury to his boats, and the breaking down of several of his men, combined to render further advance impossible, and on October 16th he fixed his winter quarters at the mouth of Pine River, 233 miles above the Falls of St. Anthony. Pike's intentions were far from passing the winter himself in a wretched cantonment, for his was a nature foreign to such isolation and inactivity as the place promised.

Elsewhere he adds: " It appears to me that the wealth of nations would not induce me to remain secluded from the society of civilized mankind, surrounded by a savage and unproductive wilderness, without books or other sources of intellectual enjoyment, or being blessed with the cultivated and feeling mind of the civilized fair."

Huts were built, canoes made, game obtained, all with great difficulty and hardship, for every burden fell on Pike, without the aid of a doctor or assistant as his second in command. In a game country, and under conditions where his insufficient food-supply must be eked out by the rifle, he was such an indifferent hunter that he did the maximum of work with the minimum of result. Unskilled in canoe-making and management, he succeeded in building three canoes, of which one sank, wetting and injuring his supply of ammunition, with the result that finally he blew up his tent in drying out the powder.

Occasionally small hunting parties of Sioux or of Menominees came to the camp, and on December 3d Mr. Dickson, who had a trading post sixty miles to the south, visited Pike and cheered him up. Dickson possessed much geographical information about the western country, and in addition to useful directions as to the best route for Pike to follow, expressed his confidence in its fullest success.

It would seem doubtful if the men shared the enthusiasm for a mid-winter trip through an unknown country filled with savages and where game must form a considerable part of their food. At all events, they managed to split a canoe which their commander relied on for the journey. Pike was dissatisfied, but not discouraged, and on December 10th started northward with eleven men, a boat, and five sleds.

At the stockade there were nine men under Sergeant Kennerman, who was given detailed written instructions as to his duties. Mindful of the possible dangers to his own party, Pike also gave orders as to the course to be pursued if his own party did not return to the cantonment by a given date the following spring.

A boat was taken along, which the freezing river soon obliged Pike to abandon and intrust to a young Indian for the winter. The journey was practically made by common sleds, dragged by men harnessed up two abreast. Often the sleds broke down, making necessary frequent changes and portages of the baggage, but they were greatly encouraged by camping at Crow-wing River, the farthest point ever reached by canoe.

In early January they ran across four Chippeway Indians, the tribe from which hostility was possible. Their anxiety was speedily relieved by finding that they were companions of Mr. Grant, a trader from the post on Sandy Lake. Grant turned back with them, and they reached the trading-post on Red Cedar Lake on January 3, 1806. Pike's satisfaction at seeing a house once more was tinctured with chagrin at finding it surmounted by a British flag. Here he tarried only a few hours and then pushed on to Sandy Lake, where he was later joined by his men, who were delayed by their heavy sleds. He was much surprised at the air of comfort at Sandy Lake, where potatoes were grown in great quantities, fish and game abundant, while the Indians furnished in trade maple-sugar, wild oats, and rice. The Sandy Lake trading-post had been established in 1794, and might be considered the headquarters of the Fond-du-Lac department, in which, in 1805, there were one hundred and nine employees, with fifty children and twenty-nine women, who were all Indian or half-breed, there not being at that time a single white woman northwest of Lake Superior.

Pike's discerning mind noted that his methods of travel were inferior to those followed in the country, so he built sleds after the Hudson Bay pattern, adopted the racket or snow-shoe for the

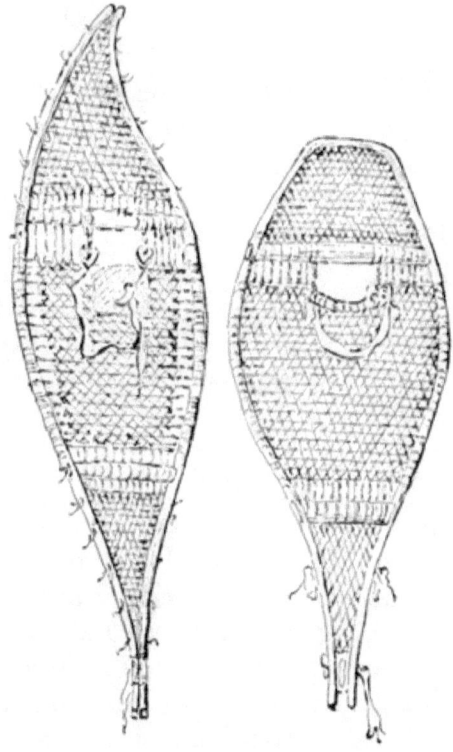

Indian Snow-shoes

winter march, and hired local Indian guides. Grant, the trader, accompanied him to Leech Lake, which Pike believed to be the main source of the Mississippi, but he could not consider it as an original discovery, as the ubiquitous Northwest Company had an establishment on this lake, under Hugh McGillis, in 47° 16' N. latitude, about twenty miles east of Lake Itasca, the true source of the Mississippi. On February 14th Pike visited Red Lake and passed to the north, which carried him to the drainage-basin of the Red River, in latitude 47° 43' N. Evidently familiar with Carver's travels, he fell into the not unreasonable error of thinking this land "to be the most elevated part of the northeast continent of America," whereas the head of the Minnesota is some four hundred feet higher.

Pike held a council with the Chippeways at Leech Lake on February 14th, when he persuaded the chiefs to give up their British flags and medals, to promise peace with the Sioux, and to send two of their young chiefs with him to St. Louis.

As to the trading establishments, he generously refrained from seizing the goods, but hauled down the British flag; required the agents of the Northwest Company to promise to issue no more flags or medals to Indians, to have no political dealings with them, but to refer them to agents of the United States; to obtain licenses for Indian trade from and pay duty to the United States for all imported goods.

On February 14th he turned his face toward home, his mind free from anxiety, though he knew the hard marches, extreme cold, and many hardships before him. He now wore snow-shoes, but on one long march the pressure of his racket-strings brought the blood through his socks and moccasins, yet he marched on, keeping pace with his guide despite the excruciating pain.

March 5th found Pike back in his stockade at Pine River, his adoption of local methods having facilitated travel to such an extent that in his return he nearly tripled the length of his outward marches. He found the garrison well and safe, but was greatly disturbed to find that his trusted sergeant, Kennerman, had indulged in riotous and extravagant living, having drank up, eaten, given away, or traded off the best of the food and the greater part of the liquor. The natural sequence of such conduct appeared in an escapade where the sentinel made a Sioux Indian drunk and then ordered him out of the tent, when the intoxicated savage fired on the sentinel, fortunately without harm. On his return he was fortunate enough, in a Menominee camp near the stockade, to see a dance, called the feast of the dead, at which "every three were served with a panful of meat, and when all were ready there was a prayer, after which the eating commenced. It was expected we would eat up our portion entirely, being careful not to drop a bone. We were then treated with soup. After the eating was finished the chief again gave an exhortation, which finished the ceremony. They gather up the fragments and threw them in the water, lest the dogs should get them. Burning them is considered sacreligious."

Leaving his cantonment at Pine River, by boat, on April 7th he descended the Mississippi without any strikingly new experiences, and on the last day of the month drew up his boat at St. Louis, with undiminished numbers, after an absence of nearly nine months.

Pike had more than carried out his orders to explore the sources of the great river, and did something more than give to the world the first definite and detailed information as to the upper river and its tributaries. He discovered the extent and importance of the British trade in that country, brought the foreign traders under the license and customs regulations of the United States, and broke up for all time their political influence over the Indians. He did much to restrain the unlawful sale of liquor to Indians by domestic traders, and not only inspired the Indians with respect for Americans, but also induced them to at least a temporary peace between themselves. He replaced a foreign flag by the ensign of his own country, and for the first time brought into this great territory the semblance of national authority and government.

II. The Upper Arkansas River and New Spain.

Pike returned to find his services in demand for a second expedition to the head-waters of the Arkansas and Red rivers. The original arrangements contemplated the detail of another officer, but Pike, at the solicitation of General Wilkinson, consented to take command of the party, commenced his preparations at once, and received his formal orders on June 24, 1806, less than two months after his return from the north. In accepting this long and dangerous service, he indicates clearly the soldierly sense of duty which actuated him. "The late dangers and hardships I had undergone, together with the idea of again leaving my family in a strange country, distant from their connections, made me hesitate; but the ambition of a soldier and the spirit of enterprise which was inherent in my breast induced me to agree."

The primary object of the expedition, according to the letter of instructions, was to conduct to Grand Osage a deputation of freed captives of the Osage Nation, while the subordinate purposes were the accomplishment of a permanent peace between the Kaws and Osages and the establishment of a good understanding with the Comanches, which latter object, the letter runs, "will probably lead you to the head branches of the Arkansas and Red rivers, approximated to the settlements of New Mexico, and there you should move with great circumspection, to keep clear of any reconnoitring parties from that province, and to prevent alarm or offence. The executive," it was added, "is much interested in ascertaining the direction, extent, and navigation of the Arkansas and Red rivers," which Pike was charged to determine by sending one party down the Arkansas, while he should return by the Red.

The written instructions were doubtless supplemented by verbal orders, for Pike says: "The great objects in view (as I conceived) were to attach the Indians to our Government and to acquire such geographical knowledge of the southwestern boundary of Louisiana as to enable our Government to enter into a definite arrangement for a line of demarcation between that territory and North Mexico."

Captain Pike's* force consisted of two officers, an interpreter, and nineteen men of the army. The officers were Lieutenant James B. Wilkinson, son of and aide-de-camp to General Wilkinson, and Doctor John H. Robinson, the latter a volunteer without pay. The party, with fifty-one Osage Indians, left Belle Fontaine, July 15, 1806, and travelling by boat up the Missouri and Osage rivers reached Grand Osage, near the head of the river, August 18th, thus accomplishing the "primary object."

Pike found no difficulty in obtaining an audience for speeches, though he was somewhat dismayed at the presence of one hundred and eighty-six warriors at an assembly, to all of whom he was obliged to give liquor. It was quite different when men and horses were wanted, and it was with the utmost endeavor that he was able to start westward on September 1st, with fifteen horses for his baggage, accompanied by only three Pawnees and four Osages.

Crossing the Grand and Verdigris he passed through a beautiful country with abundant game, but the Indians became restless, and despite his presents and persuasions, only three accompa-

---

* He obtained his captaincy in August, 1806.

nied him to the Pawnee village on the Republican fork of the Kansas.

The information here obtained and the stand taken by the Pawnee chief would have deterred a less courageous and determined man than Pike from pushing beyond. A large Spanish force, some six hundred men, had a few days before visited the Pawnees, when they had turned back on assurances from the chief that he would turn back any American force.

It appears that foreign emissaries at St. Louis had sent word to the authorities of New Spain of Pike's contemplated expedition, and steps were immediately taken to defeat its objects. The command of the Spanish force was assigned to Lieutenant Don Facundo Malgares, an officer of reputation in Indian warfare, who collected one hundred dragoons and five hundred militia at Santa Fé, N. M. Each man was mounted, had three led animals and six months' supply of ammunition. First they descended the Red River about seven hundred miles, with the expectation of meeting and turning back Pike, but learned that no force had passed that way. The Spanish commander, after holding a council with the Comanches for the purpose of winning them over to the interests of New Spain, then turned north to the Arkansas. Here Malgares put in camp two hundred and forty of his men, with the worn-out and disabled stock, and with the rest proceeded to the Pawnee village, where he distributed medals, Spanish flags, etc., and after prejudicing them against Americans and drawing the Pawnee chiefs as closely to Spain as possible returned to Santa Fé, arriving there in October. This armed invasion of the acknowledged territory of the United States and deliberate tampering with the Indian tribes probably arose from the strained relations between the two countries, which nearly resulted in hostilities on the frontiers of Texas and Orleans territory in 1806, when the local forces tacitly agreed to regard the Sabine River as the temporary boundary.

Pike first made the Osage and Kaws smoke the pipe of peace and then held a council with the Pawnees. These latter Indians, strongly impressed by the grand show made by the Spanish cavalry, regarded with doubt the small force of Americans. What Pike lacked in numbers and display, he made up in boldness of demands and in display of self-confidence. He obliged them to take down the Spanish flag and hoist the American ensign, but gave them permission to retain the foreign flag for protection if the Spaniards should return.

The chief, however, insisted that the Americans must turn back, and said that he would resist any advance by force of arms. Captain Pike, already indignant at the unauthorized raid of the Spaniards into the territory of the United States, listened with impatience to this threat, and answered that so far he had not seen any blood on his path, but the Pawnees must know that the young warriors of their great American father were not women, to be turned back by words; that they were men, well armed and prepared as braves to sell their lives dearly; that they should go on, and if the Pawnees opposed, the great American father would send other warriors to avenge the dead. This bold talk had its effect, and the onward march met with no active opposition.

Striking southwest, and following as well as he could the broad trail left by the Spaniards, Pike reached Arkansas, where he stopped long enough to build canoes, in which Lieutenant Wilkinson with five soldiers and two Osages descended the river. This officer reached the post of Arkansas on January 6, 1807, after a journey marked by many hardships, but no great dangers.

Captain Pike and Doctor Robinson pursued their route up the Arkansas with the party, now reduced to fourteen soldiers and the interpreter, Vasquez. On the 2d of November, they fell in with a large herd of wild horses, beautiful bays, blacks, and grays, whom they were unable to capture even with their fleetest coursers. Here also the buffalo were present in numbers beyond imagination, as Pike thought.

The 15th of November was a marked day, for Pike records that "at two o'clock in the afternoon I thought I could distinguish a mountain to our right, which appeared like a small blue cloud. . . . In half an hour they appeared in full view before us. When our small party arrived on the hill they with one accord gave three cheers to the Mexican mountains." The peak, first seen by Pike, remained in view from that day to the 27th of January, and in eternal commemoration of the hardships and dangers of the discoverer in that journey fittingly bears in our day the name of Pike's Peak.

Here they first strikingly realized the transparency and purity of the mountain air, which to the eye quite annihilates distance. He writes: "Marched at our usual hour, pushed with an idea of arriving at the mountains, but found at night no visible difference in their appearance from what we did yesterday." It may be added that eight days' march brought the party only to the base of the mountains.

On November 22d he fell in with an unsuccessful war-party, composed of sixty Pawnees, returning from a foray on the Comanches. The savages at first acted in a friendly manner, but receiving some small presents, demanded ammunition, corn, blankets, kettles, and indeed everything they saw. Being refused they threw away in contempt the articles given. Pike ordered the horses packed, when the Pawnees encircled the small party and commenced stealing everything they could, when Pike commanded his men to stand to arms, and to separate themselves from the savages. This done an order was given to kill the first Indian who touched any piece of baggage, when the Pawnees, realizing that further misconduct meant fight, filed off and allowed them to depart.

The party was now at the present city of Las Animas, where the Arkansas forks, and as the

Spanish troops followed the main stream instead of the Purgatory, Pike took the same route. At the Herfuano he decided to put the main party in camp while he explored the surrounding country, so he threw up a small breastwork, opening on the river, somewhat to the east of the present city of Pueblo. Starting to ascend the north fork (the main Arkansas) to the high point of a blue mountain, which he conceived would be one day's march, it took two days to reach the base and more than another day to reach its summit. He records that his men had no stockings, were clad only in light summer overalls, in every way unprovided for the inclement surroundings, the snow to their hips, the temperature nine degrees below freezing, while in forty-eight hours the four men had for food only one partridge and a piece of deer's rib, but adds that they were amply compensated for their toil and hardships by the sublimity of the view—an unbounded prairie overhung with clouds. The summit of Grand (Pike's) Peak, bare of vegetation, snow-covered, and double the height of the peak ascended, he thought no human being could then have ascended, even had it been near instead of a day's march to its base.

The December journey up the narrow, cliff-bound valley of the Arkansas is a continuous record of hardship and suffering. The horses with difficulty found grazing in the snow-covered valley, while the fearless ravens lighting on the men seized meat from them, and, despite the kicking and plunging of the horses swooped down on

them and picked their sore backs till they bled.
The thermometer fell to thirty-eight degrees below freezing, while the badness of the trail obliged
the party to cross and recross the ice-filled river,
from which several froze their feet badly. Had
the weather continued so cold "some of the men,"
says Pike, "must have perished, for they had no
winter clothing; I wore myself cotton overalls."

Here the returning Spanish expeditionary column under Malgares had turned south, skirting
the mountains until it reached a practicable pass
through the Cimarron range to Taos; but the
main Spanish trail failing in the snow-covered
plain Pike pursued a side trail to the northwest,
and crossing a dividing ridge came on an ice-covered stream, which, to his surprise, ran to the
northeast, and proved, as he thought, to be the
head-waters of the Platte, the south fork rising
in the South Park, where he then was. Here
he found evidences of the park having been
lately frequented by large parties of Indians.
Beyond this he doubtless crossed into the Middle Park, and saw the head-waters of the Colorado
Grande, and so was the second party to reach
from the Atlantic tide-water the sources of
streams draining into the Pacific.

Pike was now lost in the maze of snow-covered
mountains under most adverse circumstances, as
he recites: "Eight hundred miles from the frontiers of our country; not one person clothed for
the winter, many without blankets, having been
obliged to cut them up for socks, etc.; laying
down at night on the snow or wet ground, one

side burning, while the other was pierced with cold; endeavoring to make of raw buffalo-hide a miserable substitute for shoes;" the men falling sick, and, finally, the country so broken and precipitous, that even the Indian horse could not carry a pack, and three animals were lost from falls and bruises.

Pike was disconsolate, but not discouraged. He sent ahead the interpreter and two soldiers travelling light to find a way out, while, making five small sleds to carry the baggage and be dragged by the men, he followed. Struggling on, nearly perishing from cold, and almost famished for food, the 5th of January found Pike, greatly to his mortification, in the same old valley of the Arkansas, in sight of his camp of December 10th. Realizing that he could expect nothing further from his few worn-out horses, and burning with mortification at his egregious error in considering the Arkansas as the Red, Pike decided to try on foot that journey which had failed on horseback. He at once strengthened the small fort, left therein heavy baggage, horses, etc., with the interpreter and one man, while with the rest he started to cross the mountains with packs in search of the Red River, where he intended to send back a party to guide the pack-train to it. This in the belief that the Red River had its sources to the southwest, instead of in its true location hundreds of weary miles to the southeast.

Humboldt's map of New Spain, compiled from data in the City of Mexico in 1804, plainly indicates that the Spanish labored under the same error as Pike, they also thinking the sources of the Red River to be some two or three hundred miles northwest of their true position. This map shows that although the main Red was well known, yet the head-waters of the Canadian were believed to be, and were charted as, the northwest extension of the Red to within fifty miles of the place where Pike was later arrested. It may be added, as showing the extent of geographical knowledge in New Spain at that time, that the upper Arkansas was known under the name Rio Napestle, although its connection with the lower Arkansas was only suspected. The Pecos, Colorado, Trinity, and Sabine Rivers were also known, but the Llano Estacado, of Texas, and the plains of Colorado, Indian Territory, and Kansas, though they had been crossed here and there prior to 1805, were practically unknown lands, given over to the buffalo and savages, who were popularly and correctly associated with them.

Impressed with the belief that he finally was on the right track, Captain Pike, on January 14, 1806, started on the eventful journey that was to carry him into New Spain, and lead him into the hands of the Spaniards he was charged to avoid. They marched in heavy order, every one —man, doctor, and commander—carrying forty-five pounds of regular baggage, besides arms, ammunition, and such food as he thought proper; the average burden being seventy pounds per man, to be carried over a snow-covered and mountainous country.

The general direction followed was to the southwest, and fifty miles were made good in three days. The fourth day all wet their feet crossing a stream, and before fire could be had no less than nine of the men, including the two hunters, had their feet badly frozen; the temperature fell that night to forty-three degrees below the freezing point, while the lack of game left them without food. The next morning two men went hunting in one direction, while Pike and the doctor went in another. The latter two wounded a buffalo three times, but he escaped, when, says Pike: "We concluded it was useless to go home to add to the general gloom, and went among the rocks, where we encamped and sat up all night; from intense cold it was impossible to sleep, hungry and without cover." The next morning they struck a herd and wounded several buffalo, all of which escaped. "By this time," continues Pike, "I had become extremely weak and faint, being the fourth day since we had received sustenance. We were inclining our course to a point of woods, determined to remain absent and die by ourselves rather than to return to our camp and behold the misery of our poor lads, when we discovered a gang of buffalo." Fortunately they killed one and returned at once to camp with a heavy load of meat, Pike arriving in such a state of exhaustion that he almost fell fainting as he dropped his burden. "The men," he adds, had "not a frown, nor a desponding eye—yet not a mouthful had they ate for four days." It was found that two soldiers were so badly frozen that it was impossible for them to proceed, and indeed it was probable that one would lose his feet. To remain was apparent death for all, so Pike decided to march, and left the two men, John Sparks and Thomas Dougherty, provided with ammunition, and given all the buffalo meat except one meal for the marching column. It was like parting with the dying. Pike bade them face their possible fate with soldierly fortitude, assured them that relief would be sent as soon as possible, and then they parted, as we may well believe such comrades would, with tears—more, doubtless, from those who marched than from those who remained behind.

The main party under Pike struggled on over the barren, snow-covered mountains, and after nine days, two of which without food, a march of ninety-five miles (from the vicinity of Saguache to the neighborhood of Del Norte) brought them quite exhausted to the banks of the Rio Grande, which was, however, hailed as the long-expected Red River.

Descending the stream some distance, Pike established a picketed stockade, surrounded it by a water ditch and made it quite impregnable to any ordinary attack. On February 7th Corporal Jackson and four men were sent back across the mountain, to bring in the baggage and see if the frozen men were yet able to travel. The same day Dr. Robinson left the expedition to visit Santa Fé, ostensibly carrying the papers in a Spanish claim, but in reality to gain a knowledge of the country, the prospects of trade, the military force, etc.—in short, as a secret agent.

While Pike was strengthening his position and securing game, the party returned with word that the frozen men could not yet travel, and possibly might be crippled for life. Volunteers were called for, as the only method now was to send to the fort in the forks of the Arkansas, (near Pueblo) where the recuperated horses and the rear-guard were available to bring over the snow-clad mountains the helpless soldiers.

Regarding this last journey Pike writes: "I must here remark the effect of habit, discipline, and example in two soldiers (Sergeant William E. Meek and private Theodore Miller). Soliciting a command of more than one hundred and eighty miles over two great ridges of mountains covered with snow, inhabited by bands of unknown savages, these men volunteered it, with others, and were chosen; for which they thought themselves highly honored."

The steadfast endurance and unfailing fortitude which enabled Pike's men to withstand and overcome the horrors and hardships of famine, frost, and fatigue, form but a single page of the annals of our army. Rarely has the American soldier failed, in war or peace, for military or civic ends, to give to the accomplishment of any important trust his utmost endeavor, subordinating thereto comfort, health, and life, lavishing thereon resources of helpfulness which have so often crowned with success the most hopeless of enterprises. If the American has individuality, assertiveness, and self-reliance, he has also, in its good time and place, a spirit of obedience, subordination, and solidarity which make him the typical soldier.

On February 16th, Pike was visited by a Spanish dragoon and an Indian; and some ten days later by a Spanish officer and fifty dragoons, by whom he was escorted to Santa Fé, where he was examined by the Spanish Governor, Don Allencaster, on March 3d. Pike had been informed by the Spanish lieutenant that he would be conducted to the head-waters of the Red River, but at Santa Fé he learned that there was no intention of permitting a geographical exploration of these unknown regions. Pike was astonished to find in Santa Fé an American, a Kentuckian, named James Pursley, from Bairdstown, who had made a hunting trip to the head of the Osage in 1802, and in 1803 made a journey up the Missouri with a French trader. Sent on a trading trip on the plains with a roving band of Kioways, the hunting party was attacked and driven by the Sioux into the parks of the Rocky Mountains, at the head of the Platte and Arkansas, where Pike had seen traces of the band and their stock. From this point the Indians sent Pursley and two of their number to Santa Fé to trade. Here they arrived in June, 1805, eight months before Pike, and Pursley decided to remain.

Governor Allencaster decided to send Pike and his party to Chihuahua. Accompanied by Robinson, who rejoined him at Albuquerque, Pike passed down the valley of the Rio Grande, through El Paso, under escort of the gallant and courteous Malgares, and was taken before Salcedo, the Commandant-General of Chihuahua, on April 2d. Leaving here late that month, still under escort, he crossed the Del Norte on June 1st, passed through San Antonio, and on July 1st was within the United States, at Natchitoches, when he exclaimed "Language cannot express the gayety of my heart, when I once more beheld the standard of my country!"

It is astonishing what an amount of valuable and accurate information concerning New Spain was collected by Captain Pike during his journey through the country. If he had been permitted to return by the way of Red River his stock of knowledge would have been vastly inferior. His journey was tedious, unpleasant, and humiliating, but Pike knew how to make the best of the situation, and in so doing justified the confidence of his superiors in sending him on so dangerous and important a service.

His field notes in New Spain were made by Pike with great difficulty, as the Governor gave orders to Malgares not to permit the making of astronomical observations nor the taking of notes, Pike was determined, however, to make the best of his opportunities, and so recorded his observations while making pretext to halt, and kept his boy as a vedette while writing. Later he feared the loss of such notes as he had already made, when, he continues: "Finding that a new species of discipline had taken place, and that the suspicions of my friend Malgares were much more acute than ever, I conceived it necessary to take some steps to secure the notes I had taken, which were clandestinely acquired. In the night I arose, and, after making all my men clean their pieces well, I took my small books and rolled them up in small rolls, and tore a fine shirt to pieces, and wrapped it around the papers and put them down in the barrels of the guns, until we just left room for the tompions, which were then carefully put in; the remainder we secured about our bodies under our shirts. This was effected without discovery and without suspicions."

Pike draws a lively and striking picture of the manners, morals, customs, and politics of the people of New Spain, whom he characterized as surprisingly brave, and in hospitality, generosity, and sobriety unsurpassed by any other people, but as lacking in patriotism, enterprise, and independence of soul.

The subsequent career of Captain Pike was short and brilliant. He received the thanks of the Government, had his zeal, perseverance, and intelligence formally recognized by a committee of the House of Representatives, rose to be major, lieutenant-colonel, and deputy-quartermaster-general in rapid succession; in the reorganization of the army in 1812 was made colonel, and in the following year was appointed brigadier-general a few weeks before his death, at the capture of York (Toronto), Canada.

The day before he left for the attack on York (Toronto), General Pike wrote to his father: " I embark to-morrow in the fleet at Sackett's Harbor at the head of 1,500 choice troops, on a secret expedition. Should I be the happy mortal destined to turn the scale of war, will you not rejoice, oh my father? May Heaven be propitious, and smile on the cause of my country. But if I am destined to fall, may my fall be like Wolfe's—to sleep in the arms of victory." His wish was prophetic.

The orders issued to his troops indicate the high professional honor which ever characterized Pike's life. In part they ran thus: " It is expected that every corps will be mindful of the honor of American arms and the disgraces which have recently tarnished our arms, and endeavor, by a cool and determined discharge of their duty, to support the one and wipe out the other. The property of the unoffending citizens of Canada," he continues, "must be held sacred ; and any soldier who shall so far neglect the honor of his profession as to be guilty of plundering the inhabitants, shall, if convicted, be punished with death. Courage and bravery in the field do not more distinguish the soldier than humanity after victory ; and whatever examples the savage allies of our enemies may have given us, the general confidently hopes that the blood of an unresisting enemy will never stain the weapon of any soldier of his column."

Owing to the sickness of General Dearborn, Pike took command of the land forces, and on April 27, 1813, carried the outer battery by assault, and having silenced the fire of the main work was awaiting a white flag when the main magazine was exploded. Pike, who had a minute before assisted in making a wounded soldier comfortable, was fatally injured, but his martial spirit impelled him to yet encourage his troops. A soldier to the last, he smiled as the standard of the enemy was handed to him, and, putting it under his head, died serenely.

Laboring under the disadvantage of insufficient instruction in youth, Pike supplemented his deficiencies by assiduous application, and his journal shows him studying French and other languages in the interludes of his desperate journeys in the Northwest and Southwest. Simpleminded and warm-hearted, he won the devotion of his men without relaxing soldierly habits or impairing discipline. He was intelligent, indefatigable, brave, capable of great endurance, fertile in expedients and never distrustful of his own capabilities or of the ultimate success of his undertakings. His early death precluded judgment as to his qualities as a general, but certainly he had the power of origination, organization, and administration which are essentials to military success.

It should be recorded of his explorations that, taking into consideration his small force, and almost inadequate means, no other man ever contributed to the geographical knowledge of the United States an amount comparable to that which the world owes to the heroic efforts and indomitable perseverance of Zebulon Montgomery Pike.

VII.

CHARLES WILKES,

The Discoverer of the Antarctic Continent.

On the colored and beautifully engraved map of the world of Gulielmus Blaeuw (Amsterdam, 1642) are two side maps, one of the Arctic, the other of the Antarctic, Circle. The latter represents not only the entire Antarctic Circle as unbroken land, but also extends this great suppositious continent some distance to the northward of the sixtieth parallel and gives to it the name Magallanica Terra Australis Incognita. This mythical Magellanic continent held its place, a subject of mystery and interest to every geographer, until Captain James Cook, the greatest of navigators, either ancient or modern, attempted its definition or solution. His success here as elsewhere was marvellous, and on January 17, 1773, in the Resolution, first of all men, Cook penetrated the ice-bound wastes of the Antarctic regions, reaching 67° 15' S., on the fortieth meridian E. In the following summer he completed his circumnavigation of Southern seas in high latitudes, and penetrating the Antarctic Circle at three widely separated points,

Charles Wilkes.
(From a portrait by T. Sully.)

attained, in January, 1774, in 117° W., the extraordinary high southern latitude of 71° 10'. Cook thus "put an end to the search for a southern continent, which had engrossed the attention of maritime nations for two centuries."

Cook's discoveries led to erroneous conclusions as to the physical constituents of the Antarctic regions. Although he had reached the Great Southern Circle at four different places, and nearly attained it at the fifth, yet no land therein, either island or continent, met his eager gaze; instead there everywhere met his view a close pack of ice-floes of enormous height and extent, with a few wind-caused breaks or channels. Hence many geographers concluded that the Antarctic regions were ice-covered seas, either totally or in greater part. To-day, in the light of modern science and discovery, the opinion prevails that there is an extensive ice-clad Antarctic land, possibly rising to the dignity of a continent; and toward this conclusion no explorations have more directly and largely contributed than those of the American sailor and explorer, Charles Wilkes, of the United States Navy.

The first Antarctic land ever discovered was by an American sealer, Captain Palmer, from Connecticut. Bellingshausen, of the Russian Imperial Navy, in his voyage of 1821, that resulted in the discovery of the islands of Peter and Alexander, on the sixty-ninth parallel, fell in with the Yankee skipper immediately after he had discovered the land, to which Bellingshausen justly attached Palmer's name. Palmer's Land, extended into the Antarctic Circle by Biscoe's discoveries of 1832, merges into Graham Land of the latter explorer.

Probably incited by these discoveries, France sent forth an Antarctic expedition, under Dumont d'Irville, in 1837, and England, under Sir James Clark Ross, the discoverer of the northern magnetic pole, in 1839. Simultaneously with these expeditions was organized one by the United States, for which the exceedingly liberal appropriation of $300,000 was made.

This last expedition was authorized by the act of Congress of May 18, 1836, " for the purpose of exploring and surveying in the Great Southern Ocean in the important interests of our commerce embarked in the whale fisheries and other adventures in that ocean, as well as to determine the existence of all doubtful islands and shoals, and to discover and accurately fix the position of those which lie in or near the track pursued by our merchant vessels in that quarter." This expedition, the first of its character undertaken by the United States, grew out of the vast capital employed in whaling and trade.

The expedition was first organized under Commodore Thomas Ap Catesby Jones, United State Navy, but finally the President of the United States appointed Lieutenant Charles Wilkes to command the squadron, and he was formally assigned to this duty under instructions of Secretary Paulding, dated August 11, 1838.

Charles Wilkes was born in New York City,

April 3, 1798, and entering the United States Navy as a midshipman at the age of nineteen was promoted to be lieutenant in 1826. He had long served in the department of charts and instruments and was especially qualified for the proposed astronomical and surveying work connected with the expedition.

An anomalous feature of the expedition was the acceptance of appointment as second in command by Lieutenant William L. Hudson, whose naval rank was above that of Wilkes's. The squadron, then consisting of the sloops of war Vincennes and Peacock, the store-ship Relief, the brig Porpoise, and tenders Sea Gull and Flying Fish, left Norfolk, Va., August 13, 1838. Associated with Wilkes were a number of lieutenants destined to later distinguish themselves in their country's service, among whom may be mentioned T. P. Craven, James Alden, S. P. Lee, G. F. Emmons, and A. L. Case, all of whom afterward rose to be rear admirals, and H. J. Harstene, later associated with the relief of Kane. Under its instructions the expedition was to visit Rio de Janeiro, Cape Frio, the Rio Negro, Terra del Fuego, the Antarctic Ocean southward of Powell's group to Cook's farthest, Valparaiso, the Navigators' Group, the Feejee Islands, the Antarctic regions south of Van Dieman's Land, whence it would return home by way of the Sandwich Islands, San Francisco, Singapore, and the Cape of Good Hope. No ship had steam-power, nor was any vessel of the squadron fitted with appliances for protection in ice navigation; indeed, the squadron was a makeshift, ill-suited for so long and dangerous a voyage. Eventually the Sea Gull was lost in a gale off the coast of Chili, the Flying Fish proved of little use, and the extreme slowness of the Relief delayed the voyage.

Wilkes sailed for the Antarctic regions from Orange Bay, near Cape Horn, on February 24, 1839, but owing to the lateness of the summer accomplished little, and spent thirty-six days in attempting to visit Palmer's Land, which was only sighted.

A second attempt at Antarctic exploration was made by Wilkes from Sidney, N. S. W., which was left December 21, 1839. A compact barrier of field ice, with frequent large bergs, was fallen in with on January 11, 1840, and from this time on the ships were often in imminent danger owing to continuous ice, impenetrable fog, bad weather, and occasional embayment of the vessels in the ice-pack. It is scarcely needful to enter into the details of Wilkes's perilous voyage from longitude 95° E. to 155° E. and in latitudes ranging from the Antarctic Circle to the neighborhood of the seventieth parallel. It may be mentioned, however, that the Peacock narrowly escaped entire destruction by collision with a heavy iceberg, which seriously injured the ship. Fortunately she cleared the berg in time to escape crushing by the falling of detached ice masses from the overhanging floe berg. Heavy gales and the bad sanitary condition of the ship caused the medical

officers of the Vincennes to specially report to
Wilkes that such continued exposure would so
weaken the crew by sickness as to hazard the ship
and the lives of all on board. Wilkes, however,
had sighted the long-looked-for Antarctic land,
and, disregarding the warning, followed the coast-
line eastward, keeping his squadron as near it as
the conditions would permit. The land was a

The Ice-Barrier.
(From a sketch by Captain Wilkes.)

series of lofty mountain ranges, often snow-
capped, frequently broken by indentations, and,
worst of all, shut out from immediate approach
by an almost continuous ice-barrier, which in its
extent, height, and appearance struck every be-
holder with admiration not unmixed with apprehension. This barrier rose perpendicularly from
the deep sea to a height varying from one hundred to two hundred feet above the level of the

water, which gave no bottom in soundings ranging from one hundred and fifty to two hundred and fifty fathoms. Despite this great depth of water, the perpendicular icy barrier was evidently grounded, thus indicating ice of a thickness of about one thousand feet.

Regarding the land discovered the first reliable observations were those of January 16th, when land was seen by Lieutenant Ringgold, of the Porpoise, and by Midshipmen Eld and Reynolds, of the Peacock, their statement running as follows: "The mountains could be distinctly seen stretching over the ice to the southwest." On the 19th land was again visible from the Vincennes, Alden reporting it twice to Wilkes, and on the same day high land was seen by all the crew of the Peacock. The ships were then in longitude 154° E., 66° 20′ S., practically on the Antarctic Circle. On February 2d high bold land bordered by the ice-barrier was visible to the Vincennes and Porpoise in longitude 137° E., latitude 66° 12′ S. Five days later the westerly trend of the land as previously seen was confirmed by a well-defined outline of high land rising above the perpendicular ice-barrier, the Vincennes being in longitude 132° E., latitude 66° 8′ S. On February 9th, in longitude 123° E., latitude 65° 27′ S., the land is spoken of as being indistinct. At 8 A.M. of the 12th land was reported again, in longitude 112° E., latitude 64° 57′ S., the land being in about 65° 20′ S. and trending nearly east and west.

Wilkes says of the land and of his efforts to reach it: "The solid barrier prevented our further progress. Land was now distinctly seen from eighteen to twenty miles distant, bearing from S.S.E. to S.W., a lofty mountain range covered with snow, though showing many ridges and indentations." Two days later he writes: "The 14th was remarkably clear and the land very distinct. By measurement we made the extent of coast of the Antarctic continent then in sight seventy-five miles and by approximate measurement three thousand feet high."

In longitude 97° E., Wilkes found the ice trending to the northward, well out of the Antarctic Circle, and after following it near to where Cook was stopped in February, 1773, Wilkes took his course for Sydney, where he learned that an English sealer, Captain Balleny, had discovered land in longitude 165° E., south of and near the point where Wilkes found the ice-barrier, and had attained a latitude of 69° S. in longitude 172° E. Here Wilkes, hearing of the prospective arrival of Sir James Clark Ross, forwarded for his benefit a tracing of the chart prepared as the American squadron had passed along the barrier, supplemented by the discoveries of Balleny. Ross publishes a copy of this chart in his "Voyage to the Southern Seas," together with Wilkes's letter, giving information not only as to discoveries, but also as to winds, currents, and the probable position of the magnetic pole.

Most unfortunately, on the chart transmitted to Ross by Wilkes, he entered, without distinguishing marks, land between longitudes 160° E. and 165° E., near the sixty-sixth parallel, which should have been marked with the legend of "probable land," it being most probably the supposed land of Lieutenant Ringgold, of the Vincennes, who on January 13, 1840, in longitude, 163° E., latitude 65° 8′ S., to use Ringgold's own words, "thought he could discern to the southeast something like distant mountains." As a matter of fact, Ross found no bottom at six hun-

The Vincennes in a Storm.
(From a sketch by Captain Wilkes.)

dred fathoms over this charted land, and naturally enough pointed out that he had sailed over a clear ocean where Wilkes had laid down land. This lack of caution on the part of Wilkes led to an acrimonious controversy which had no good end, but tended to discredit among the ill-informed the discoveries of land actually made by the expedition. Ross, evidently somewhat nettled, had the questionable taste to omit from his general South Polar Chart all of Wilkes's discoveries. This course, it is hardly necessary to say, has not commended itself to the best geographers, for in the standard atlas of Stieler, issued by the famous publishing house of Justus Purthes, the discoveries claimed by Wilkes are entered, with the legend, "Wilkes Land," extending from longitude 95° E. to 160° E. It is gratifying, moreover, to note as an evidence of the impartial justice of the Royal Geographical Society, that it acknowledged the accuracy and extent of the discoveries of Wilkes and of the value of his detailed narrative of the expedition, and therefor that society awarded to him its founders' medal.

Ross, it may be added, reached the highest known latitude in the Antarctic Circle, 78° 11′ S., where he discovered Victoria Land, tracing its coast from 70° to 79° S. latitude, along the meridian of 161° W., which proved to be a bold, mountainous country, practically inaccessible and having within its limits an active volcano about twelve thousand feet high—Mount Erebus.

On the subject of an Antarctic continent Ross says: "There do not appear to me sufficient grounds to justify the assertion that the various patches of land recently discovered by the American, French, and English navigators on the verge of the Antarctic Circle unite to form a great southern continent."

The investigations and deductions of a great scientist, the late W. B. Carpenter, give the latest word on this subject. Carpenter says: "The Antarctic ice-barrier is to be regarded as the margin of a polar ice-cap whose thickness at its edge is probably about two thousand feet. . . . These vast masses have originally formed part of a great ice-sheet formed by the cumulative pressure of successive snow-falls over a land area," etc. Elsewhere he adds: "That the circumpolar area is chiefly land and not water seems to be farther indicated," etc. The periphery of the ice-cap is estimated to be about ten thousand miles.

Thus the ordinary man may safely believe in the existence of an Antarctic continent whose outer margins were first skirted and recognized as part of a great land by Charles Wilkes, of the United States Navy.

After quitting the Southern seas, Wilkes voyaged through the Pacific Ocean, in accordance with his original orders. In the Feejee group, however, his experiences were most unfortunate. The pillaging of a grounded cutter by the natives resulted in Wilkes destroying one of their villages and capturing several of their chiefs, causing ill-feeling which a few days later culminated in an attack on a boat's crew, whereby Lieutenant Underwood and Midshipman Henry were killed by the natives and others of the party were severely wounded. An attack of a retaliatory character was made by Wilkes, who destroyed two native towns, laid waste plantations, killed about sixty of the savages and wounded many others.

View of the Antarctic Continent.
(From a sketch by Captain Wilkes.)

At every port Wilkes and his staff of officers and scientific assistants were most assiduous in making surveys and in acquiring knowledge of the countries and their inhabitants. Even the most prolonged voyage must end, and with pleasure officers and men saw again the shores of their country, where Wilkes landed, at New York, June 10, 1842, after four years of absence.

As might be expected, there were officers of the squadron who felt that their merits had not been properly recognized by Lieutenant Wilkes during this voyage of four years, and in consequence charges of a voluminous character and under a large number of heads were brought against him. The court which considered them acquitted Wilkes except as regards the punishment of several of his men, which in some cases appeared to have been more summary and severe than the regulations of the navy justified, for which action a reprimand was administered.

The collections made by the expedition, and the scientific volumes published in connection therewith, were very important additions to the scientific knowledge of the world. Professor Henry, in 1871, says: " The basis of the National Museum is a collection of the specimens of the United States Exploring Expedition under Captain, now Admiral, Wilkes. . . . The collections made by the naval expeditions—1838 to 1842—are supposed greatly to exceed those of any other similar character fitted out by any government; no published series of results compare in magnitude with that issued under the direction of the joint Library Committees of Congress." Sixteen quarto volumes were issued, five of narrative and eleven of a scientific character, while other parts were unfortunately destroyed by fire.

The beginning of the great civil war again brought Wilkes into striking and international prominence. Sent to the coast of Africa for the United States steamship San Jacinto, Wilkes promptly brought her into West Indies waters. Here he learned that the Confederate Commissioners, John Slidell and J. M. Mason, had run the blockade and landed in Cuba, and he decided, without consultation or orders, to capture them. The San Jacinto was then cruising for the Confederate privateer, the Sumter, but visited frequently the Cuban ports. Wilkes apparently accepted the prevailing opinion that Mason and Slidell were safe from interference, but, keeping his views to himself, he was frequently seen by one of his subordinates to be deeply engaged in perusing international law books, doubtless occupied in seeking for precedents in justification of his contemplated action.

On November 1, 1861, Lieutenant J. A. Greer, navigating officer, brought word that Mason and Slidell were booked for England by the steamer Trent, which was to leave Havana on the 7th. On November 4th Wilkes took station in the narrow channel of Old Bahama, through which the Trent would naturally pass and where she could not escape being seen by the lookout. Early on the morning of the 8th Wilkes ordered the ship cleared for action, and when the Trent was sighted at noon, Wilkes gave his executive officer, Lieutenant D. M. Fairfax, written instructions to board the steamer Trent, with two armed cutters, when he was to make prisoners of Messrs. Mason, Slidell, and their secretaries, and seize any despatches which he might find. A round shot

In an Ice-Field.

failed to stop the Trent, but a shell exploding in front of her bows brought her to. After protest, Mason and Slidell accepted the arrest, went on board the San Jacinto, whence they were taken to New York and later confined as prisoners at Fort Warren.

When Wilkes landed in New York he found

himself again famous, the central figure toward which, even in that time of war, the attention of all was turned. He was lauded by almost every citizen, praised by nearly every journal, and was the recipient of most flattering attentions. Complimentary banquets were given to him in New York, Boston, and elsewhere.

The Secretary of the Navy, in a letter dated November 30, 1861, wrote: "Especially do I congratulate you on the great public service you have rendered in the capture of the rebel emissaries. . . . Your conduct in seizing these public enemies was marked by intelligence, ability, decision, and firmness, and has the emphatic approval of this Department." With reference to the omission of Wilkes to capture the Trent, the Secretary says: "The forbearance exercised in this instance must not be permitted to constitute a precedent hereafter for infractions of neutral obligations."

Congress was not then in session, but it met a few weeks later, when almost the first act of the House of Representatives was to pass a joint resolution which declared that "the thanks of Congress are due, and are hereby tendered, to Captain Wilkes, of the United States Navy, for his brave, adroit, and patriotic conduct in the arrest and detention of the traitors, James M. Mason and John Slidell."

The hostile attitude of Great Britain, which country to many Americans appeared quite ready on slight pretence to acknowledge the Southern Confederacy, gave great anxiety to the administration. The astute Lincoln and the diplomatic Seward, supported by the patriotic Sumner in the Senate, and other conservative men in the House of Representatives, after due correspondence acceded to the demands of Great Britain that the prisoners should be released. Seward, however, justified Wilkes's action in the main as legal, but said that he erred in releasing the Trent; and by constituting himself as a court, and in not bringing the steamer before an admiralty court as guilty of carrying articles contraband of war, had acted irregularly. The United States declined to apologize, as no offence to Great Britain was intended, and forbore from claiming against England the right of search which that nation had so persistently exercised.

The Naval Committee of the Senate reported without amendment the resolution of thanks to Wilkes, but deemed it best to postpone it indefinitely. The ordinary citizen did not share the conservative, and it may be said the very wise, course of the administration, and the sentiment throughout the country was very generally one of national pride that under doubtful circumstances an American sailor had dared rather too much than too little for the dignity and safety of his country. Wilkes, himself, when told that possibly this act would cause him to lose his commission, said that he deemed his seizure of the commissioners simply a patriotic duty, and if needs be was willing to be sacrificed for his country. He continued to perform efficient service during the war, despite his advancing years.

In 1862, while in command of the Potomac flotilla, he shelled and destroyed City Point, and in command of a special squadron to maintain the blockade, captured and destroyed many blockade-runners.

With the closing of the war, and his retirement from active service, Wilkes returned to the scientific pursuits which had always engrossed his mind, and full of years and honor, died at Washington, February 8, 1877.

Of his early scientific labors it may be said that they had contributed in no small degree to the establishment of a national institution of international repute, the Naval Observatory.

For his important additions to the knowledge of the world, and especially for his ever-zealous war services, the memory and life of Charles Wilkes will ever abide fresh and honored in the hearts of his countrymen.

VIII.

JOHN CHARLES FRÉMONT,

THE PATHFINDER.

THE discovery and exploration of the trans-Mississippi region had many phases, the outcome of different conditions and varying individual efforts to determine the extent, possibilities, and resources of the undeveloped half of the American continent. The seamanship of Gray, the enthusiasm of Lewis, the courage of Clarke, the assiduity of Pike, the enterprise of Ashley, Wyeth, Sublette, Bonneville, and other trappers and traders, had done much to make known to the pioneer and settler the advantages and promise of the great West, and had roughly delineated the routes of travel best suited for the emigrant in his westward march.

In time many urged that the government of the United States, so long shamefully negligent of its magnificent acquisitions by purchase, discovery, and settlement, should enter in and possess its own. This, however, necessitated, first, a systematic examination of the physical features of the West to such an extent as to render possible its general and authoritative description; second, the granting of lands or homesteads to such of its daring citizens as might be willing to venture their lives as settlers in these remote regions.

Among public men who urged most strongly such action was one of the most distinguished of our Western statesmen, Thomas H. Benton, first Senator from the new and growing State of Missouri. He persistently advocated the settlement of the lower Columbia by Americans, the enforcement of the title of the United States to the Pacific Coast region from California northward to the forty-ninth parallel, and in 1825 he presented in the Senate a bill authorizing the use of the army and navy to protect American interests in Oregon.

In season and out of season Benton opposed the joint occupation of Oregon by England and America, unfailingly supporting every measure which promised to fill its fertile valleys with American settlers. So dominant was this idea in Benton's career that artistic skill has fittingly shaped his statue in St. Louis with its bronze hand pointing *west*, with his prophetic words carved on the pedestal, "There is the *east*. There is India."

In his efforts to put his ideas into practical shape, Benton threw the great weight of his influence as a Senator toward the employment in such explorations of a member of his family by marriage, John Charles Frémont, whose ability and inclinations specially suited him for the scientific examination and exploration of the trans-Mississippi region.

Born January 21, 1813, at Savannah, Ga., Frémont entered Charleston College, where his disregard of discipline prevented his graduating, although the faculty later honored him with the degrees of Bachelor and Master of Arts. Well

John Charles Frémont.

grounded in the classics and familiar with the ordinary astronomical methods of determining latitude and longitude, Frémont visited South America on the United States ship Natchez, as a teacher. Later, appointed a professor of mathematics in the navy, he declined the position to accept more congenial service as assistant engineer of the United States Topographic Corps, where he had experience in preliminary surveys of railroads and also in a military reconnoissance among the Cherokees in Georgia. Commissioned in the United States Army, in 1838, as second lieutenant in the Topographic Corps, his

Jessie Benton Frémont.

initial service was fortunately as principal assistant to I. N. Nicolet, in the survey of the country between the Mississippi and the Missouri. Nicolet, an able and distinguished engineer, was the first explorer in America who made general use of the barometer for determining elevations of the great interior country, and his map of this region was one of the greatest contributions ever made to American geography.

In 1841 Frémont married Jessie Benton, a daughter of Senator Benton, through whose influence Frémont was assigned to the command of the expedition ordered to explore the country between the Missouri River and the Rocky Mountains on the line of the Kansas and Platte Rivers.

In May, 1842, while Frémont was on the frontier making preparations for the journey, there came, as Mrs. Frémont relates, an order recalling him to Washington. Mrs. Frémont sent a special messenger to her husband, advising him to move immediately for good and sufficient reasons, to be given later. Meanwhile, holding the letter, she wrote the colonel who had given the order for the recall that she had neither forwarded the order nor informed Frémont of it, as she knew that obedience thereto would ruin the expedition. On such a small thread of circumstances hung the fate of his first separate command, which brought Frémont into such great prominence in connection with the exploration and development of the Pacific Coast region.

The journey of Frémont lay up the North Fork of the Platte, through South Pass, into Wind River Valley, his march being marked by the usual experiences of hardship and suffering inseparable from the time and region. The most notable event of the journey was the ascent of the main and highest peak of the Wind River range, now known as Frémont's Peak. Their first attempts were unsuccessful, the party suffering from great cold, excessive fatigue, and mountain fever resulting from the rarity of the air. Frémont, however, persevered and succeeded. He describes the final ascent as follows:

"We reached a point where the buttress was overhanging, and there was no other way of surmounting the difficulty than by passing around one side of it, which was the face of a vertical precipice of several hundred feet. Putting hands and feet in the crevices between the blocks I succeeded in getting over it, and when I reached the top found my companions in a small valley below. Descending to them, we continued climbing and in a short time reached the crest. I sprang upon the summit and another step would have precipitated me into an immense snow-field five hundred feet below. At the edge of this field was a sheer icy precipice, and then, with a gradual fall, the field sloped off for about a mile until it struck the foot of another lower ridge. I stood on a narrow crest about three feet in width. As soon as I had gratified the first feelings of curiosity I descended, and each man ascended in turn, for I would only allow one at a time to mount the unstable and precarious slab, which it seemed a breath would hurl into the abyss below. We mounted the barometer in the snow at the summit, and fixing a ramrod in the crevice, unfurled the national flag to wave in the breeze where never flag waved before." The elevation of this summit, as determined by Frémont, was 13,570 feet.

His success on this expedition caused his most favorable reception by the War Department on his return to the States.

218   EXPLORERS AND TRAVELLERS

Frémont's second expedition contemplated the connection of his first explorations with those

Ascending Frémont's Peak.

made by Captain Wilkes on the Pacific Coast, so as to give a connected survey across the interior of North America. The party, which left Kansas City May 29, 1843, consisted of forty men, equipped with twelve carts for transportation and a light wagon for scientific instruments. The route followed was up the valley of the Kansas River, thence by the South Fork of the Platte to the vicinity of the present city of Denver. After considerable hesitation a northerly route was taken, skirting the westerly limits of the great Laramie plain, which brought Frémont to the emigrant trail in the vicinity of the South Pass. The volume of travel toward the Pacific Coast even at that early date may be estimated from his description of the Oregon trail as "a broad smooth highway where the numerous heavy wagons of the emigrants have entirely beaten and crushed the mountain sage."

Crossing Green River and following up Ham's Fork, Frémont reached the valley of Bear River, the principal tributary of Great Salt Lake, which was filled with emigrants travelling to the lower Columbia River. Frémont expressed his surprise at the confidence and daring of the emigrants as he met in one place "a family of two men and women and several children travelling alone through such a country so remote from civilization." Turning south from this point and quitting the travelled road Frémont visited the Great Salt Lake, of which he says: "Hitherto this lake had been seen only by trappers, who were wandering through the country in search of new beaver streams, caring very little for geography; its lands had never been visited, and none were to be found who had entirely made the circuit of its shores, and no instrumental observations or geographical survey of any description had ever been made anywhere in the neighboring region. It was generally supposed that the lake had no visible outlet, but among the trappers, including those in my own camp, were many who believed that somewhere on its surface was a terrible whirlpool, through which its waters found their way to the ocean by some subterranean communication."

The lake was eventually reached from the lower part of Bear River in an india-rubber canoe, by means of which Frémont also landed on a mountainous island near the centre of the lake, where from an elevation of eight hundred feet he was able to determine with considerable accuracy the contours and extent of this remarkable body of water. Instead of a tangled wilderness of shrubbery teeming with an abundance of game, as the party expected, the island proved to be broken, rocky land, some twelve miles in circumference, on which there was neither water nor trees; a few saline shrubs and other hardy plants formed the only vegetation. The lake is described as being enclosed in a basin of rocky mountains, which sometimes leave grassy fields and extensive bottoms between them and the shore, while in other places they come directly down to the water in bold and precipitous bluffs. He speaks of the water of the lake being at a low stage and the probabilities that the marshes and low ground are overflowed in the season of high water. Frémont says that "we felt pleasure in knowing that we were the first who in the traditional annals of the country had visited the island and broke with joyful sounds the long solitude." But in view of the dissipation of his dream of fertility he named it Disappointment Island.

Turning northward Frémont reached, on September 18, 1843, Fort Hall, Idaho, then a post under British control, whose original importance as an Indian trading-post had been greatly enhanced by its location on the emigrant route to Oregon, at a distance of over one thousand three hundred miles from the then frontier settlement of Westport, Mo. Following closely the emigrant trail Frémont, on October 8th, passed Fort Boisé, then occupied by the Hudson Bay Company, and on the 25th of the month arrived at another trading establishment of this company, at the junction of the Walla Walla and Columbia Rivers. This was considered by emigrants as the practical termination of their overland journey since navigation down the river was rapid and convenient.

Frémont found many American emigrants at Fort Vancouver on his visit to that post and also learned that others already occupied the adjacent lowlands of the Willamette Valley. Moreover, these pioneers were not confining their efforts to Oregon, for while small parties were pushing southward through that valley to settlements in Northern California, still others, making detours near Fort Hall, reached, by a more direct route through passes in the Sierra Nevada, the banks of the Sacramento.

On November 10, 1843, Frémont left Vancouver to return to the United States, having in view an entirely new route whereby he might be able to complete the exploration of the great interior basin between the Rocky Mountains and the Sierra Nevada. His party then consisted of twenty-five. Leaving the Columbia at a point above The Dalles, Frémont followed Des Chutes River to its source, and passing over to Lake Klamath, contemplated a journey to and a winter camp on either Mary's Lake or the mythical Buenaventura River. His trail brought him to Lake Klamath, and later to Goose Lake, the source of the Sacramento. Winter had now commenced; the weather in the mountains proved to be extremely cold, snow-storms became frequent, and his search for Mary's Lake and Buenaventura River proved fruitless and dangerous.

These mythical water-courses, which had been eliminated from the domain of geography by Bonneville's map of 1837, proved indeed to be veritable waters of the desert, mere mirages that nearly led Frémont to an untimely fate. Frémont's frequent allusions in his field journal to these imaginary streams show his then belief in their existence, which appears extraordinary in view of existing publications. In Bonneville's maps are charted with general accuracy the great interior basins of the Great Salt, Mud, and Sevier Lakes, the Humboldt and Sevier Rivers. The general extent and direction of the Willamette, Sacramento, and San Joaquin Rivers are indicated, and the non-existence of the Buenaventura and other hypothetical streams was conclusively determined. The existence of these maps was generally known, and their absence from Frémont's topographic outfit is remarkable; a most unfortunate omission, as Benton in his "Thirty Years' View" describes Frémont's charts and geographic information as "disastrously erroneous."

Struggling along in the snow through a forest of unknown extent, Frémont halted, on December 16th, on the verge of a rocky precipice, from which the party looked down more than one thousand feet upon a broad lake, the most westerly waters of the great interior basin, which, from its pleasing contrast to the wintry weather of the Sierra Nevada, they called Summer Lake. Attempting to travel in an easterly direction Frémont found himself beaten back by an impassable country, there being rocky, sterile mountains on either side which obliged him to keep to the south through a wild, barren, and uninhabited region. Frémont, describing the country, says: "On both sides the mountains showed often stupendous and curious-looking rocks, which at several places so narrowed the valley that scarcely a pass was left for the camp. It was a singular place to travel through—shut up in the earth, a sort of chasm, the little strip of grass under our feet, the rough walls of bare rock on either hand, and the narrow strip of sky above."

The year 1844 opened with the party in a forlorn and dispirited condition, as they were practically lost in the tangle of the valleys and mountains. The grass had become so scanty and unwholesome that the overtaxed animals fell ill; some died and others were stolen by Indians, so that the party lost fifteen head of stock by the time they reached Pyramid Lake, where they camped from the 10th to the 16th of January. Here they found grass abundant, firewood plentiful, and from an Indian village they obtained salmon trout, a feast to the famished men. The Indians indicated the general direction of the route out of the desolate country, but no one would consent to accompany the party as guide. The region traversed continued so rough and lamed the animals so badly that on the 18th Frémont determined to abandon the easterly course, thinking it advisable to cross the Sierra Nevada to the valley of the Sacramento by the first practicable pass. Now and then a few Indians were met, and finally a guide was obtained, who led them to the southward, over a low range of mountains through a snow-covered pass into what proved to be Carson Valley. The snow deepened and the country became so broken as to make progress difficult, long, tedious detours necessary, and soon travel was only possible along high and exposed ridges, which were comparatively snow free. Finally it became necessary to abandon their mountain howitzer at an impracticable cañon that led into a valley which Frémont at first erroneously supposed to be to the westward of the Sierra Nevada. Continuing on without a guide they met other Indians, who stated it was impossible to cross the mountains on account of the deep snow, but after much persuasion, and by means of large presents, an Indian guide was finally induced to undertake the journey. Frémont, fully conscious of the desperate conditions, which entailed the possible death of all, endeavored to encourage his men by reminding them of the contrast between the fast falling snow of the surrounding Sierra Nevada and the flower-clad meadows in the adjacent valley of the Sacramento, and informed them that his astronomical observations showed that they were only sixty miles distant from Sutter's great establishment.

Their provisions were now practically exhausted; neither tallow, grease, nor salt remained, and even their hunting dogs were killed for food. Making the best of the situation their clothing and outfit were put in the best of order, and on February 2d, crossing the frozen river on the ice, the party commenced the ascent of the mountain, the men, Frémont relates, being unusually silent over the hazardous and doubtful enterprise. Ten men, mounted on the strongest horses, broke the road, each man in succession opening the path, either on foot or on horseback, until he and his horse became exhausted, when he dropped to the rear. The very deep snow made it impossible to follow the main valley, and they necessarily worked along steep and difficult mountain-sides. On the third day the snow had become so deep that their best horses gave out entirely, refusing to make further effort; the day ended with the party at a stand-still and the camp equipage strewed along the route. Too exhausted to make huts, they camped that night without shelter and suffered bitterly from the unusual cold, as the temperature fell to twenty-two degrees below freezing. Two Indians who had

Kit Carson.

joined the party expatiated on the impossibility of crossing at this point, and the guide, influenced by them, deserted the party the next morning.

Having obtained snow-shoes from the Indians,

on February 6th, Frémont, accompanied by Carson and Fitzpatrick, made a reconnoissance and reached a high peak, from which Carson saw a little mountain to the westward which he recognized as one seen by him fifteen years before, so that confidence was somewhat restored. On examining the general depth of the snow it was found to be five feet, but in places it proved to be twenty. As this snow was plainly impracticable for the pack-train, sledges were made for transporting the baggage, which was dragged forward by the men with the expectation that the horses without load could break a path for themselves. Unfortunately the weather turned bitterly cold, and the temperature falling thirty-five degrees below the freezing-point, a number of the men were frost-bitten.

Frémont, and indeed the whole party, now realized that the crossing of the mountains into the valley of the Sacramento was a struggle for life, but this in no wise disorganized the party. This desperate march lasted during the whole of February. Finally Frémont with the advance party reached Sutter's ranch on March 6th in a state of complete exhaustion; help was immediately sent to the main party, which arrived a few days later. Frémont's route across the mountains was practically through the pass now crossed by the Central Pacific Railway, the descent into the Sacramento being through the valley of the American River. In crossing the Sierras not less than thirty-four out of the sixty-seven horses died of exhaustion or were killed for food, the meat of these animals being the only resource against starvation.

One of the party, DeRossier, became insane on March 1st, and Frémont says: "Hunger and fatigue joined to weakness of body and fear of perishing in the mountains had crazed him. The times were severe when stout men lost their minds from extremity of suffering, when horses died, when mules and horses ready to die of starvation were killed for food, yet there was no murmuring or hesitation."

Sutter's Fort, on the Sacramento, was then the most important American establishment in California; the fort itself was an adobe structure defended by twelve pieces of artillery. Sutter had a large force in his employ engaged in farming his extensive wheat-fields, in milling operations, in blacksmith- and other work-shops.

One might have thought that Frémont would have delayed long in the delightful climate and conditions that obtained at Sutter's, but such was not the nature of the man. The entire party were reunited at Sutter's Fort on March 8th, and under Frémont's well-directed efforts, in the short space of fourteen days the starving band was reorganized, remounted, and equipped fully for instant march. The return journey was to be through the pass at the head of the San Joaquin River, discovered by Walker, whose name was affixed to it by Frémont. Crossing the Sierra Nevada the party struck the Spanish trail, which was then followed by all wagon-trains or mounted parties travelling to and fro between Los

Angeles and Santa Fé. The region over which they passed was desolate in the extreme, the road rough and rocky, grass scanty and poor, while water was found only in holes and at long distances. In pointing to it, Fremont's Spanish guide well states: "There are the great plains; there is found neither water nor grass—nothing; every animal which goes upon them dies."

The party had to undergo not only terrible discomforts arising from the physical conditions of the country, but was also harassed by hostile Indians, who stole some of their stock. The expedition fortunately escaped with the loss of only one man, although parties in advance and in their rear were plundered and slaughtered. Speaking of their travelling alone in twenty-seven days a distance of five hundred and fifty miles through this inhospitable region, Frémont comments, that although their lonely journey gave them the advantage of more grass, yet they "had the disadvantage of finding also the marauding savages who had gathered down upon the trail, waiting the approach of their prey. This greatly increased our labors, besides costing us the life of an excellent man. We had to move all day in a state of watch and prepare for combat, scouts and flankers out, a front and rear division of our men, and baggage animals in the centre. At night camp duty was severe; those who had toiled all day had to guard by turns the camp and horses all night. Frequently one-third of the whole party were on guard at once, and nothing but this vigilance saved us from attack.

We were constantly dogged by bands and even whole tribes of the marauders."

Reaching, in Southern Utah, the head-waters of the Virgin River, where Santa Fé trains usually halt to recruit the strength of their animals in its grassy meadows, Frémont was joined by the famous trapper, Joseph Walker, who consented to serve as guide in the departure to the northeastward, as they now quitted the Spanish trail. Frémont then skirted the eastern edge of the great interior basin and visiting Sevier and Utah Lakes, thus completed practically the circuit of the basin. He then turned eastward through the valleys of the DuChesne and Green Rivers, tributaries to the Colorado, and pushing through the very heart of the Rocky Mountains, by the way of the pass near Leadville, at an elevation of eleven thousand two hundred feet, he reached the Arkansas Valley June 29, 1844.

His journey eastward across the great Kansas plains was of an easy character, and the 31st of July, 1844, saw his expedition safe at Independence, Mo. He had been absent fourteen months, during which time he had travelled some six thousand five hundred miles, the greater part of his journey being through the most barren and inhospitable regions of North America.

The character and extent of Frémont's astronomical and other physical observations on this long, arduous, and dangerous journey constituted the great value of his exploring work. In few instances did it fall to Frémont's lot to first explore any section of the country, but it was his good fortune, as it was his intent, to first contribute systematic, extended, and reliable data as to climate, elevation, physical conditions, and geographical positions. The hypsometrical work begun by Frémont culminated, indeed, in the un-

Lake Klamath.

paralleled collation of elevations by Gannett; his climatic observations have been perfected by the Signal Corps; his astronomical and geological data have been overwhelmed by the magnificent collections and field work of the United States Coast and Geodetic and Geological Surveys; but it is to be noted that Frémont's observations, which he gave in detail, were so honest and good that they have withstood successfully the test of hostile examination. Frémont's scientific spirit was strikingly exemplified in this terrible mid-winter journey through the mountains of Nevada, when observations for time, latitude, elevation, or temperature were daily and regularly made despite snow, extreme cold, and physical weakness from semi-starvation.

On the recommendation of General Winfield Scott, in a special report, the unprecedented honor of double brevets—of first lieutenant and captain—was conferred on Frémont for gallant and highly meritorious services in connection with these two expeditions.

Frémont's third expedition consisted of sixty men. They left Bent's Fort, on the Arkansas, August 16, 1845. Its object, as far as exploration was concerned, included a survey of the head-waters of the Arkansas, Rio Grande, and Rio Colorado, the basin of the Great Salt Lake and the practicable passes of the Cascade and southern Sierra Nevada.

It was during this journey that Frémont quite fully surveyed the southern shores of Salt Lake. The water was then at an unusually low—possibly at its lowest known—level, and having been informed by the Indians that it was fordable to Antelope Island, Frémont with Kit Carson rode to the island, the water nowhere reaching above the saddle-girths of their horses.

Dividing his party Frémont crossed the Utah desert between the thirty-eighth and thirty-ninth parallels, while his subordinate, Walker, explored the valley and sink of the Humboldt. Rendezvousing at Lake Walker and again separating, Frémont reached Sutter's Fort through the American River route, while Walker and the main party crossed the Sierras into the extreme southern part of the San Joaquin Valley, opposite Tulare Lake. Of the survey and explorations made by the expedition it may be briefly said that they added very greatly to a knowledge of Upper California, and resulted in the publication in 1848 of the most accurate map of that region extant.

There was, however, another and more important phase to the third expedition than that of mere exploration. Frémont before leaving Washington was informed that war with Mexico was possible, and received general unwritten instructions looking to such a contingency. The forecast of trouble proved correct, and the preliminary and extensive disturbances in California interfered most materially with the progress of his surveys. Frémont's explorations westward of the Arkansas River had been through and over Mexican territory. In order to place himself in proper position as a non-invader he proceeded to Monterey, Cal., at the earliest practicable moment and applied to the commanding general, Don José Castro, for permission to extend, in the interests of science and commerce, the geographical survey of the nearest route between the United States and the Pacific Ocean. The request was granted promptly and courteously. Scarcely had Frémont commenced his survey in Northern California than he was peremptorily ordered by General Castro, who later appears to have been acting under orders from the Mexican Government, to quit the department; the message being coupled with an intimation that non-compliance would result in expulsion by an armed force. The message was delivered in such manner and language as incensed Frémont and caused him to peremptorily refuse. Withdrawing a short distance he erected a stockade and awaited expulsion by arms. The Mexican force made several forward movements, but carefully avoided an attack. Frémont finally judged it advisable to quit Mexican territory, as his remaining might be detrimental to the United States. He consequently withdrew slowly toward Oregon, surveying and exploring as he moved northward.

On May 7, 1845, Frémont was overtaken in the valley of the upper Sacramento by Lieutenant Archibald H. Gillespie, of the marine corps, who brought from Washington important despatches which were destined to settle the fate of California as a Mexican state. Frémont was informed through Gillespie that war with Mexico had been declared, that the government counted upon him to ascertain and conciliate the disposition of the people of California toward the United States, and especially to conserve American interests by ascertaining and counteracting any scheme looking to the cession of California to Great Britain. Frémont was then surrounded by hostile Klamaths, who killed several of his party and with whom he had several engagements, which resulted in the de struction of the principal village, fishing appliances, etc., of the offending tribe.

Frémont, turning promptly southward, his heart set on the important mission intrusted to him, saved from ravage the American settlements in the valley of the Sacramento, which were in imminent danger of destruction between the proclamation of the Mexican authorities ordering confiscation and expulsion and the threatening attitude of the Indian allies, incited by unscrupulous officials to activity. Aided by volunteers from the American settlers Frémont freed California permanently from Mexican domination, his actions receiving mention and approval from the President in his Annual Message to Congress, in December, 1846.

Commodore Stockton, United States Navy, charged with the control of affairs on the Pacific Coast, appointed Frémont Governor and military commander of California. When controversies arose between Commodore Stockton, of the navy, and General Kearney, of the army, each having authority from Washington to conquer California and organize its government, Frémont adhered to Stockton, his first commander. In consequence serious complications arose, which finally resulted in the trial of Frémont, and, although the findings of the court were partly disapproved and the sentence remitted, he resigned from the army.

His courage, persistency, and success in these expeditions gained for Frémont world-wide reputation. At home he was named The Pathfinder; abroad he received the Founders' Medal from the Royal Geographical Society of England and many other well-deserved marks of appreciation from geographers.

Devoted to California and to its exploration Frémont immediately fitted out, at his own expense, another expedition, the fourth. In October, 1848, with thirty-three men and a large train he crossed the Rocky Mountains, undeterred by his fearful experiences in 1844, and again attempted the passage of the snow-covered Sierras in mid-winter. The snow was deep, the guide inefficient, and the winter unusually cold. One-third of his men and all his animals perished after suffering cold, hunger, and fatigue of the most appalling character, and the remnant of the expedition returned to Santa Fé. Unappalled by this overwhelming disaster Frémont reorganized at Santa Fé a new party, and after a long, perilous journey reached Sacramento in the spring of 1849.

Frémont's experiences during his surveys of the great valleys of the San Joaquin and Sacramento caused him to fall under the fascinating spell which California exercises over the greater number of its Eastern settlers. The vast domain of its virgin forests, the luxuriance of its vegetation, the extent and fertility of its valley lands, and its incomparable climate were speedily recognized by Frémont as so many physical conditions calculated to insure unparalleled prosperity when once it should be occupied by Americans. He saw this vast region practically a waste; its magnificent harbors unvexed, unbroken by the keels of commerce; its unrivalled valleys awaiting the hand of intelligent labor to transform them from mere pastures for scattered herds of cattle into fruitful granaries, orchards, and vineyards capable of feeding a continent. Imbued with these ideas he cast in his lot with California, and was a potent power in making it a free State, and was honored by election as its first Senator, unfortunately, however, drawing the short term in the United States Senate.

Failing, through the defeat of his party, of re-election, Frémont visited Europe for a brief and well-earned rest, which was broken by the authorization of Congress for a survey of a trans-continental railway, which awoke his dormant exploring spirit. Returning promptly to the United States he organized an expedition under private auspices, which started westward in September, 1853. He travelled by the central route through the mountains of Colorado, passing over the Sierra Blanca, through the Sandy Hill Pass and the valley of the Grand River. Turning southward into Utah and crossing the Sawatch Mountains, Frémont's march brought him to the Sierra Nevada near the end of winter, and their passage was attempted near the thirty-seventh parallel. Thereof he writes: "I was prepared to find the Sierra here broad, rugged, and blocked with snow, and was not disappointed in my expectations." The snow being impassable and food failing he made a detour of some seventy miles to the southward and reached the Kern River Valley through Walker Pass. The march entailed endless suffering and extreme privations on the party, which was pushed to the direst extremities to preserve life. They were often without food of any kind for an entire day and for many weeks had only the flesh of their emaciated and exhausted horses. The disastrous outcome of this expedition impaired Frémont's reputation, it appearing, then as now, surprising that, aware by bitter experience of the impracticability of such a journey, he should have so timed his march as to be again overwhelmed by the dreadful winter snow of the Nevada range.

This sketch has in view the treatment neither of Frémont's career as a soldier nor as a politician, which phases of his life, viewed by ordinary circumstances, may be considered as unsuccessful. It need not be here dwelt on that his name became a watchword of the ever-growing spirit of human freedom, and that as the standard-bearer of an idea he astonished the country and the world by obtaining the suffrages of nearly one and a half millions of his countrymen for the highest office in the gift of the people. His unwavering, if impractical, devotion to freedom was forcibly illustrated by his emancipation proclamation in Missouri, which he declined to recall, even at the request of the President who revoked it.

It is undoubted that Frémont's non-success in business and political ventures has tended to diminish his reputation as an explorer, a reputation which, it is safe to say, must continue to grow steadily in the future with the development of the great trans-Rocky Mountain region to which he gave the enthusiasm of his youth, the maturity of his manhood, and for which he sacrificed his profession and his private fortune. While Frémont loved all the great West, it was to California especially that he gave the best he had of mind, heart, and body, never sparing himself in any effort for the upbuilding of her future. So it is that in the scene of his activities on the shores of the golden Pacific, rather than on the coast of the Atlantic, should be more appreciated the labors and ever grow brighter and brighter the name of John C. Frémont, the Pathfinder.

IX.

ELISHA KENT KANE,

Arctic Explorer.

Among the picturesque and striking figures of Arctic explorers none abides more firmly in the minds of Americans than that of Elisha Kent Kane, whose career and fame largely relate to the fate of the lost explorer, Sir John Franklin.

Kane was born in Philadelphia, February 3, 1820. In 1842 he graduated in medicine at the University of Pennsylvania, and the following year, while waiting for a vacancy in the medical corps of the navy, for which he had passed an examination, sailed on the frigate Brandywine, as physician to the embassy, to China, under Caleb Cushing, Minister Plenipotentiary. Later, commissioned as an officer of the medical corps of the United States Navy, he served on the west coast of Africa, in Brazil, in the Mediterranean, and on special duty with the army in Mexico. This brief statement of his duties conveys, however, no idea of the intense energy and restless activity of Kane in his eager efforts to acquire personal knowledge of the very ends of the earth.

Indeed, considering Kane's very short life (he

died at thirty-seven), there is no man of modern times to whom the words of Tennyson, in his strong poem of Ulysses, more fittingly apply:

> "I cannot rest from travel, . . .
> For always roaming with a hungry heart
> Much have I seen and known: cities of men
> And manners, climates, councils, governments,
> Myself not least but honored of them all."

Suffice it here to say that before Kane was thirty he had visited in America the greater part of the eastern half of the United States, the city of Mexico, Cuba, and Brazil from Rio de Janeiro to the eastern Andes; in Africa, along the Gold and Slave Coasts, to Dahomey, Cape Colony, and up the Nile to the Second Cataract; in Europe, the eastern, southern, and central countries; in Asia, the coast of China, Ceylon, India from Bombay to the Himalayas, Persia, and Syria. Elsewhere he had travelled in the islands of Cape Verde, Singapore, Java, Sumatra, and Luzon of the Philippines. This incessant travel is the more remarkable as he was always sea-sick, was a man of delicate physique, and nowhere passed six months without being prostrated by severe illness. As to personal experiences, he had been wounded in Egypt by a Bedouin who strove to rob him, narrowly escaped death in saving captured Mexican officers from slaughter at the hands of renegade irregulars, and barely survived his unique experiences in the crater of a volcano.

His descent into the volcano of Tael, in the

Philippines, illustrates Kane's utter disregard of dangers whenever he desired to investigate any phenomena. As related by Dr. Elder, Kane not

Elisha Kent Kane

only was lowered two hundred feet below the point usually visited, but descended to the very surface of the burning lake and dipped his specimen bottles into the steaming sulphur water. This feat nearly cost him his life, for although he was able to crawl to and fasten the bamboo ropes around his body, yet his boots were charred in pieces on his feet, sulphurous air-currents stifled him into insensibility, and he would have perished had it not been for the strenuous exertions of Baron Löe, his companion.

The turning-point in Kane's life came in 1850, when, induced by the persistent petition of Lady Franklin, President Taylor recommended to Congress an appropriation for an expedition in search of Sir John Franklin and his missing ships. Kane immediately volunteered for Arctic service, pressing and urging his application by every means at his command. Congress acted tardily, so that the whole expedition was fitted out in eighteen days, and Kane at the last moment, when his hopes had failed, received orders as surgeon of the Advance, the flagship, which he joined May 20, 1850.

The expedition owed its existence to the enterprise and generosity of Henry Grinnell, whose philanthropic mind planned, practical energy equipped, and munificence endowed it. Without Grinnell's action Congress would have failed to fit out the expedition, and the grateful chapter of American co-operation with England in its Franklin search would have been unwritten. Such practical displays of sympathy in matters of general and national interest, now considered the most hopeful signs of international fellowship, may be said to have been inaugurated by the despatch of the first Grinnell expedition on its errand of humanity.

Under a joint resolution of Congress, passed May 2, 1850, the President was authorized "to accept and attach to the navy two vessels offered by Henry Grinnell, Esq., to be sent to the Arctic seas in search of Sir John Franklin and his companions." These vessels—two very small brigs, the flagship Advance and the Rescue—were placed under command of Lieutenant Edwin J. DeHaven, an officer of Antarctic service under Wilkes. The vessels had detachable rudders, modern fittings, were admirably strengthened and fully equipped; in short, they were thoroughly adapted to the difficult navigation in prospect. Where Grinnell's forethought and liberality ended there was, says Kane, another tale: the strictly naval equipment could not be praised, and the "crews consisted of man-of-war's-men of various climes and habitudes, with constitutions most of them impaired by disease or temporarily broken by the excesses of shore life;" but he commends them as ever brave, willing, and reliable.

The squadron touched at various Greenland ports and then entered the dreaded ice-pack of Melville Bay, in which the sailing vessels made slow progress; but in their besetment of three weeks the only dangerous experience was a "nip," which nearly destroyed the Advance. The movement of the ice-floes is thus graphically told by Kane: " The momentum of the assailing floe was so irresistible that as it impinged against the solid margin of the land ice there was no recoil, no interruption to its progress. The elastic material corrugated before the enormous pressure, then cracked, then crumbled, and at last rose, the lesser over the greater, sliding up in great inclined planes, and these again, breaking by their weight and their continued impulse, toppled over in long lines of fragmentary ice."

DeHaven entered Lancaster Sound, near the end of August, in company with half a dozen English ships bound on the same humane errand, and on the 24th Master Griffin, of the Rescue, participated in the search with Captain Ommaney, which resulted in the discovery, on Beechy Island, of vestiges of an encampment. Two days later DeHaven and Kane shared in the joint search, wherein Captain Penny discovered the graves of three of Franklin's crew. These discoveries proved that Franklin's expedition had wintered there during 1845-46, and later innumerable traces of their stay were noted, indicating the good condition and activity of the expedition. On September 10th DeHaven's squadron was off Griffith Island in company with eight English search ships. Consulting with Griffin, DeHaven concluded that they had not attained such a position as promised advantageous operations in the season of 1851, and so decided to extricate the vessels from the ice and return home.

Strong gales and an unusually early advance of winter prevented such action and resulted in the ships being frozen up in the pack, where they drifted helplessly to and fro, a condition they were destined to undergo for many months.

The Arctic Highway.

Beset in the middle of Wellington Channel, the American squadron, with varying movements to and fro, first drifted under the influence of southerly gales to the north-northwest, attaining latitude 75° 25′ N., longitude 93° 31′ W. In this northerly drift the expedition discovered Murdaugh Island and quite extensive masses of land to the northwest of North Devon, to which the name of Grinnell was given. This land was further extended the following year by the discoveries of Captain Penny, and most unwarrantable efforts were made by ungenerous and unappreciating officials in England to take from the American squadron its ewe lamb of 1850, an attempt that, properly refuted, failed of its purpose.

October 2, 1860, the direction of the drift changed to the south and later to the east. Their involuntary course lay through Wellington Channel, Barrow Strait, and Lancaster Sound into Baffin Bay, where release came, near Cape Walsingham, June 5, 1851. The drift covered ten hundred and fifty miles and lasted eight and a half months. The sun was absent twelve weeks. It is impossible to adequately describe the physical and mental sufferings of the party during this protracted ice imprisonment. It was a constant succession of harassing conditions, each, if possible, seeming worse than the former. Now the ships were so firmly imbedded in the cemented ice-pack that extrication appeared impossible; again the complete disruption of the pack threatened, or the instant destruction of their vessels impended, with prospects of a winter on the naked floe under such conditions of darkness, sickness, lack of shelter, and suitable nutrition as would render a lingering death unavoidable. No single week passed with a feeling of security; for days at a time there was no hour free from terrible suspense as to what fate might immediately befall, and four times in one day the entire party prepared to abandon ship at order. The cold became extreme, the mean of one week in March being thirty-one degrees below zero; seal and other fresh meat could be got only in small quantities, and scurvy, the bane of Arctic explorers, affected all save six of the crew, DeHaven being put off duty by this disease. In all these terrible experiences, which were borne with a fortitude, courage, and patience most creditable, Kane was first and foremost in sustaining the heroic efforts of Griffin, master of the Rescue, on whom the executive duties devolved during DeHaven's illness. It may be said that not only Kane's medical skill, but also his cheeriness, activity, and ingenious devices contributed largely to conserve the health, spirits, and morale of the crew in these dark hours when despair seemed justified.

Released from the pack, DeHaven patched up his injured ships and attempted to return and prosecute further the Franklin search; but, stopped in his return journey by ice in the upper part of Melville Bay, he judiciously decided to return to the United States, which was safely reached September 30, 1851.

The following extracts from Kane's very vivid account of the expedition illustrate some of the most striking phases of their experiences as recorded in his journal.

Of the conditions and experience of the Advance in the moving ice-pack he says:

"We were yet to be familiarized with the strife of the ice-tables, now broken into tumbling masses and piling themselves in angry confusion against our sides; now fixed in chaotic disarray by the fields of new ice that imbedded them in a single night; again, perhaps, opening in treacherous pools, only to close around us with a force that threatened to grind our brig to powder."

"A level snow-covered surface was rising up in inclined planes or rudely undulating curves. These, breaking at their summits, fell off on each side in masses of twenty tons' weight. Tables of six feet in thickness by twenty of perpendicular height, and some of them fifteen yards in length, surging up into the misty air, heaving, rolling, tottering, and falling with a majestic deliberation worthy of the forces that impelled them."

The following descriptions indicate the narrow escapes of the ships from destruction during disruptions of the ice-pack:

"The separated sides would come together with an explosion like a mortar, craunching the newly formed field and driving it headlong in fragments for fifty feet upon the floe till it piled up against our bulwarks. Everything betokened a crisis. Sledges, boats, packages of all sorts were disposed in order; contingencies were met as they approached by new delegations of duty; every man was at work, officers and seamen alike. The Rescue, crippled and thrown away from us to the further side of a chasm, was deserted, and her company consolidated with ours. Our own brig groaned and quivered under the pressure against her sides."

"The ice came in with the momentum before mentioned as irresistible, progressive, and grand. All expected to betake ourselves sledgeless to the ice, for the open space around the vessel barely admits of a foot-board. The timbers and even cross-beams protected by shores vibrated so as to communicate to you the peculiar tremor of a cotton-factory. Presently the stern of the brig, by a succession of jerking leaps, began to rise, while her bows dipped toward the last night's ice ahead. Everybody looked to see her fall upon her beam-ends and rushed out upon the ice."

"On the 13th the hummock ridge astern advanced with a steady march upon the vessel. Twice it rested and advanced again—a dense wall of ice, thirty feet broad at the base and twelve feet high, tumbling huge fragments from its crest, yet increasing in mass at every new effort. We had ceased to hope, when a merciful interposition arrested it, so close against our counter that there was scarcely room for a man to pass between. Half a minute of progress more and it would have buried us all. As we drifted along five months afterward this stupendous memento of controlling power was still hanging over our stern."

The discomfort of the prescribed out-of-door exercise in extreme cold appears from the following:

"Close the lips for the first minute or two and

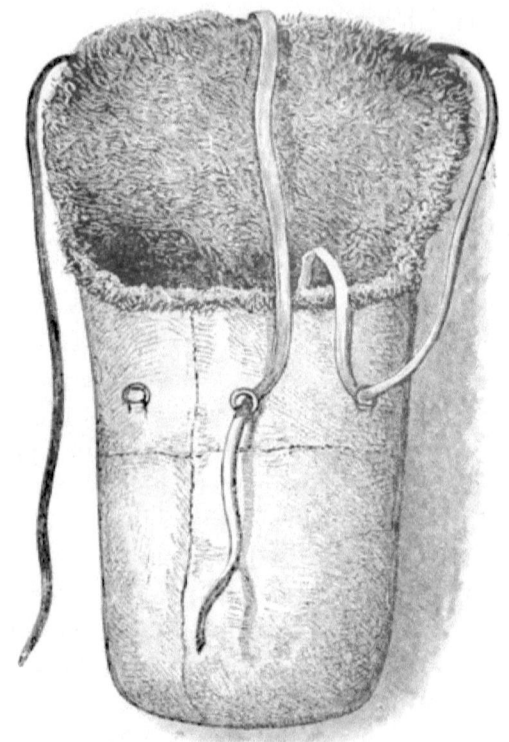

A Sleeping bag for Three Men

admit the air suspiciously through nostril and mustache. Presently you breathe in a dry, pungent but gracious and agreeable atmosphere. The beard, eyebrows, eyelashes, and the downy pubescence of the ears acquire a delicate white and perfectly enveloped cover of venerable hoar-frost. The mustache and under lip form pendulous beads of dangling ice. Put out your tongue and it instantly freezes to this icy crusting, and a rapid effort and some hand aid will be required to liberate it. The less you talk the better. Your chin has a trick of freezing to your upper jaw by the luting aid of your beard; even my eyes have often been so glued as to show that even a wink may be unsafe."

The unfortunate physical condition of the party made Kane's duties most onerous and wearing. In mid-winter he says:

"Scurvy advanced steadily. This fearful disease, so often warded off when in a direct attack, now exhibited itself in a cachexy, a depraved condition of system sad to encounter. Pains diffuse and non-locatable were combined with an apathy and lassitude which resisted all attempts at healthy excitement. These, of course, were not confined to the crew alone: out of twenty-four men but five were without ulcerated gums and blotched limbs. All the officers were assailed."

The expedition safe in port, the recollection of the horrors and privations of his mid-winter drift through the polar pack did not deter Kane from again braving the danger of Arctic exploration, and he was soon busily engaged in stimulating public opinion to the support of another expedition. To this end he especially addressed the American Geographic Society, of which Henry Grinnell was president, presenting a well-intended but fallacious and illogical plan for continuing the search for Franklin.

Kane was personally aware, from the experiences of his previous voyage with DeHaven, that Franklin had wintered at Beechy Island, in 74° 43′ N., 91° 33′ W., and that his positive orders from the admiralty required him to push southward from the vicinity of Cape Walker to Behring Strait. A search for him by the way of Smith Sound, four degrees of latitude to the *northward* and seventeen degrees of longitude to the *eastward* of his last known position, rested on the violent assumption that Franklin had not only directly disobeyed his positive orders to go *west* and *southwest*, but had done so after one-third of the distance from Greenland to Behring Strait had been accomplished.

Again there had lately been made public in England the last direct report from the Franklin expedition—a letter from Captain Fitzjames— who relates that Franklin showed him part of his instructions, expressed his disbelief in an open sea to the north, and gave " a pleasant account of his expectations of being able to get through the ice on the coast of America." Dr. Rae had also reported finding drift material on the north coast of America, which, having the broad arrow and red thread of the government, could come from the quarter where Franklin's orders sent him, thus confirming the belief that he had gone southwest from Cape Walker. Moreover, the squadrons of Belcher and Collinson were actively engaged in the search northward of America.

It was finally decided that a second expedition should be sent, the United States co-operating, as before, with private enterprise; and to the command of this expedition Kane was assigned, by orders from the Secretary of the Navy, in November, 1852. The expedition was fitted out through the liberality of two Americans, Henry Grinnell, who again placed the brig Advance at the disposal of the government, and George Peabody, the American philanthropist, who contributed $10,000, a sum that practically covered all other expenses of the voyage.

Kane's faith in the existence of an open polar sea and his intention of reaching it were clearly asserted. Combined with the proposed search for Franklin was a declared purpose to extend northward the discoveries of Inglefield, in 1851, on the west coast of Greenland, where, as Kane says, he contemplated reaching "its most northern attainable point, and thence pressing on toward the Pole as far as boats or sledges could carry us, examine the coast lines for vestiges of the lost party."

The expedition sailed from New York May 30, 1853, consisting of eighteen men, all volunteers, although ten belonged to the United States Navy. Except as regards scientific instruments, the equipment of the expedition was in most respects inadequate and unsuitable for Arctic service, the bulk of the provisions, for instance, being hard bread, salt beef, and pork, with no canned meats or vegetables.

The Greenland ports were visited, where a

moderate amount of fur clothing and fifty Esquimau dogs were purchased. On June 27th the Advance entered Melville Bay, and standing boldly to the westward, although hindered by the loose drifting ice, was favored by an offshore gale, and in ten days passed into the open sea west of Cape York, known to Arctic voyagers as the "North Water," the only misfortune being the loss of a whaleboat. In order to secure retreat Kane, fortunately for himself as it afterward proved, cached his metallic life-boat, filled with boat stores, on Littleton Island. Favored by the conditions of the ice Kane rounded Cape Hatherton, when the main pack setting southward obliged him to seek shelter in Refuge Harbor, a land-locked cove. Later the Advance was able, as the ice opened, to make sail and pass around Cairn Point, but a violent gale broke her from her moorings and nearly wrecked her. The ice conditions were now so adverse that seven of his eight officers addressed to him written opinions in favor of a return to a more southern harbor. Such retrograde movement would have removed them from the contemplated field of operations, and Kane declined. Every favorable opportunity of warping the brig—she could be moved in no other way—was availed of, and despite most difficult conditions of ice and water, the brig being on her beam-ends at low tide and jammed by floes at high water, she was moved a number of miles to the eastward, and on September 9th was put into winter-quarters in Rensselaer Harbor, 78° 37' N., 71° 14' W., which, says

Kane, "we were fated never to leave together— a long resting-place to her, for the same ice is around her still."

Scarcely were they moored than signs of coming winter crowded fast one after another; the flowers were blackened by frost; long lines of flying water-fowl trended southward, leaving sol-

The Coming Arctic Night.

itary the hardy snow-bird; the sun grew lower from day to day with startling rapidity, and the young ice cemented the separated old floes into one solid roadway for the sledgemen. Kane set about exploring the country and travelled some fifty miles to Mary Minturn River, whence from adjoining high land he had a view of Washington land, the vicinity of Cape Constitution. During this journey he first observed the peculiar ice formation now known as the ice-foot, but then novel. It is best described in his words: "We were on a table or shelf of ice which clung to the base of rocks overlooking the sea, . . . with huge angular blocks, some many tons in weight, scattered over its surface." Hayes and Wilson travelled some fifty miles into the interior till their further progress was stopped by the edge of the inland ice. McGary and Bonsall, with sledge party of seven, made three caches to the northeast, the farthest being in 79° 12′ N., 65° 25′ W., under the face of an enormous glacier, to which the name of Humboldt was given.

The winter passed quietly, the officers making tidal, astronomical, magnetic, and meteorological observations, while the men, engaged in ordinary pursuits, kept in health. Unfortunately fifty-seven, nearly all, of the dogs died, thus depriving Kane of his main reliance for field operations. The extreme cold—the mean temperature for December to March, inclusive, being thirty-two degrees below zero—had reduced the fuel so that the allowance was three buckets a day. Other supplies commenced to show their need or inadequacy; oil for lamps failed, as did fresh meat from game, and unfortunately there was no canned meat, only salted.

Despite his loss of dogs Kane decided on laying out new depots, and with the advance of March he watched eagerly the temperature. From the 10th to the 19th the cold averaged seventy-six degrees below the freezing-point. He started his man-sledge on the 20th, under charge of Brooks, first officer, with seven others at the drag-ropes. Unfortunately the equipment was either somewhat defective or some of the party were inexperienced in the methods needful for self-preservation in such extreme cold. Kane gives no details of the causes of the calamity save to say that "a heavy gale from the north-northeast broke upon the party, and the temperature fell to fifty-seven below zero."

The first news of the disaster came from Sontag, Ohlsen, and Petersen, who suddenly appeared in the cabin, at midnight of March 31st, swollen, haggard, and hardly able to speak. Kane continues: "They had left their companions in the ice, risking their own lives to bring us the news; Brooks, Baker, Wilson, and Pierre, were all lying frozen and disabled. Where? They could not tell; somewhere among the hummocks to the northeast; it was drifting heavily around them. Irish Tom had stayed to care for the others. It was vain to question them, for they were sinking with fatigue and hunger, and could hardly be rallied enough to tell us the direction."

Kane instantly organized a relief party of ten men, which, despite his delicate physique, he headed himself. Taking Ohlsen, the most rational of the sufferers, in a fur bag, and as lightly equipped as was possible, the rescuers moved out in a temperature seventy-eight degrees below freezing. Ohlsen fell asleep, but on awakening was of no use as guide owing to his delirious condition. Reaching a large level floe Kane put up his tent and scattered his party to find traces of the lost men. Eighteen hours had now elapsed and Kane's own party was in a deplorable state, partly owing to the extreme cold and partly to extreme nervousness arising from anxiety and sympathy. He says: "McGary and Bonsall, who had stood out our severest marches, were seized with trembling fits and short breath, and in spite of all my efforts I fainted twice on the snow." Fortunately Hans, the Esquimau, found a sledge-track which led to the camp in a few hours, where Kane found the four men on their backs, whose welcome greeting, "We expected you: we were sure you would come," proved how great was their confidence in their commander. The day was extremely cold and most providentially clear and sunny, but even with these favoring conditions it was almost a miracle that they were able to drag the frozen men to the brig. "The tendency to sleep," says Kane, "could only be overcome by mechanical violence; and when at last we got back to the brig, still dragging the wounded men instinctively behind us, there was not one whose mind was found to be unimpaired." Baker and Schubert died; Wilson and Brooks finally recovered, losing, however, part of their feet by amputation.

Kane determined to lead the next party himself, and near the end of April, 1854, with seven men he attempted to lay down an india-rubber boat high up on the Greenland coast. He had, however, sadly overrated the strength of his men and of himself. About eighty miles from

the brig, near Dallas Bay, one man broke down
entirely and four others were partly disabled, and
their cache was made at that point with many

Esquimau Boys Fishing.

misgivings, as bears had destroyed the stores
laid down the previous autumn. The troubles
of the party now commenced, for Kane, fainting
while making an observation, had to be hauled
back by the disabled men. Despite the moder-

ate temperature Kane's left foot froze, his limbs became rigid and badly swollen, fainting spells were more frequent, and he fell into alternate spells of delirium and unconsciousness, in which state his broken-down sledge crew conveyed him by forced marches to the brig, where, says Hayes, the surgeon, he arrived nearly insensible and so swollen by scurvy as to be hardly recognizable, and in such a debilitated state that an exposure of a few more hours would have terminated his life. Kane's wonderful recuperative powers speedily restored him from his nearly helpless condition to a state of comparative good health, but he could not conceal his evident inability to personally attempt further sledge journeys that spring.

In this emergency he decided to send his surgeon, Dr. I. I. Hayes, to explore the western shore of Smith's Strait, from Cape Sabine northward, and for this purpose detailed Godfrey with the seven best dogs available.

The ice over Smith's Sound was extremely rough, so that progress was slow and tedious. Finally, with his provisions nearly exhausted, Hayes reached land in the vicinity of Dobbin Bay and made his farthest at Cape Hayes, which, according to his observations, was in about 79° 45′ N. Hayes was stricken with snow-blindness; the journey was extremely exhausting; Godfrey broke down, and the dogs were so nearly worn out that at the last camp they abandoned sleeping-bags, extra clothing, and everything except arms and instruments. Kane says that both men were snow-blind on arrival at the brig, and the doctor, in a state of exhaustion, had to be led to his bedside to make his report.

Impressed with Hayes's success on the west shore of Smith's Sound, Kane decided to send Morton northward on the Greenland side so as to determine the extent of the frozen channel seen by Hayes from his farthest. Morton was supported by a sledge party of four men, who reached Humboldt glacier after ten days' travel, and were here joined by Esquimau Hans with a dog-sledge. On the 18th the supporting party turned homeward, while Morton and Hans, with a dog-sledge, started northward, travelling about five miles distant from and parallel with the face of Humboldt glacier.

On June 24th Morton's northward progress was stopped by very high, perpendicular cliffs washed by open water and free from the customary ice-foot. All efforts to pass around the projecting cliff, to which the name of Cape Constitution was given, proved unavailing. Morton says: "The knob to which I climbed was over five hundred feet in height, and from it not a speck of ice was to be seen as far as I could observe; the sea was open, the swell came from the northward, . . . and the surf broke in on the rocks below in regular breakers."

Morton, in his report, described two islands opposite Cape Constitution; Kennedy Channel as about thirty-five miles wide, running due north and having an unbroken mountainous land along its western limits. Twenty miles, estimated, due south of Cape Constitution, Morton made the latitude, by meridian altitude of the sun, 80° 41' N., which by dead reckoning made the cape 81° 1'. Kane gives its latitude, corrected by triangulation, as 81° 22' N.

These discoveries, strengthening Kane's belief in an open polar sea, caused him to put forth on his return such statements and generalizations as drew forth sharp criticisms, wherein the correctness and value of all the field work of his expedition were impugned.

It would be most gratifying to Americans if adverse criticisms as to distances travelled and astronomical positions determined could be refuted. It is, however, a matter of fact, not of opinion, that nearly all the given latitudes are much too far to the north, while no considerable distance was travelled which was not overestimated from fifty to one hundred per cent. These blemishes on Kane's great work doubtless arose from two causes: first, his implicit confidence in the ability and accuracy of his subordinates, and, second, to his poetic temperament, which transformed into beauty the common things of life and enhanced their interest by striking contrasts of high lights and deep shadows.

Subsequent expeditions have surveyed and charted Kennedy Channel with an accuracy leaving little to be desired, and as a result it is now known that the open "sea" seen by Morton was simply the ice-free water of the southern half of Kennedy Channel, which condition obtains during a great part of each year. The descriptions of the region by Morton in his report, though simple, are yet so accurate and free from

An Arctic Stream.

exaggeration as to prove conclusively his entire honesty. When, however, his astronomical observations and estimates of distances are considered,

Morton's incompetency is apparent, as they are, in common with most of the other field work, erroneous and misleading. The latitude of Cape Constitution was overstated fifty-two geographic miles by Kane and thirty-one miles by Morton, while Kennedy Channel, instead of being thirty-five miles wide, ranges only from seventeen to twenty-five. The farthest mountain seen was Mount Ross, on the north side of Carl Ritter Bay, about 80° 58′ N., more than ninety miles to the southward of its assumed position. Kane's personal knowledge of Morton's honesty was so complete that he placed equal confidence in his ability and accuracy, an error of judgment arising largely from Kane's great affection for his subordinate.

In the meantime the Etah Esquimaux, most fortunately for Kane, had discovered and visited the Advance, and through their friendly offices the expedition profited largely.

The summer of 1854 disclosed the error of wintering in Rensselaer Harbor, for it passed without freeing the brig from ice. The situation, Kane relates, was most unpromising, and near the middle of July he determined on a desperate attempt to communicate with the English expeditionary vessels supposed to be at Beechy Island, several hundred miles to the southwest. Kane with five others started in a whaleboat, but owing to the bad ice returned unsuccessful after an absence of eighteen days.

On August 18th Kane regards it as an obvious fact that they must look another winter in the face, and says: "It is horrible—yes, that is the word—to look forward to another year of disease and darkness to be met without fresh food or fuel. The physical energies of the party have sensibly declined; resources are diminished; there are but fifty gallons of oil saved from the summer seal hunt; we are scant of fuel; our food consists now of ordinary marine stores and is by no means suited to dispel scurvy; our molasses is reduced to forty gallons and our dried fruits seem to have lost their efficiency."

Under these discouraging circumstances came the most trying experiences of the expedition. The majority of the party entertained the idea that escape to the south by boats was still practicable despite the lateness of the summer, although Kane's own experience in the previous month had shown the futility of such an effort. Conscious, however, that he could control only by moral influence the majority who were of this opinion, he decided to appeal to them. On August 24th he assembled the entire crew, set forth eloquently that such an effort must be exceedingly hazardous, escape southward almost improbable, and strongly advised them to forego the project. However, he ended by freely according his permission to such as were desirous of making the attempt, provided that they would organize under an officer before starting and renounce in writing all claims upon the expedition. Nine out of the seventeen, headed by Petersen, the Danish interpreter, and Dr. Hayes, the surgeon, decided to attempt the boat journey and left the vessel August 28th. Kane fitted them out liberally, provided every possible appliance to facilitate and promote their success, and gave them a written assurance of a hearty welcome should they be driven to return. One of the party, Riley, rejoined Kane within a few days, and well into the Arctic winter, on December 7th, Bonsall and Petersen returned through the aid of the Esquimaux. They reported to Kane that their associates were some two hundred miles distant, their energies broken, provisions nearly gone, divided in their counsel, and desirous of returning to share again the fortunes of the Advance. Kane immediately sent supplies to the suffering party by the natives, and took active measures to facilitate their return, and on December 12th had the great joy of seeing the entire expedition reunited. In this connection Kane properly notes the humane actions of the Esquimaux, saying: "Whatever may have been their motives, their conduct to our friends was certainly full of humanity. They drove at flying speed; every hut gave its welcome as they halted; the women were ready without invitation to dry and chafe their worn-out guests."

Kane, it may be added, did not allude in his official report to the Secretary of the Navy to this temporary division of his command, which, however, is told, both in his own narrative and in that of Dr. Hayes, in his " Arctic Boat Journey."

As winter went on they hunted unavailingly for game, and the abundant supplies hitherto obtained from the Etah Esquimaux failed, owing to the unfavorable ice conditions, which caused a famine among the natives and reduced them to the lowest stages of misery and emaciation. Scurvy with its varying phases also sapped the energies of the crew, while Hayes was disabled from amputation of a portion of his frozen foot.

When practically the entire crew must be said to have been on the sick-list, Blake and Godfrey decided to desert and take their chances with the Esquimaux. The plan being detected by Kane, Blake remained, but Godfrey deserted, and with Hans, the Esquimau, remained absent nearly a month. Godfrey, however, contributed to the support of the expedition by sending supplies of meat, and later returned under duress.

With the returning spring of 1855 the necessity of abandoning the brig was apparent to all; the ship was practically little more than a shell, as everything that could possibly be used without making her completely unseaworthy had been consumed for fire-wood. There remained in April only a few weeks' supply of food and fuel, while the solidity of the ice in the vicinity of Rensselaer Harbor indicated the impossibility of an escape by vessel. It was no slight task to move the necessary stock of provisions and stores to their boats and to the open water in the vicinity of Cape Alexander. This was, however, safely accomplished by the middle of June, the vessel having been formally abandoned on May 17th. The final casualty in the party occurred near

Littleton Island, when Ohlsen, in a tremendous and successful effort to save a loaded sledge from loss in broken ice, so injured himself internally that he died within three days. During this retreating journey Kane records the invaluable assistance of the Esquimaux, who "brought daily supplies of birds, assisted in carrying boat-stores, and invariably exhibited the kindliest feelings and strictest honesty." Leaving Cape Alexander on June 15, 1854, Cape York was passed on July 21st, and, crossing Melville Bay along the margin of its land ice in five days, Kane reached the north coast of Greenland on August 3d, forty-seven days from Cape Alexander.

At Disco the party met Lieutenant Hartstene, whose squadron, sent to relieve Kane, had already visited Cape Alexander, and learning from the natives of Kane's retreat by boat to the south turned promptly back to the Greenland ports. Surrounded by all the comforts and luxuries which the means or thoughtfulness of their rescuing comrades of the navy could furnish, Kane and his men made a happy journey southward to meet the grand ovation that greeted them from their appreciative countrymen in New York, on October 11, 1855.

Neither the anxiety of countless friends nor the skill of his professional brethren could long preserve to his family, to the navy, and to the country the ebbing life of the gallant Kane. The disease which for twenty years had threatened his life now progressed with rapidity, and on February 16, 1857, he died at Havana, Cuba.

No single Arctic expedition of his generation added so greatly to the knowledge of the world as did that of Kane's. In ethnology it contributed the first full account of the northernmost inhabitants of the world, the Etah Esquimaux; in natural history it supplied extensive and interesting information as to the flora and fauna of extreme western Greenland, especially valuable from its isolation by the surrounding inland ice; in physical sciences the magnetic, meteorological, tidal, and glacier observations were extremely valuable contributions; in geography it extended to a higher northerly point than ever before a knowledge of polar lands, and it opened up a practical and safe route for Arctic exploration which has been more persistently and successfully extended poleward than any other.

Of Kane's conduct under the exceptionally prolonged and adverse circumstances attendant on his second Arctic voyage, it is to be said that he displayed the characteristics of a high and noble character. Considerate of his subordinates, assiduous in performing his multifarious duties as commander, studying ever to alleviate the mental and physical ailments of his crew, and always unsparing of himself whenever exposure to danger, hardships, or privations promised definite results. It is not astonishing that these qualities won and charmed all his associates, equals or subordinates, and that they followed him unhesitatingly into the perils and dangers that Kane's enthusiastic and optimistic nature led him to brave, with the belief that to will was to do.

The career of Kane cannot be more beautifully and truthfully summarized than was done in the funeral sermon over his bier: "He has traversed the planet in its most inaccessible places; has gathered here and there a laurel from every walk of physical research in which he strayed, has gone into the thick of perilous adventure, abstracting in the spirit of philosophy, yet seeing in the spirit of poesy; has returned to invest the very story of his escape with the charms of literature and art, and dying at length in the morning of his fame, is now lamented with mingled affection and pride by his country and the world."

X.

ISAAC ISRAEL HAYES,

And The Open Polar Sea.

History affords many examples wherein neither the originator nor the early advocate of a striking idea has reaped fame therefrom, and their names give way to some persistent, tireless worker who forces the subject on public attention by his ceaseless efforts. Among Arctic theories none has more fully occupied and interested the mind of the general public than that of an open, navigable sea in the polar regions. In connection with this theory the minds of Americans turn naturally to Dr. I. I. Hayes, who, not the originator, inherited his belief therein from the well-known Professor Maury, through the mediation of Kane, Hayes's Arctic commander. DeHaven thought he saw signs of Maury's ice-free sea to the northward of Wellington Strait, Kane through Morton found it at Cape Constitution, Hayes recognized it a few miles farther up Kennedy Channel, but Markham turned it into a frozen sea in 83° 20′ N. latitude, and Lockwood, from Cape Kane, on the most northerly land of all time, rolled the frozen waste yet to the north, beyond the eighty-fourth parallel, to within some three hundred and fifty miles of the geographical Pole.

Isaac Israel Hayes was born in Chester County, Pa., March 5, 1832. He gained the title of doc-

Isaac Israel Hayes.

tor by graduation in the University of Pennsylvania, in 1853, in which year, at twenty-four hours' notice, he accepted the appointment, procured his outfit, and sailed as surgeon of Kane's Arctic expedition. An account of this voyage appears in the sketch of Dr. Kane, but some further reference to it is now necessary. Hayes, it will be remembered, was the surgeon, a position which exempted him from field-work. However, when Kane and others broke down, Hayes volunteered, and was sent with Godfrey, a seaman, and a team of seven dogs to explore the west coast of Smith Sound. The journey lasted from May 20 to June 1, 1853, and, all things considered, such as defective equipment, rough ice, and attacks of snow-blindness, the results were unusually creditable.

The rough ice travelled over is thus described by Hayes: "We were brought to a halt by a wall of broken ice ranging from five to thirty feet in height. . . . We had not a foot of level travelling. Huge masses of ice from twenty to forty feet in height were heaped together; in crossing these ridges our sledge would frequently capsize and roll over and over—dogs, cargo, and all." Hayes finally reached land on May 27th, at a bluffy headland "to the north and east of a little (Dobbin) bay, which seemed to terminate about ten miles inland." This point, called later Cape Hayes, was placed by him by observations in 79° 42' N., 71° 17' W. From his farthest Hayes mentions the sea-floe as continuing in a less rough condition to the northward, and correctly describes the interior of Grinnell Land as a great mountain-chain following the trend of the coast.

His broken sledge and nearly exhausted provisions obliged Hayes to return, and in so doing he crossed Dobbin Bay to, and passed under the shadow of, the noble headland of Cape Hawks, where they gave their dogs the last scrap of pemican. Hayes resolved to here abandon all his extra clothing, sleeping-bags, etc., some forty pounds, a rash act, as they must have been between sixty and seventy miles from the brig, and in case of a storm would have perished. The first day's return journey the dogs were fed with seal-skin, from old boots, and a little lamp-lard, and the day following with bread crumbs, lard scrapings, and seal-skin off mittens and trousers. The travellers got scanty rest, dozing in the sun on the sledge, and finally reached Rensselaer Harbor snow-blind and utterly exhausted.

Hayes was thus the first white man to put foot on the new land, to which Kane affixed the name of Grinnell. It is impossible to understand Kane's failure to properly recognize this successful and arduous journey of Hayes, and one looks in vain for confirmation of Kane's claim that he "renewed and confirmed," in April, 1854, the work of Hayes and Godfrey, for his own account shows that Kane's April journey failed completely to reach Grinnell Land.

Two months after his journey to Grinnell Land, Hayes was called on to decide whether he would remain with Kane at Rensselaer Harbor, where the unbroken ice plainly claimed the brig Advance as its own for another year, sharing the hardships and dangers of a second Arctic winter, or, fleeing south without his commander, seek safety and shelter through a boat journey down Smith Sound, and across Melville Bay, to

the northern Danish settlement, Upernivik, in
Greenland. Hayes, unfortunately for his reputation, yielded to the majority, and nine of the
party, headed by Petersen, Sontag, and Hayes,
decided to go, while only six white men and Esquimau Hans remained. It is true that Kane had

Upernivik.

only two weeks before returned from an unsuccessful attempt to reach Beechy Island, as difficult a task as the voyage to Upernivik, which he
had quitted his brig to lead in person; but such
action should not have been viewed as a justification for again separating the party.

Hayes alleges in extenuation that Kane had

previously announced to the crew that their labors would thereafter be directed homeward, that the attempted journey to Beechy Island was solely to procure aid, that the "boat journey" simply changed the direction of their efforts, save that it was led by Petersen and not by Kane. Further, that the departure of the majority of the crew would give augmented health-conditions, space, and food to those who remained.

Accepting Kane's permission, freely accorded, as he says, to make the boat journey, liberally equipped with such supplies as the brig had, and assured of a hearty welcome should they return, the boat party left Rensselaer Harbor, August 28, 1853, confident of its ability to succeed.

Sudden cold, sledging accidents, and bad ice soon caused Riley to return to the brig; but despite sea-soaked bedding, injured limbs, and exhausting labor, the rest of the boat party persevered with sledge to the open water, and, launching their whaleboat, proceeded rapidly till a closed ice-pack stopped them at Littleton Island.

It is unnecessary to detail despairing delays or delusive hopes which changing conditions of ice and weather alternately aroused, during their southward journey, nor to recite the hardships and perils arising from violent gales, drifting snow, the disruption and closing of the pack, the severe cold of a rapidly advancing winter, their lack of shelter and insufficiency of proper food. Suffice it to say that, confronted by impassable ice-floes, they were finally forced, with damaged boat, depleted supplies, and impaired strength, to establish winter quarters south of Cape Parry, midway between Whale and Wostenholme Sounds.

The preservation of stores, construction of shelter, and accumulation of means of subsistence now engrossed their entire energies. The construction of a hut, although facilitated by a rocky cavern, proved to be exhausting in the extreme from the difficulty of obtaining material from the frozen soil. Their most skilful hunters kept the field continually, but game failed, and from day to day food supply diminished with, to them, startling rapidity. Eventually reduced to the verge of starvation, they would have perished but for food obtained from the Esquimaux, which, though scanty and irregular, yet sustained life.

Affairs went from bad to worse, and with the increasing cold and diminishing light of December it was decided that they must either perish or return to the brig; either alternative had its advocates. To decide was to act. Petersen negotiated with the Esquimaux, and by judicious admixture of persuasion, command, and force, succeeded in having the entire boat party transported by sledge to the Advance, where they were received with fraternal kindness. Hayes relates, "Dr. Kane met us at the gangway and grasped me warmly by the hand. . . . Ohlsen folded me in his arms, and, kissing me, threw me into his warm bed."

The boat journey to Upernivik, which proved dangerous and impracticable to his small party in advancing winter, proved, with the returning summer of 1855, not difficult to the reunited party of Kane, and so ended the boat journey of Hayes and his first Arctic service.

The loss of a portion of his foot, extreme sufferings from exposure, and his great privations in the Kane expedition failed to abate Hayes's enthusiasm in Arctic exploration. Immediately on his return to the United States, in October, 1855, he advocated a second expedition, with the object of completing the survey of the north coast of Greenland and Grinnell Land, and to make explorations toward the North Pole. His strenuous efforts to excite public interest failed at first; but Hayes devoted himself to lecturing on Arctic subjects, and finally enlisted in his support most of the scientific societies of the country. The advocacy of Professors Bache and Henry, and the support of Grinnell, gave an impulse which finally resulted in the organization of an expedition, under Hayes's command, and on July 6, 1860, he left Boston on the sailing schooner United States, with a crew of fourteen.

It is not needful to dwell on his outward voyage farther than to say that, in addition to the complement of dogs and stock of furs usually obtained in Greenland, Hayes there recruited dog-drivers, interpreters, and hunters. At Cape York he also added Hans Hendrik, Kane's dog-driver, who, smitten with the dusky charms of the daughter of Shang-hu, had chosen to remain with the Etah Esquimaux rather than return to

Danish Greenland with the Kane retreating party in 1855. Now, five years later, he showed an equal willingness to quit his adopted tribe for expeditionary purposes.

Profiting by the experience of his predecessor, Hayes was unwilling to push a sailing vessel northward into Kane's Basin, beyond the seventy-eighth parallel, and wisely decided to establish

Hayes's Winter-Quarters.

his winter-quarters in Foulke Fiord, near Littleton Island, twenty miles to the south, and about forty miles west, of Kane's quarters. Game proved abundant both at sea and on land, pleasant relations were established with their neighbors, the Etah Esquimaux, an observatory built, and scientific observations inaugurated. Indeed everything looked most promising for the future.

An autumnal journey of special interest was Hayes's visit to "My Brother John Glacier," near Port Foulke, which, up to that time, was the most northerly and one of the most successful attempts to penetrate the glacier-covering of Greenland, known commonly as the "Inland Ice." With seven men he penetrated some forty miles or more on the ice, when the temperature, sinking to thirty-four degrees below zero, with wind, compelled their immediate return. The ice changed gradually, as they went inland, from rough to smooth, and the angle of rise decreased from six to two degrees at their highest, over five thousand feet. A snow-storm broke on them, and, as Hayes describes, "fitful clouds swept over the face of the full-orbed moon, which, descending toward the horizon, glimmered through the drifting snow that hurled out of the illimitable distance, and scudded over the icy plains—to the eye, in undulating lines of downy softness; to the flesh, in showers of piercing darts."

Suddenly misfortunes came on them. Peter, an Esquimau dog-driver, brought from Upernivik, deserted. Hans Hendrik, in his interesting "Memoirs," says: "In the beginning of the winter Peter turned a Kivigtok, that is, fled from human society to live alone up the country. We were unable to make out what might have induced him to do so. Searching for him, at last I found his footprints going to the hills." The poor native was never seen alive, but it eventually transpired that he sought shelter in a remote and rarely visited Esquimau hut, where he died of starvation, his body being found in a very emaciated condition by an Etah native the following spring.

Next the dogs began to die of distemper, which led up to the death of Sontag, the astronomer. By the 21st of December only nine remained of thirty fine dogs, and in this contingency it was decided to open up communication with the Esquimaux of Whale Sound, some one hundred and fifty miles to the south, for the purchase of dogs. For this journey Sontag volunteered, and with him went Hans as dog-driver. Hayes waited week after week, but no news came from either Sontag or Hans. Then feelings of uneasiness gave place to alarm and fear; for a journey of Dodge, first mate, proved that the travellers had gone outside Cape Alexander, where the floe had broken, so that possibly they had been lost on drifting ice. Hayes was projecting a personal search on January 29th, when two Esquimaux visited the ship and reported that Sontag was dead. They proved to be advance-couriers of Hans, who arrived a few days later, with only five of his nine dogs remaining.

In his " Memoirs " Hans relates as follows : " It still blew a gale and the snow drifting dreadfully, for which reason we resolved to return. . . . The ice began breaking up, so we were forced to go ashore and continue our drive over the ice-foot. At one place the land became impassable, and we were obliged to return to the ice again. On descending here my companion (Sontag) fell through the ice, which was nothing but a thick sheet of snow and water. I stooped, but was unable to seize him, it being very low tide. As a last resort I remembered a strap hanging on the sledge-poles; this I threw to him, and when he had tied it around his body I pulled, but found it very difficult. At length I succeeded in drawing him up, but he was at the point of freezing to death, and now in the storm and drifting snow he took off his clothes and slipped into the sleeping-bag, whereupon I placed him on the sledge and repaired to our last resting-place. Our road being very rough, I cried for despair from want of help; but I reached the snow-hut." He recites that Sontag remained unconscious to his death, and that the breaking up of the ice around Cape Alexander, confirmed by Dodge's journey, prevented his return to the ship at that time. There was much talk about Sontag's death, but Hans's account is doubtless correct.

Sontag was the only trained scientific observer in the party; and in addition, from his skill, experience, and enthusiasm in Arctic work, was almost indispensable to Hayes. His death was a great blow to the party, socially as well as professionally.

In early spring Hayes succeeded in obtaining the co-operation of the Etah Esquimaux in sledging, and in a preliminary journey visited his old winter-quarters, where he had served with Kane six years before. Where they had abandoned the Advance, surrounded by the solid pack, he found ice nearly as high as were her mastheads; no vestige of the vessel remained except a bit of plank, and its fate was a matter of conjecture, though little doubt exists that she was ultimately crushed by the disruption of the pack during some violent gale. It was during this journey that Hayes experienced an intense degree of cold. Stating that the thermometer which hung inside the hut against the snow-wall indicated thirty-one degrees below zero, Hayes says: "We crawled out in the open air to try the sunshine. 'I will give you the best buffalo skin in the ship, Jansen, if the air outside is not warmer than in that den which you have left so full of holes.' And it really seemed so. Human eye never lit upon a more pure and glowing morning. The sunlight was sparkling all over the landscape and the great world of whiteness; and the frozen plain, the hummocks, the icebergs, and the tall mountains made a picture inviting to the eye. Not a breath of air was stirring. Jansen gave in without a murmur. I brought out the thermometer and set it up in the shadow of an iceberg near by. I really expected to see it rise; but no, down sank the little red column of alcohol, down, down almost to the bulb, until it touched sixty-eight and a half degrees below zero, Fahrenheit, equal to one hundred and a half degrees below the freezing-point of water. It struck me as a singular circumstance that this great depression of temperature was not perceptible to the senses, which utterly failed to give us even so much as a hint that here in this blazing sunlight we were experiencing about the coldest temperature ever recorded."

After this preliminary journey Hayes laid

down supplies at the nearest point on the Greenland shore south of, and facing, Cape Hawks. This place, called Cairn Point, was to be the base of his summer's campaign to the north. Finally everything was ready for the main journey, and the party started on the night of April 3, 1861. Twelve men, the entire available force, were put

Adrift on a Berg.

into the field: Jansen with an eight-dog sledge, Knorr with a six-dog sledge, and a ten-man sledge on which was mounted a twenty-foot metallic life-boat, with which Hayes hoped to navigate the Polar Sea. The journey lay directly to the north over the frozen surface of Kane Sea, where the difficulties of travel through the broken hummocky ice were so great, and the unfitness of some of the men for Arctic travel so speedily developed, that Hayes was forced to abandon his efforts to get the boat across the frozen sea, which, he says, " could not have been done by one hundred men." On April 24th Hayes records that he had been twenty-two days from the schooner, and was now distant only thirty miles from Cairn Point. Four days later, still struggling across the rough ice of Kane Sea, the party was practically broken down, being, as Hayes chronicles, " barely capable of attending to their own immediate necessities without harboring the thought of exerting themselves to complete a journey to which they can see no termination, and in the very outset of which they feel that their lives are being sacrificed."

In this critical condition Hayes changed his plans, and sent back the entire party to the brig, except Knorr, Jansen, and McDonald, whom he selected as best fitted to make the northern journey, which he had decided to make with fourteen dogs and two sledges. Turning northward with renewed confidence and vigor, though yet struggling with various misfortunes through a tangle of broken hummocks, Hayes reached Cape Hawks on May 11th. The condition of the ice may be judged from the fact that he had been thirty-one days in making a distance of eighty miles, a little more than two miles a day. Three days' farther march took him to Cape Frazier, where the flagstaff erected by him in 1853 yet stood erect. At the end of the next march, where they were driven to the sea ice owing to the impossibility of following the ice-foot, Hayes ascended the hillside, whence, he says, " No land was visible to the eastward. As it would not have been difficult through such an atmosphere to see a distance of fifty or sixty miles, it would appear therefore that Kennedy Channel is somewhat wider than heretofore supposed."

On May 15th Jansen was disabled for travelling by a sprained back and injured leg, and the next morning was scarcely able to move. Hayes decided to leave the disabled man in charge of McDonald and proceed with Knorr, his purpose being "to make the best push I could and travel as far as my provisions warranted, reach the highest attainable latitude and secure such a point of observation as would enable me to form a definite opinion respecting the sea before me."

Rough ice and deep snow so impeded his progress the first day that he only made nine miles in as many hours. Ten hours' march compelled them to again camp, and four hours of the third day brought them to the southern cape of a bay which he determined to cross. After travelling four miles the rotten ice and frequent waterchannels proved that the bay was impassable, and therefore they went into camp. The next day Hayes climbed to the top of the cliff, some eight hundred feet high, whence, he says, " the sea beneath me was a mottled sheet of white and dark patches multiplied in size as they receded until the belt of the water-sky blended them together. . . . All the new evidence showed that I stood upon the shores of the polar basin, and that the broad ocean lay at my feet. . . . There was seen in dim outline the white sloping summit of a noble head-land, the most northern known land upon our globe. I judged it to be in latitude 82° 30' N., or four hundred and fifty miles from the North Pole. . . . There was no land visible except the coast on which I stood."

Hayes, before returning to his ship, deposited in a cairn a record, dated May 19, 1861, setting forth his trip, stating that his observations placed him in 81° 35' N. latitude, and 70° 30' W. longitude; that his further progress was stopped by rotten ice and cracks; that he believed the polar basin was navigable during the months of July, August, and September, and that he would make an attempt to get through Smith's Sound when the ice broke that summer.

The extent and scope of Hayes's discoveries, as set forth in his account of the expedition in "The Open Polar Sea," gave rise to persistent and adverse criticism both as to the soundness of his judgment and also as to the accuracy of his observations. Three expeditions, by their later surveys, have demonstrated that the astronomical position assigned by Hayes to his "farthest" on the east coast of Grinnell Land is impossible. There is unmistakably an error either of latitude or of longitude. Cape Joseph Goode, it is to be remarked, is in the longitude assigned by Hayes, while Cape Lieber is no less than six and a half degrees to the eastward; reversely, Lieber corresponds nearly to Hayes's latitude, while Cape Joseph Goode is a degree and a half to the

south. Grave and undisputable errors in other
latitudes, all being too far to the north, indicate
that the mistake in this instance is also of latitude.
In justice to Hayes it should be said that
the latitude of his "farthest" depended solely
on a single observation with a small field sextant
of the meridian altitude of the sun. While
this is the common method on shipboard it is
exceedingly objectionable in Arctic land determinations.
It depends not only on the honesty
of the observer, but on the condition of the sextant
and also on the manner in which it is
handled; either of these three qualities being
faulty the observation is incorrect. The tendency
of the sextant to "slip," as it is turned
over for reading, and the almost invariably benumbed
condition of the hands of the traveller,
indicate the extreme difficulty of making any
single reading with accuracy. Again, with haste
demanded so often by adverse circumstances, the
index of a very small sextant may be misread a
whole degree. It is unquestioned that one or
the other of these accidents happened to Hayes,
for the independent investigations of Bessels,
Schott, and others lead to the inevitable conclusion,
which any scientist may verify by examination
of Hayes's widely separated data, that
his "farthest" is placed too far north. The concensus
of opinion in the Lady Franklin expedition
pointed to Cape Joseph Goode, $80° 14'$ N.,
as Hayes's "farthest," as it agreed better with
Hayes's description than any other point; it may
be added that from this cape Hayes could not

see the Greenland coast above Cape Constitution, which he leaves blank on his chart, and again, here the unusually heavy spring tides, of nearly twenty-five-foot range, break up the southern half of the floes of Kennedy Channel, thus forming early in the year large water-spaces —the Open Polar Sea of Hayes and Morton.

Even if Hayes's sight of the Open Polar Sea proved visionary, and certain unskilled observations failed of verification, yet his adventurous voyage was not barren of geographical results. He was the first civilized man to land on the shores of Ellesmere Land, along the coasts of which, between the seventy-seventh and seventy-eighth parallels, he made important discoveries; while farther to the northward, Hayes Sound, Bache Island, and other unknown lands and waters were added to our maps through his strenuous exertions.

Breaking out his schooner on July 10, 1861, an unprecedentedly early date for an Arctic ship, he quickly decided that he could hope for no further northing in a sailing vessel. However, he crossed the strait to the unvisited shores of Ellesmere Land, where he made such an examination of the coast as was practicable, and then turned his face homeward.

Hayes was fully alive to the absolute necessity of steam-power for complete Arctic success, but strictly limited means obliged him to go in a sailing vessel or not at all. He plainly foresaw the magnificent success awaiting the first expedition that should carry steam-power into Smith

Sound, and full of dreams of future Arctic work he impatiently returned to the United States. It was not to be. Civil war raged, and the country called its loyal sons to arms. Hayes was not the man to falter at such a juncture. He at once tendered his schooner to the government for such use as was possible, and volunteered for the war, where his activity as the head of a great war hospital taxed to the utmost the mental and physical powers which had so long been occupied in arduous efforts to solve the riddle of the ice-free sea.

Hayes visited Greenland a third time, in 1869, with the Arctic artist, William Bradford, in the steam-sealer Panther. Arctic scenery was their quest, and so they visited the fiord of Sermitsialik, where the inland ice, which covers the greater part of Greenland, pushes down into the sea as an enormous glacier, with a front two and a half miles wide.

Here Hayes witnessed the birth of an iceberg, of which he says: "It would be impossible for mere words alone to convey an adequate idea of the action of this new-born child of the Arctic frosts. Think of a solid block of ice, a third of a mile deep, and more than half a mile in lateral diameter, hurled like a mere toy away into the water, and set to rolling to and fro by the impetus of the act. Picture this and you will have an image of power not to be seen by the action of any other forces upon the earth. The disturbance of the water was inconceivably fine. Waves of enormous magnitude were rolled up with great violence against the glacier, covering it with spray; and billows came tearing down the fiord, their progress marked by the crackling and crumbling ice which was everywhere in a state of the wildest agitation for the space of several miles."

The famous mine of cryolite, the only valuable mineral deposit in Greenland; the Hope Sanderson of John Davis's great voyage of 1587, with its lofty crest and innumerable flocks of wildfowl; Tessuissak, the most northerly settlement of Greenland; Duck Islands, the haunts of the eider, and the chosen rendezvous of ice-stayed whalers; Devil's Thumb, the great, wonderful pillar, to the base of which Hayes struggled up thirteen hundred feet above the ice-covered sea, and Sabine Island, all saw the Panther, in its pleasure-seeking journey. If no geographical results sprang from this voyage, it had a literary outcome in Hayes's book, "The Land of Desolation," and in a series of detached sketches, which in beauty and interest are unsurpassed as regards life in Danish Greenland.

Hayes died in New York City, December 17, 1881. To the last he maintained a lively interest in Arctic exploration, and ever and again he favored polar research, always with an alternative scheme of his old harbor, Foulke fiord, as the base of operations. He resented the appellation "Great Frozen Sea" as properly characterizing the Arctic Ocean to the north of Greenland, and to the last held fast to the ideal of his youth, the belief of his manhood, "The Open Polar Sea."

XI.

CHARLES FRANCIS HALL,

AND THE NORTH POLE.

AMONG the many exploring expeditions that have crossed the Arctic Circle with the sole view of reaching the North Pole, one only has sailed entirely under the auspices of the United States. This expedition was commanded neither by an officer of one of the twin military services nor by a sailor of the merchant marine, but its control was intrusted to a born Arctic explorer, Charles Francis Hall. Born in 1821, in Rochester, N. H., Hall early quitted his native hills for the freer fields of the West, as the Ohio Valley was then called, and later settled in Cincinnati. There was ever a spirit of change in him, and as years rolled on he passed from blacksmith to journalist, from stationer to engraver. Through all these changes of trades he held fast to one fancy, which in time became the dominating element of his eventful career: in early youth, fascinated with books of travel relating to exploration in the icy zones, he eagerly improved every opportunity to increase his Arctic library, which steadily grew despite his very limited resources. His interest in the fate of Franklin was so intense that he followed with impatience the slow and uncertain efforts for the relief of the lost explorer. Not content with mere sympathy he also planned an American search, to be conducted in

Charles Francis Hall.

Her Majesty's ship Resolute. Learning in 1859 that this Arctic ship was laid up and dismantled he originated a petition asking that it be loaned for such purpose. The return of McClintock with definite news of the death of Franklin, and the retreat and loss of his expeditionary force, put an end to the petition. Hall, however, despite the admirable and convincing report of McClintock, persisted in the belief that some members of Franklin's crew were yet alive, and he determined to solve the problem by visiting King William Land, the scene of the final disaster. He issued circulars asking public aid, diligently sought out whalers and explorers who could give him their personal experiences, and finally determined that he must go and live with the Esquimaux, and, conforming to their modes of travel and existence, work out his Arctic problem on new lines.

The inauguration of the plan presented difficulties, for Hall was without means; but his persistent action created confidence, and the modest outfit for the voyage was procured through friendly contributions, while passage on a whaler for himself and baggage was tendered.

On July 30, 1860, with a whale-boat and scanty supplies, Hall landed alone on the west coast of Davis Strait, in Frobisher Bay. His base of operations was Rescue Harbor, 63° N., 65° W., whence he made a series of sledge journeys during the two years passed in this region. He re-examined the coasts visited by Frobisher in his eventful voyages of 1575 to 1579, and found the famous gold mine on Meta Incognita, whence 1,300 tons of ore were carried to England, where, as the chronicles relate, " in the melting and refining 16 tonnes whereof, proceeded 210 ounces of fine silver mixed with gold."

An extensive collection of relics of Frobisher's

expedition was made, which later was given to the Royal Geographical Society. The expedition of Hall was mainly fruitful in training him for other Arctic work, for though his knowledge was self-acquired and instruments imperfect, yet his indefatigable industry and practice in scientific observations made him a reliable observer by the time of his return. It may be added that his careful and detailed description of the habits and life of the Esquimaux of the west coast of Davis Strait are of decided value from his rigid truthfulness, which caused him to record what he saw without exaggeration.

Hall's success in obtaining so many relics of Frobisher's voyage of three centuries previous, and the fact that the Esquimaux yet had traditionary knowledge of that voyage, encouraged Hall and his friends to a confident belief that a voyage to the shores of King William Land would result in the discovery of records, relics, possibly survivors, and in any event rescue the story of the retreat of Crozier from oblivion by hearing it from Esquimau eye-witnesses.

Future search operations were to be promoted through his Esquimau followers, commonly known as Joe and Hannah, who returned with him to the United States, and further, Hall relied upon his knowledge of the Esquimau language, in which he had acquired considerable facility during his long sojourn with them.

Hall's return was in 1862, and in 1864 he was ready for his second voyage. On August 20th he was landed, with his two natives, a whale-boat, tent, and a moderate amount of provisions, on Depot Island, in the extreme northern part of Hudson Bay, in 63° 47′ N., 90° W., where Hall began his life and quest that were to last five weary years.

Preliminary autumnal journeys extended his knowledge, but they were marked by no definite progress, and the summer of 1864 was spent by the natives in securing game for the coming winter, thus postponing Hall's chances of a westward sledge-trip to King William Land yet another year. Despairing of assistance from natives near the whaling rendezvous, Hall decided to make his winter-quarters in Repulse Bay, at Fort Hope, 60° 32′ N., 87° W., occupied, 1846-47, by the famous explorer, Dr. Rae. Here he hoped to secure the friendship of the neighboring Esquimaux and lay up stores of game for the final expedition, and there he wintered in 1865-66, during which he secured about one hundred and fifty reindeer, some salmon, and ptarmigan. With returning spring the Esquimaux promised to make the journey, and with quite a party and several dog-sledges Hall's heart was full of joy and expectation as they moved northward across Rae Peninsula, on March 30, 1866. His discouragements commenced with the long halts and frequent detours for hunts, and his disappointment was complete when the natives decided to turn back from Cape Weynton, 68° N., 89° W., after having, in twenty-eight days, only travelled as far with dogs as Rae had gone on foot in five days. Hall simply records: "My King William party is ended for the present; disappointed but not discouraged."

The journey and time were not fruitless, for near Cape Weynton he fell in with four strange Esquimaux, who gave him most valuable information as to the subject nearest his heart. They related that some of their people had visited the search ships and had seen Franklin. What was more to the point, they produced a considerable number of articles that had once belonged to members of Franklin's party. The most important were silver articles, such as spoons, forks, etc., which bore the crest of Franklin and other officers of the lost expedition. These veritable evidences of the passage of Crozier and others of Franklin's expedition through this region were fortunately secured by Hall, and were later supplemented by many others.

Unable to obtain Esquimau assistance the following year, Hall made journeys here and there wherever it was possible; one, in February, 1867, to Igloolik, the winter-quarters of Parry in 1822, on Boothia Felix Land, and a second, in 1868, to the Strait of Fury and Hekla, discovered by Parry in 1825; furthermore, he surveyed the northwest coast of Melville Peninsula, and filled in the broken line of the Admiralty chart for the northwest of that peninsula.

Visiting whalers urged on Hall the impossibility of succeeding in reaching King William Land by aid of natives, and more than one captain offered to carry him and his party back to the United States. Never despairing of final success, Hall determined to pass another winter at Fort Hope, Repulse Bay. Here, learning by experience, and acquiring food supplies during the winter, he succeeded, in March, 1869, in again starting westward with ten Esquimaux— men, women, and children—with well-loaded

Igloos, or Esquimau Huts.

dog-sledges. Progress was slow and delays frequent, but still the journey was continued.

Their course from Repulse Bay lay overland, by nearly connecting lakes and rivers, across Rae Peninsula to Committee Bay, thence by another similar overland route over the south end of Boothia Felix Land, to James Ross Strait, where King William Land lies some sixty miles to the west.

Hall, singularly enough, was never able to appreciate the attitude of the natives in making such a long, dangerous journey merely to please him, for he quaintly complains that the Esquimaux had no appreciation of his mission and continually lost valuable time by stopping to smoke and talk. They now objected to go west of Pelly Bay, but by persuasion proceeded to Simpson Island, 68° 30′ N., 91° 30′ W., where a successful hunt for musk-oxen so restored their spirits that they went on.

At Point Ackland, on the eastern shore of James Ross Strait, Hall fortunately fell in with natives, with whom he remained nine days, and from whom he obtained important information. In-nook-poo-zhee-jook proved to be the chief man of the party, and from him and others were purchased relics, such as silver spoons, plain and with the crest of Franklin. Hall was told that these articles came from a large island where a great many white men died, and that five white men were buried on an island known to the chief. This Esquimau finally agreed to accompany Hall and guided him direct across James Ross Strait to a group of small islets to the east of King William Land, where, on Todd Island, part of a human thigh-bone was found; snow covering the ground to such a depth as to make thorough search impossible without long delay.

On May 12, 1869, Hall had the supreme pleasure of putting foot on King William Land, the object and end of his five years' life among the

Esquimaux. The only tangible result of the search thereon was the discovery of a human skeleton, and he reluctantly set out on his return. Esquimaux were fallen in with in Pelly Bay, 68° 30′ N., 90° 30′ W., and an old man, Tungnuk, on inquiry regarding Franklin relics in their possession, told Hall that the natives had found a ship beset near Ki-ki-tuk, King William Land, and that in getting wood out of it they made a hole in the ship, which soon after sank. Ko-big, another native, said that all the white men perished, except two at Ki-ki-tuk, whose fate was unknown.

Hall felt satisfied, from the stories of the Esquimaux and other evidences, that he was able to determine the fate of seventy-nine out of the one hundred and five men of Crozier's party, which retreated in 1848 from the abandoned ships. The Esquimaux told him that Crozier, Franklin's second in command, had passed near their huts; that he had a gun in his hand and a telescope around his neck, and that his men were dragging two boats. Crozier told the natives that they were going to Repulse Bay. The Esquimaux admitted that they had deserted Crozier owing to the fact that his party was in a starving condition and their food was scarce.

As far as Hall could make out, Crozier, late in July, 1848, passed down the west coast of King William Land with forty men dragging two sledges, and near Cape Herschel fell in with four Esquimaux families, who, after communicating with Crozier, fled from the starving party during

the night. From native accounts Hall was also
able to enumerate in detail the points at which
the retreating party had died and been buried.

Among other relics collected by Hall were
portions of one of the boats, an oak sledge-runner, a chronometer box with the Queen's broad
arrow engraved thereon, Franklin's mahogany

In Winter-Quarters.

writing-desk, and many pieces of silver, forks,
spoons, knives, and parts of watches. It was
claimed by the natives that one of Franklin's
ships made the northwest passage with five men
on board, and in the spring of 1849 was found
by them near O'Reilly Island (68° 30′ N., 99° W.).

Hall had now passed five years among the Esquimaux, in which time he had made sledge
journeys aggregating more than three thousand
miles; acquired a thorough knowledge of the

language and methods of life of the natives, and proved the possibility of a white man living the same life and making the same sledge journeys as the natives; but at the same time he became conscious that no very extended sledge-work could be done by Esquimau aid alone. His five years of arduous Arctic life ended in 1869 by his returning home on an American whaler, bringing with him his faithful Esquimaux, Joe and Hannah.

Hall's return to the United States was simply, however, to pursue another and greater voyage, in which he believed he would be able to reach the North Pole.

After strenuous efforts he succeeded in interesting the President, the Cabinet, and a large number of Congressmen in his project, and on July 12, 1870, Congress appropriated $50,000 for the purpose of the expedition; authorized the employment of any suitable vessel in the navy, and provided that the National Academy of Sciences should prescribe the scope of the scientific observations. An old tug of nearly four hundred tons burden, rechristened under the name of Polaris, was selected, overhauled, and strengthened.

Hall sailed from New York June 29th, the party consisting of Captain Buddington, sailing-master; Dr. Emil Bessel, chief of the scientific staff; R. W. D. Bryan, astronomer; Sergeant Frederick Meyer, Signal Corps, meteorologist; seven petty officers, and a crew of fourteen, together with his faithful servants, Joe and Hannah.

The Polaris was provisioned and equipped for

an absence of two and a half years, and her voyage was destined to be over the route made famous by the expeditions of Kane and Hayes, through Davis Strait and northward along the west coast of Greenland, although Hall was at first uncertain whether he would not enter Jones's Sound, instead of Smith's Strait. The usual visits to the Greenland ports were made, with resulting stores of furs, dogs, sledges, and other paraphernalia for exploration in the far North. To this point the expedition was convoyed by the man-of-war Congress, which bade the Polaris Godspeed as she left Godhaven on her lonely journey.

Hans Hendrick, the Esquimau dog traveller, whose services with Kane and Hayes commended him to Hall, accompanied the expedition with his wife and children. It was a strange meeting between Morton, the second mate, and Hans, the Esquimau, who, twenty years before, as subordinates of Kane, had made together the memorable sledge journey from Rensselaer Harbor, along the Humboldt Glacier, to Cape Constitution.

The Polaris was favored by an unusually open sea; Melville Bay was crossed in forty-eight hours and the "North Water" beyond was so free of ice that the Polaris kept her way unchecked until she reached Hakluyt Island; even here the ice-pack was so open that the Polaris easily forced her way. Littleton Island was passed on the evening of August 27, 1870, and later, crossing the parallel of Rensselaer Harbor,

An Arctic Fiord.

the Polaris attained a higher latitude than any
former vessel on this route. Kane Sea and
Kennedy Channel proved equally free of ice, so
that the Polaris, steaming uninterruptedly northward, entered the Arctic Ocean, hitherto inaccessible, where she was finally stopped by an impenetrable pack, in 82° 26′ N. This point was
more than two hundred miles directly north of
the farthest reached by Kane's vessel, the Advance. From this vantage-ground it was seen
that the eastern coast-line of Grinnell Land extended somewhat farther to the north before
turning to the west, and that, on the other hand,
the coast of Northern Greenland trended very
nearly eastward. Strenuous, though unavailing,
efforts were made to push the Polaris further
northward; failing this, attempts were then
made to find a safe harbor to the eastward,
but none was accessible. In the meantime the
main ice-pack of the Arctic Ocean, setting
southward to its normal position, carried the
Polaris steadily to the south, through Robinson
Channel, a distance of nearly fifty miles, and
nearly caused her destruction by forcing her
on the Greenland coast. Fortunately the pack
opened somewhat, so that the vessel was enabled to change her position and secure safe
anchorage. This place, later named Thank God
Harbor, in 81° 37′ N., 61° 44′ W., was sheltered by a bold cape to the north, while the
Polaris was protected from the polar pack by an
immense ice-floe, called Providence Berg. This
enormous floe-berg, grounded in a hundred

fathoms of water, was by direct measurement four hundred and fifty feet long, three hundred feet broad, and towered sixty feet above the level of the sea.

Preparations were at once made to put the crew in winter-quarters, and on shore an observatory was built for scientific purposes. To the surprise and delight of the party, seals proved to be quite abundant, and a small herd of musk-oxen was found, the first of these animals ever seen on the west coast of Greenland.

Leaving his chief of the scientific staff and his sailing-master to their respective duties, Hall decided on a preliminary sledge journey in order to determine the best route for his contemplated journey of the next spring toward the pole. A heavy fall of snow insured good sledging and enabled him to leave Thank God Harbor on October 10th, he being accompanied by the first mate, Chester, the Esquimaux, Joe and Hans Hendrick, with two dog-sledges and fourteen dogs. In a journey of six days he attained Cape Brevoort, in 82° N., on the north side of Newman Bay, a considerable distance to the southward, however, of the point reached by the Polaris in the Arctic Ocean. In a despatch written at this point, Hall says, "From Cape Brevoort we can see land extending on the west side of the strait to the north, a distance of about seventy miles, thus making land, as far as we can discover, about 83° 5′ N." To illustrate the accuracy of Hall's judgment and his freedom from making extravagant claims, it may be stated that the detailed surveys of the British Arctic expedition of 1876 show the most northerly point on the east coast of Grinnell Land, Cape Joseph Henry, which possibly could be seen by Hall, was in 82° 55', or within ten miles of the position assigned it from a distance of seventy miles.

Hall returned to the Polaris on October 24th,

A Woman of the Arctic Highlanders. Sketched from life.

speaking most encouragingly of his prospects and planning another sledge journey for the autumn. Within an hour, however, he was taken violently ill, and upon examination, Dr. Bessels announced that he had been stricken with apoplexy, that his left side was paralyzed, and that his sickness might prove fatal. After an illness, with delirium, for several days, he improved materially, and was even able, through his clerk, to arrange the records of his late sledge journey, but a recurrence of the attack caused his death, on November 8, 1871.

The death of Hall left the expedition without a head. However, Captain Buddington, the sailing-master, and Dr. Bessels, the chief of the scientific staff, signed an agreement to do all in their power to fulfil the ultimate object of Hall's ambition. Desultory efforts to go northward by boat were made without success the following year, and the only expedition which had definite result was one on foot by Sergeant Meyer, of the Signal Corps of the United States Army, during which he reached Repulse Harbor, $82°$ $9'$ N., on the shores of the frozen Polar Sea, at that time the most northerly land ever attained.

The future of the Polaris expedition does not strictly pertain to Hall. However, the winter was marked by a series of valuable physical observations, made by Dr. Bessels and Mr. Bryan, the astronomer. In August, 1872, it was decided to return to the United States. Pushed into an impenetrable pack, anchored to a floe, the Polaris drifted with the main ice-pack down Kennedy Channel, through Kane Sea, and into Smith Sound, where, on October 15, 1872, off Northumberland Island, the pack was disrupted by a violent gale, which freed the Polaris. Part of her crew, left upon the ice-pack, experienced the horrors of a mid-winter drift southward of thirteen hundred miles, and were picked up off the coast of Labrador by the sealer Tigress, in the spring of 1872. The Polaris drifted to land in Lifeboat Cove, near Littleton Island, where the party built winter-quarters on shore, known as Polaris House. In the succeeding summer they built boats from the remains of their ship, by means of which they reached Cape York, where their contemplated journey across Melville Bay was rendered unnecessary by falling

Esquimau Woman. Sketched from life.

in with the whaler Ravenscraig, which took them to England.

The geographical results of Hall's last expedition were extensive and valuable. Not only was the Polaris navigated to the highest point then ever attained by a vessel, but the very shores of the Polar Sea were visited and explored. Hall carried northward and completed the exploration of Kennedy Channel; outlined the coast of Hall Basin and Robinson Channel; extended

Grinnell Land northward nearly two degrees of latitude to practically its extreme limit; added materially to the northern limits of Greenland, and charted a very extensive portion of its northern coast. Unfortunately for the general credit of the expedition, the accurate observations and conservative estimates of Hall were not adhered to, and in their stead were published, under government auspices, a chart of Hall's discoveries which proved misleading in many of its details, extravagant and unreliable in its claims of new northern lands.

The fidelity, accuracy, and importance of Hall's Arctic work is recognized, especially by his American and British successors in Smith Sound. Nares, in his official report to Parliament, states that the east coast-line of Grinnell Land agreed "so well with Hall's description that it was impossible to mistake their identity. Their bearing also, although differing upward of thirty degrees from those of the published chart, agreed precisely with his published report." Thus Hall merited the commemorative inscription on the brass tablet which the British polar expedition of 1875, with a generous appreciativeness creditable to its own brave men, erected to Hall's memory over his lonely northern grave. It recognizes Hall as one "who sacrificed his life in the advancement of science," and further recites that they, "following in his footsteps, have profited by his experience."

XII.

GEORGE WASHINGTON DE LONG,

AND THE SIBERIAN ARCTIC OCEAN.

OF all the routes followed by explorers attempting to extend northward our knowledge of unknown lands, there is one which, more than all others, seems to have been closed by nature to the daring enterprise of man. While successful voyages to the northward of America, and along the meridian of Spitzbergen, have been of frequent occurrence, yet it has been the fortune of one expedition only to penetrate the vast ice-pack that covers the Arctic Ocean to the north of Siberia, and give an account thereof.

This expedition, organized through the munificence of James Gordon Bennett, Jr., and known to the world as the Jeannette Expedition, was commanded by De Long, then a lieutenant-commander of the United States Navy.

George Washington De Long was born in New York City, March 22, 1844, and entered the United States Navy, by graduation from the Naval Academy, in 1865. He rose to be a lieutenant-commander and rendered ordinary naval service until 1873, when special duty fell to his lot which turned his thoughts to Arctic research.

George Washington De Long.

The rescue of the drift party of the Polaris naturally caused great alarm as to the safety of the remainder of her crew, and with the despatch of the Tigress into the waters of Smith Sound, came orders for the Juniata, to which De Long was attached, to visit the coasts of western Greenland for additional search for the missing explorers. The Juniata proceeded to Upernivik, as far as it was deemed safe for the man-of-war to venture, but its brave and sagacious commander, Captain D. L. Braine, of the Navy, thought it most necessary to search the fast inshore ice of Melville Bay, along which he correctly surmised they would conduct a retreat by boats. For this duty—novel, hazardous, and difficult — De Long promptly volunteered. For this dangerous trip the steam-launch Little Juniata, some 32 feet long and 8 wide, was selected. Her crew consisted of Lieutenant Chipp, Ensign May, ice-pilot Dodge, who had served with Hayes, and four others, while she was equipped and provisioned for sixty days. In this small craft De Long, following the fast ice, reached a point immediately off Cape York, when he was struck by a violent gale. The sea was so heavy that his only chance of safety lay in carrying sail, steam being useless, to keep the boat under control. The violence of the wind disrupted the inshore ice, threatening the launch continually; owing to fog the presence of immense icebergs made navigation more dangerous than ever; high seas constantly broke over her, soaking everything on board and harassing the crew with the imminent danger of swamping. Thirty hours the gale lasted, leaving the party in the last stages of exhaustion, wet to the skin and benumbed with cold, with closed floes to the north and east and the dangerous "middle pack" to the west. Under these conditions De Long reluctantly abandoned the search and returned.

This brief experience created an interest in northern work which never abated, and as a result, De Long, the voyage ended, approached James Gordon Bennett, Jr., who was favorable to his projects. Nothing, however, was done until November, 1876, after the return of the Nares's expedition, when the exploration was decided on; but no vessel could be procured. Eventually Sir Allen Young, an Arctic explorer of note, was persuaded to sell the Pandora, in which he had twice made polar voyages.

The ship was, by Act of Congress, given an American register under the name of Jeannette, strengthened under naval supervision, and put in commission under the orders and instructions of the Secretary of the Navy, with full discipline in force; but the expense of the expedition—repairs, equipment, and pay—was met by Bennett.

On July 8, 1879, the Jeannette sailed from San Francisco, commanded by De Long, and officered by Lieutenant Chipp, Master Danenhower, Chief Engineer Melville, Doctor Ambler, an ice-pilot, two scientists, twenty-four petty officers and men. The route selected by De Long was via Behring Strait, apparently under the impression that Wrangel Land was continental in extent, an idea supported by the German geographer Petermann, whose advice De Long had sought, and along the shores of which coursed the northern current that swept forever out of the vision of man such whalers as were fully beset by the ice-pack north of Asia.

Before pursuing his own exploration De Long, in compliance with instructions from the Navy Department, made search for the Vega, in which ship Nordenskiold, circumnavigating Europe and Asia, had wintered at Cape Serdze Kamen, in $67° 12'$ N. latitude, on the northwestern coast of Asia. On reaching this point he learned that the Vega had comfortably wintered and had passed south, thus confirming the report he had gained from the natives at St. Lawrence Bay.

They at once steamed northward, thankful, as De Long records, "that Nordenskiold was safe, and we might proceed on our way toward Wrangel Land." Ice was soon fallen in with, and, after preliminary efforts to proceed directly to the north, which impenetrable floes prevented, De Long, on September 5, 1879, "got up a full head of steam and entered the pack through the best-looking lead in the general direction of Herald Island," which was plainly visible at a distance of forty miles.

It was De Long's intention on leaving San Francisco to explore this land the first winter, but completely beset by heavy floes, in $71° 35'$ N. latitude, $175°$ W. longitude, his ship never escaped. In hopes that information of value might be had from a visit to Herald Island, an unsuccessful attempt was made to reach it by dog-sledge over the fast-cementing pack, but the party was turned back by impassable leads.

It soon became evident that the Jeannette was drifting steadily with the entire pack. First, the

Herald Island.

direction was to the north, taking the ship out of sight of Herald Island, but next it changed to the southwest, bringing that land again in view. While the drift was by a devious and very irregular course, yet it was in the general direction of northwest, from 71° 35′ N., and 175° W., at besetment, to 77° 15′ N., and 155° E., when the ship was finally crushed by the pack. In investigating the cause of the drift, De Long says: "As to the currents in this part of the Arctic Ocean, I think our drift is demonstrating that they are the local creation of the wind for the time being. As our drift in resulting direction has been northwest since our besetment, so the greater amount of wind has been from the southeast; our short and irregular side-drift east and west, and occasionally to south, being due to correspondingly short and irregular winds from northwest or east."

The party settled down to their regular life, which though very monotonous soon had an element of excitement and danger introduced that never passed away in entirety. This was the threatened disruption of the pack, which, seemingly without cause, would change its form and position with such suddenness and violence as to endanger the safety of the ship. On November 13, 1879, without warning, the pack separated on a line with the ship's keel, the port snow-wall being carried with the pack one hundred and fifty feet away, leaving open water, that fortunately froze over before other violent changes took place.

De Long writes: "This steady strain is fearful; seemingly we are not secure for a moment. . . . Living over a powder-mill, waiting for an explosion, would be a similar mode of existence. . . . I sleep with my clothes on, and start up anxiously at every crack . . . of the ship's frame."

Almost by intervention of Providence, as it seemed, the Jeannette escaped destruction from these violent disruptions, which, except that of January 19, 1880, left her, during the first winter, comparatively unharmed. On that day, with terrible groaning and grinding, the main pack was fearfully agitated; no large openings were seen and the ice acted as though its entire periphery was subjected to steady and irresistible pressure, which being toward the centre caused the whole surface to buckle up irregularly. Enormous pieces of ice piling up under the stern of the Jeannette brought a tremendous longitudinal pressure on the ship and broke her fore-foot, which caused a serious leak. It was only through the indomitable energy and great professional skill of Melville that the leak was got under control, and later cared for, without taxing greatly their precious stock of fuel.

The winter passed with all in health save Danenhower, whose eyes becoming diseased necessitated several operations and permanently placed him off duty for the voyage. The summer of 1880 came, found them fast embedded in the ice, and went without release. Autumn passed, winter came, and even the opening year of 1881 found them with conditions unchanged, as De Long recites: "A disabled and leaking ship, a seriously sick officer, an uneasy and terrible pack, constantly diminishing coal-pile and provisions, and far from the Siberian coast." A break came, however, with the discovery of new land in May, along the north coast of which the Jeannette drifted slowly. On May 31st a party was sent to examine the island, for such it proved to be, Melville being in command, as Chipp was then on the sick-list. Melville, despite the open condition of the ice, succeeded in landing on June 3, 1881, his third day out. He was obliged to carry his instruments and provisions, at the risk of his life, through the moving pack. It proved to be a desolate, ice-capped, rocky islet, almost destitute of vegetation and inhabited only by dovekies, who nested in the inaccessible cliffs adjoining the discharging glaciers. Another island appearing, De Long named the two; Jeannette, in 76° 47′ N., 159° E., and Henrietta, in 77° 08′ N., 158° E.

The end of the besetment came at last. On June 12, 1881, in 77° 15′ N., 155° E., the pack showed signs of great pressure, the immense floes seeming to be alive in their motion, and despite all efforts the Jeannette was terribly nipped, her bows being thrown high in air. It was evident that escape was hardly possible. Steps were immediately taken to abandon ship, and everything of value or use was speedily withdrawn, with boats, sledges, etc., to a safe distance. Early the next morning the ice opened a little, and the Jeannette immediately sank, with colors flying, in thirty-eight fathoms of water.

De Long and his party thus found themselves adrift in the Polar Sea, more than three hundred miles from the nearest point of the mainland of Asia, and about one hundred and fifty miles from the New Siberian Islands. While the condition of affairs seemed desperate, De Long never despaired. Lieutenant Danenhower being disabled, and Chipp sick, De Long's main dependence was in his chief engineer, Melville, who was well, strong, energetic, and fertile in expedients.

They had five boats (two very small), nine sleds,

In the Pack.

provisions for sixty days, ammunition, instruments and records; a terrible load for the party, as five men were off duty, and several others too weak to do their share in the drag-ropes. There remained, however, twenty dogs, whose utility was questionable, as they soon consumed more in weight than they ever hauled. The ice was very rough, large openings were frequent, snow often impeded progress, roads had to be made, and on occasion all the stores and men had to be ferried across wide water-lanes. At the beginning there was so much baggage that seven separate loads were hauled, causing the men to travel thirteen times over the same road, but this was soon unnecessary, as weights were gradually reduced.

To add to De Long's discouragement he discovered that they were under the influence of a northwest drift, and after six days' travel due south were twenty-eight miles further north than when the ship sunk. He refrained from discouraging the men by this information, but changing his course to the southwest, got out of the drift.

On July 11th land was discovered, and turning toward it the shipwrecked and exhausted men reached it July 28, 1881; it was in 76° 38′ N., 148° E., and was called Bennett Island. Landing was effected by ferrying and crossing heavy, fast-moving floes, and the danger was greatly enhanced by the low water, which made it extremely dangerous work to attain the surface of the overhanging ice-foot. The cliffs were alive with birds, which was a welcome change of diet, to the sick men especially. The island was quite mountainous, with several grass-covered valleys; a seam of coal was found and signs of considerable animal life.

Recuperated by their nine days' rest, the party started south on August 8th, and landed on

Where the Bodies were Found.

Thaddeus Island, of the New Siberian group, August 20, 1881. It is unnecessary to dwell on the dangers and hardships which this unprecedented journey entailed on the members of this party, which were met with fortitude, courage, and energy that made its successful issue one of the most notable efforts in the history of man, overcoming obstacles almost insurmountable.

This remarkable journey had been so far made alternately by sledge and boat, owing to the broken condition of the Polar pack; from Thaddeus Island, however, an open sea enabled them to proceed in boats, which were respectively commanded by De Long, Chipp, and Melville. On September 12th a severe storm separated the boats off the Lena Delta; Chipp with eight men were lost, while Melville, with nine others, reached a small village through one of the eastern mouths of the Lena.

De Long landed, in 77° 15′ N., 155° E., September 17th, with Dr. Ambler and twelve men, having been obliged to abandon his boat, owing to the shallowness of the river. He took with him the ship's records, arms, ammunition, medicines, necessary camp equipments, and four days' provisions, which were carried on the men's shoulders. Fuel proved abundant, and Alexey, their interpreter, killed two deer, thus improving the situation. Retarded by the presence of sick men and by the weight of cumbersome records, they followed slowly southward the barren shores of the Lena, travelling through snow and over ice which broke readily. Their feet were soon in terrible condition, and eventually an ulcer on Ericksen's foot rendered partial amputation necessary on September 29th. De Long then records the terrible situation: They were confronted by a tributary of the Lena which must freeze before they could cross, and as to Ericksen, if forced along, he could not recover, and "if I remained here and kept everybody with me, Ericksen's days would be lengthened a little at the risk of our all dying from starvation." Ice formed in a couple of days, and they proceeded, dragging Ericksen on a sled.

October 3d, food entirely failing, their dog was killed and cooked, giving them strength the following day to reach a deserted hut large enough to hold the party. Here they were storm-stayed two days; Ericksen dying, Alexey hunting unsuccessfully, the drifting snow and piercing cold—all these served to plunge the party into despair. De Long writes: "What, in God's name, is going to become of us?—fourteen pounds of dog meat left and twenty-five miles to a possible settlement. . . . Read the burial service and carried our departed shipmate's body to the river, where he was buried." Their last food was eaten October 7th, and nothing remained except old tea-leaves and two quarts of alcohol; but Alexey shot a ptarmigan, of which a thin soup was made.

On October 9th the exhausted condition of some of the men and an open, unfordable creek debarred further progress of the party as a whole. In this contingency De Long sent Nindermann and Noros ahead for relief, with orders to keep the west bank of the Lena until they reached a settlement. Later De Long advanced

Noros and Nindermann.

a mile and camped in a hole in the bank; Alexey killed four ptarmigans and the party resorted to their deer-skin clothing for subsistence, but without avail. The last entry in De Long's diary, October 30, 1881, records all dead except

Collins, who was dying, Ah Sam and Dr. Ambler, of whom no mention was made.

Noros and Nindermann, after a march of one hundred and twenty miles, reached Bulcour, which they found deserted. Seeking shelter in one of the vacant huts, they were discovered by a native, who took them to an adjacent encampment. The natives either did not understand Nindermann or were unwilling to go northward, for despite his incessant and urgent entreaties they carried the two seamen southward to Bulun, where they arrived on October 29th, and met Melville and his party.

This energetic officer, exhausting all practicable means, pushed his relief parties northward to the extremity of the Lena Delta, but without success. He reached the Arctic Ocean, recovered the log-books, chronometer, and other articles on November 14th, when a severe storm obliged him to abandon the search. Renewing his efforts, in March, 1882, he discovered, on the 23d of that month, the bodies of his companions.

An official inquiry as to the general conduct of the expedition caused the board of officers to express their opinion that the general personnel were entitled to great praise for their solidarity and cheerfulness, their constancy and endurance. The zeal, energy, and professional aptitude of Melville were noticed, and special commendation given to De Long for the high qualities displayed by him in the conduct of the expedition.

The scientific observations of the Jeannette

expedition must be of considerable value, involving as they do hydrographic, magnetic, and meteorological observations over an extended portion of the earth's surface previously un-

Finding the Bodies.

known, and it appears surprising that after all these years they remain undiscussed.

In addition may be noted the importance of De Long's hydrographic contributions, covering some fifty thousand square miles of polar ocean, which indicate with equal clearness the character of fifty thousand other square miles of area to the south, and thus prove the Siberian Arctic Ocean to be a shallow sea, dotted with islands.

The geographic results are represented in part by the attainment of the highest latitude ever reached in Asiatic seas, and in the discovery of Jeannette, Henrietta, and Bennett Islands. Discoveries, however, are both direct and indirect, and to positive results should be added successes of an inferential though negative character. Through De Long's northwest drift the long-sought-for Wrangel Land shrank from its assumed dimensions as a continent, connecting, under the Petermann hypothesis, Asia with Greenland, to its reality—a small island.

It is to be said that this reduction of Wrangel Land into a little island doomed De Long's expedition to certain failure and closed Behring Strait as a promising route to high latitudes; for the arctic canon of Parry yet obtains, that without a sheltering coast no vessel can hope to navigate safely the Polar Ocean.

With the march of time it is not to be expected that geographic problems connected with the vast ice-covered ocean to the north of Siberia will be left unsolved. These coming explorers may be more fortunate than was De Long, and while profiting by his experiences they will surpass his efforts, yet their successes cannot make greater demands on the courage and constancy of them and their subordinates than were shown by the gallant De Long and his associates in the fateful voyage of the Jeannette.

XIII.

PAUL BELLONI DU CHAILLU,

Discoverer of the Dwarfs and Gorillas.

Among the thousands of vigorous and adventurous men whom chance brought to light in foreign climes, but who by choice have cast their lot with America, by becoming citizens of the United States, there are few whose explorations and discoveries have excited more popular interest and discussion than have those of Du Chaillu, the discoverer, in modern times, of the dwarfs and the capturer of the gorilla.

Born in Paris, July 31, 1835, the early environments of Paul Belloni Du Chaillu fostered and forecast his taste for African exploration, for his father was one of the adventurous Frenchmen whose consular appointment and commercial enterprises led him to settle at the mouth of the Gaboon, on the west coast of Africa, where his distinguished son passed his boyhood. While young Du Chaillu was, doubtless, well grounded in ordinary sciences by his instructors, the learned Jesuit fathers, of Gaboon, yet apart from regular educational institutions he imbibed other wealth of learning by observation of the rich tropical world around him, and also through

Paul Belloni Du Chaillu.

familiar intercourse with neighboring tribes acquired a knowledge of native tongues and craft, of savage habits and character, which insured his after-success in African exploration.

Commercial pursuits brought Du Chaillu to the United States, in 1852, when he was so strongly impressed by American institutions that he became a naturalized citizen of the United States.

Du Chaillu was brought prominently before the American public by a series of striking and interesting articles on the Gaboon country, which from their favorable reception strengthened his belief in the importance of thoroughly exploring certain portions of the west coast of Africa. The region selected for his investigations was under the burning sun of the equator, somewhat to the north of the Congo country, in the basins drained by the Muni, Ogowe, and Rembo Rivers, which, owing to difficulty of access, extreme heat, prevailing fevers, and deadly climate, were practically unknown. Between 1856 and 1859 Du Chaillu journeyed upward of eight thousand miles through this country, travelling on foot, with no white companion, and, with the aid of natives, cursorily explored nearly one hundred thousand square miles of virgin territory. Working with the ardent zeal of a naturalist, his enormous ornithological collection aggregated thousands of specimens, and in this collection alone he added some sixty new species of birds to the domain of science. Among the quadrupeds, he discovered no less than twenty new species, and among the most important animals brought to light were the very remarkable nest-building ape, with its unknown and its almost equally extraordinary brother the koo-loo-lamba, and his observations of the almost unknown gorilla were most interesting and valuable.

In ethnology he accumulated a number of invaluable native arms and implements, which now adorn the British Museum. Space fails in which to recite his intense sufferings, during these explorations, from semi-starvation, the wild beasts of the dense forests, the venomous reptiles of the river valleys, the attacks of ferocious ants, and other intolerable poisonous insects which infest the interior.

There are many interesting accounts of curious quadrupeds in Du Chaillu's book, "Adventures in Equatorial Africa," but none appeals more strongly to most readers than that of the gorilla. Traditions from antiquity, the relation of Hanno, the Carthaginian navigator of 350 B.C., set forth the existence of such an animal, but no white man had ever seen a gorilla, except Andrew Battell, early in the seventeenth century. Nearly ten years before the explorations of Du Chaillu the gorilla had been, however, brought to the notice of naturalists by Dr. Savage, of Boston, who had received a skull from the Rev. J. L. Wilson, an American missionary on the Gaboon.

From boyhood up Du Chaillu had heard from the natives of Gaboon fearful stories of the cunning, strength, and ferocity of this ape, which is the most dreaded animal on the west coast of Africa. For years he had longed for an opportunity to hunt the gorilla, and when he first saw its tracks, which threw his native hunters into alarm, he relates that his sensations were indescribable, his feelings so intense as to be painful, and his heart-throbs so violent that he actually feared the animal would be alarmed by them.

Du Chaillu chronicles the end of his first successful hunt as follows:

"Before us stood an immense male gorilla. He had gone through the jungle on his all-fours; but when he saw our party he erected himself and looked us boldly in the face. He stood about a dozen yards from us, and was a sight, I think, never to forget. Nearly six feet high (he proved two inches shorter), with immense body, huge chest, and great muscular arms; with fiercely glaring, large, deep-gray eyes, and a hellish expression of face, which seemed to me like some nightmare vision, thus stood before us this king of the African forests. He was not afraid of us. He stood there and beat his breast with his huge fists till it resounded like an immense bass-drum—which is their mode of offering defiance—meantime giving vent to roar after roar. The roar of the gorilla is the most singular and awful noise heard in these African woods. It begins with a sharp bark, like an angry dog, then glides into a deep bass roll, which literally and closely resembles the roll of distant thunder along the sky, for which I have sometimes been tempted to take it where I did not see the ani-

The Gorilla. (*Troglodytes Gorilla.*)

mal. So deep is it that it seems to proceed less from the mouth and throat than from the deep chest and vast paunch. He again sent forth a thunderous roar, and now truly he reminded me of nothing but some hellish dream-creature—a being of that hideous order, half-man half-beast, which we find pictured by old artists in some representations of the infernal regions."

The explorer relates that flying gorillas so resembled men running for their lives, and their discordant cries seemed so human, that he felt almost like a murderer as he shot them.

Having obtained a number of specimens, he now used his utmost endeavors to obtain an ape alive, and speaks of his success as "one of the greatest pleasures of my life;" to his great grief, however, the intractable and savage brute soon died. Regarding it, Du Chaillu writes:

"Some hunters who had been out on my account brought in a young gorilla alive. I cannot describe the emotions with which I saw the struggling little brute dragged into the village. All the hardships I had endured in Africa were rewarded in that moment. It was a little fellow of between two and three years old, two feet six inches in height, and as fierce and stubborn as a grown animal could have been."

Several were captured from time to time, but all died after short confinement. Every effort to subdue their ferocity, whether by force or by persistent kindness, utterly failed: they were never other than morose, bellicose, and treacherous.

Another very interesting animal is the nest-building ape, a before unknown species, which was discovered by our explorer almost by accident. Du Chaillu says:

"As I was trudging along, rather tired of the sport, I happened to look up at a high tree which we were passing, and saw a most singular-looking shelter built in its branches. I asked Aboko whether the hunters here had this way to sleep in the woods, but was told, to my surprise, that this very ingenious nest was built by the *nshiego mbouve*, an ape. The material is leafy branches with which to make the roof, and vines to tie these branches to the tree. The tying is done so neatly, and the roof is so well constructed that, until I saw the nshiego actually occupying his habitation I could scarce persuade myself that human hands had not built all. It sheds rain perfectly, being neatly rounded on top for this purpose. The material being collected, the male goes up and builds the nest, while the female brings him the branches and vines."

Yet another member of the ape family, discovered by our explorer, deserves passing notice in his own words:

"The koo-loo-lamba has for distinctive marks a very round head; whiskers running quite around the face and below the chin; the face is round; the cheek-bones prominent; the cheeks sunken; the jaws are not very prominent—less so than in any of the apes; the hair is black, long on the arm, which was, however, partly bare. This ape, whose singular cry distinguishes it at once from all its congeners in these wilds, is remarkable as bearing a closer general resemblance to man than any other ape yet known. It was very rare, and I was able to obtain but one specimen of it. This is smaller than the adult male gorilla, and stouter than the female gorilla. The head is its most remarkable point. This struck me at once as having an expression curiously like an Esquimau or Chinaman."

Among the worst pests of Africa are ants, especially the bashikouay, which travel in a line about two inches wide and often miles in length. Du Chaillu says: "They devour and attack all with irresistible fury. The elephant and gorilla fly, the black men run for their lives. In an incredibly short time a leopard or deer is overwhelmed, killed, and eaten. They seem to travel day and night. Often have I been awakened out of sleep and obliged to rush from my hut and into the water to save my life. A bashikouay army makes a clean sweep, even ascending to the tops of the highest trees in pursuit of their prey."

The results of his four years of research in the interests of ethnography, geography, and natural history, were placed before the public in a valuable work entitled "Explorations and Adventures in Equatorial Africa." The book gave rise to bitter, harsh, unjust criticisms, and engendered endless discussions. Du Chaillu's journey to the interior was entirely discredited, and his accounts of the animals and natives were characterized as mere fabrications. Discoveries necessarily develop discrepancies between the realities brought to light and existing beliefs produced through inference or imagination; then, as has many another discover in science or geography, Du Chaillu learned how slow is the willingness of a jealous mind to relinquish its favorite error for a conflicting truth.

Justification came speedily, for the explorations of Serval and Bellay, of the very next year,

proved the accuracy of Du Chaillu's account of
the great Ogowe River, and indicated the general correctness of his map of the Ashira country.
Burton confirmed his reports regarding the cannibalistic habits of the Fans, and other statements
were speedily corroborated.

Stung to the quick by the adverse criticisms
Du Chaillu, although suffering from the effects
of fevers contracted in his long residence in
Western Africa, determined to repeat the journey with such precautions regarding his observations as would be absolutely convincing
as to their truthfulness; especially he determined to capture and bring to Europe a living
gorilla. To ensure accuracy he went through a
course of instruction in the use of instruments,
learning to make, test, and reduce astronomical
and hypsometrical observations, and acquired
proficiency in the then difficult art of photography. As regards geographical explorations
he had a vague hope that he might reach from
the west coast of Africa some unknown tributary
of the Nile, down which he might be able to
reach the main river and the Mediterranean Sea.

Leaving England in August, 1863, Du Chaillu's
first destination was the mouth of Fernand Vaz
River, about one hundred and ten miles south of
the Gaboon, this point being selected both because he knew the natives and also because that
river valley being unknown afforded him virgin
ground from the beginning of his journey.

In landing through the terrible surf that makes
entrance into the Fernand Vaz so dangerous, Du

Chaillu was nearly drowned and all his astronomical instruments and medicines were lost or damaged. This necessitated his delay in that region until other instruments could be had from England; but the time was not lost, for he had ample opportunity of further studying the

A Village of Dwarfs.

habits of the gorillas, which abound there; fortunately he captured four, an adult and three young, one of which he shipped alive to London, but it died during the voyage.

Du Chaillu started on his journey with ten Commi negroes, previous servitors, as his bodyguard, and fifty porters in place of the hundred needed, thus making double trips necessary for a while. Following up the Fernand Vaz River to its tributary, the Rembo, he left this latter stream at Obindshi and travelled southeasterly to Olenda. Here a council was held by the local chief, who forbade him to enter the Apingi country, but allowed him to proceed to the Ashira region, where he was long delayed and robbed by the natives. In crossing the Ngunie River, on his way eastward to the Ishogo country, he was surprised to obtain ferriage in a large, flatbottomed canoe, which carried baggage and party across in seven journeys.

Near the end of June, while traversing a tract of wild forest near Yangue, Du Chaillu came suddenly upon a cluster of most extraordinary and diminutive huts, which he was told were occupied by a tribe of dwarf negroes. In his previous journey in the Apingi country he had given no credence to exaggerated descriptions and reports that had often come to his ears concerning dwarf tribes, assuming the stories to be fables. Now, however, with these curious huts before him he pressed on eager to obtain personal information concerning these little folks, whose existence had been vouched for centuries before by Pomponius Mela, Herodotus, and Strabo, and who were described in a fairly accurate way, by Andrew Battell, in 1625. In answer to Du Chaillu's inquiries the natives said that there were many such villages in the adjacent forests, and that the tiny men were called the Obongos.

He found the huts entirely deserted, but from scattered traces of recent household effects, it was quite evident that the Obongos, alarmed at the approach of strangers, had fled for safety to the dense jungle of the neighboring forest. He thus describes their habitations: "The huts were of a low, oval shape, like a gypsy tent; the highest part, that near the entrance, was about four feet from the ground; the greatest breadth was about four feet also. On each side were three or four sticks for the man and woman to sleep on. The huts were made of flexible branches of trees, arched over and fixed into the ground at each end, the longest branches being in the middle, and the others successively shorter, the whole being covered with heavy leaves."

On June 26, 1864, Du Chaillu entered Niembouai, a large village in Ashango Land, in the vicinity of which, he learned with great joy, was situated an inhabited encampment of the Obongos, or hairy dwarfs, as he terms them. The Ashango natives offered to accompany him, at the same time intimating that it was likely the village would be found deserted; for, said they, the Obongos (the dwarfs) are shy and timid as the gazelle, and as wild as the antelope. To see them, you must take them by surprise. They are like to the beasts of the field. They feed on the serpents, rats, and mice, and on the berries and nuts of the forest.

Du Chaillu made his first visit to an Obongo encampment with three Ashango guides, and with great precaution they silently entered a village of twelve huts to find it long since deserted. Fortune was more favorable at the second village, where, however, no one was to be seen on entrance. The curling smoke, calabashes

A Pigmy Warrior.

of fresh water, and a half-cooked snake on living coals indicated that the alarmed inhabitants had fled on their approach. A search of the huts resulted in disclosing the presence of three old women, a young man, and several children, who were almost paralyzed with fear at the sight of an unknown monster—a white man. By judicious distribution of bananas, and especially of beads, Du Chaillu succeeded in allaying their fears, and later made several visits, but confidence was never firmly established, and it was impossible to see the men except as they fled at his approach, or at a distance when they visited the Ashango village for purposes of barter.

During his several visits he carefully measured six dwarf women, whose average height proved to be four feet six and one-eighth inches; the shortest was four feet four and one-half inches, and the tallest five feet and one-quarter of an inch; the young man, possibly not full grown, measured four feet six inches in height.

Du Chaillu says: "The color of these people was a dirty yellow, and their eyes had an untamable wildness that struck me as very remarkable. In appearance, physique, and color they are totally unlike the Ashangos, who are very anxious to disown kinship with them. They declare that the Obongos intermarry among themselves, sisters with brothers. The smallness and isolation of their communities must necessitate close interbreeding; and I think it very possible this may cause the physical deterioration of their race."

Their foreheads were very low and narrow, cheek-bones prominent, legs proportionately short, palms of hands quite white, and their hair short, curly tufts, resembling little balls of wool, which, according to the young man seen by Du Chaillu, grew also, in plentiful, short, curly tufts on his legs and breast, a peculiarity which the Ashangos declared was common to the Obongo men.

These dwarfs feed partly on roots, berries, and nuts gathered in the forest, and partly on flesh and fish. They are very expert in capturing wild animals by traps and pitfalls, and in obtaining fish from the streams; and the surplus of flesh is exchanged for plantains and such simple manufactured articles as they stand in need of.

Concerning their settlements and range of migration Du Chaillu adds: "The Obongos never remain long in one place. They are eminently a migratory people, moving whenever game becomes scarce, but they do not wander very far. These Obongos are called the Obongos of the Ashangos; those who live among the Njavi are called Obongo-Njavi, and the same with other tribes. Obongos are said to exist very far to the east, as far as the Ashangos have any knowledge."

In his "Journey to Ashango Land" Du Chaillu gives quite a number of words of the Obongo language; he considers their dialect to be a mixture of their original language with that of the tribe among whom they reside. It appeared that none of the dwarf women could count more than ten, probably the limit of their numerals. Their weapons of offence and defence were usually small bows and arrows, the latter at times poisoned.

Leaving Mobano, 1° 53′ S. latitude, and about 12° 27′ E. longitude, by dead reckoning, Du

Chaillu passed due east to the village of Mou-
aou Kombo, where, by accident, while firing
a salute, one of his body-guard unfortunately

A Dwarf Prisoner.

killed a villager. An effort to atone for the accident by presents would doubtless have been
successful, but, most unfortunately, and despite
Du Chaillu's strict orders, his body-guards and

porters had already irritated the Ashangos by offensive conduct. Overtures for "blood-money" were interrupted by an offended chief denouncing the exploring party. Almost instantly the natives commenced beating their war-drums, and Du Chaillu, realizing the danger and loading his men with his most valuable articles, retreated westward toward the coast. Before they reached the forest he and one of his men were wounded by poisoned arrows. Pursued by the infuriated savages Du Chaillu restrained his men from shooting, when, demoralized by the situation, many of his porters threw away their loads, which consisted of note-books, maps, instruments, photographs, and natural history collections. Curiously enough the instruments and goods thus abandoned by Du Chaillu in 1864, were found in 1891, by an African trader, in the jungle where they had been thrown down by the retreating carriers, having remained all these years untouched by the Ashangos, who believed they were fetich and so regarded them with superstitious dread.

After retreating a few miles and finding that inactivity and self-restraint meant self-destruction, Du Chaillu took the offensive, and drawing up his men in a favorable position, repelled his pursuers with considerable loss. The wounds from poisoned arrows being external, if subjected to immediate treatment, healed in a few weeks.

Further explorations under these circumstances were impossible, for Du Chaillu depended entirely for his success on friendly relations with the natives; in consequence he returned to the sea-coast, and on September 27, 1865, quitted the shores of Western Equatorial Africa.

Although the second voyage of Du Chaillu into the unknown regions of Western Equatorial Africa rehabilitated his reputation as a reliable observer, as far as related to geography and natural history, yet his description of the Obongo dwarfs gave rise to further discussion and aspersions. It is needless to say that the discoveries of Stanley in his last African expedition have definitely settled this question in Du Chaillu's favor, and that the studies of Lenz, Marche, and Bastian, in and near the region visited by Du Chaillu, confirm the accuracy of his descriptions. Indeed the Obongos of Ashango Land rise in proportion to undersized negroes when compared with the dwarf queen found by Stanley on the eastern edge of the great equatorial forest, who measures only two feet nine inches in height.

Thus in time has come complete vindication of all of Du Chaillu's statements as to the wonders of the Ashira and Ashango Lands, which portions of Western Equatorial Africa he was the first to explore. If the geographical extent of his explorations give way to that of other African travellers, yet it must be admitted that he stands scarcely second to any in the number, importance, and interest of his contributions and collections in connection with ethnography and natural history of Equatorial Africa.

In later years Du Chaillu has devoted his attention to the northern parts of Sweden, Norway, Lapland, and Finland, and although his travels in these regions had no important geographical outcome, yet they resulted in lately placing the general public in possession of many interesting details of these countries, as given in his book called "The Land of the Midnight Sun." His important work, "The Viking Age," is an elaborate presentation of his theory that the ancestors of the English-speaking races were Vikings and not Anglo-Saxons, and has awakened much comment in the scientific world. "Ivar the Viking," his latest book, is a popular account of Viking life and manners in the third and fourth centuries.

Arrows of the African Pigmies.

Henry M. Stanley.

XIV.

STANLEY AFRICANUS AND THE CONGO FREE STATE.

THE largest, the richest, and the least known of the great continents is Africa. Despite its vast area, numerous tribes, and complicated interests it may be said that its potential influences as regards the rest of the world have been alternately retarded and advanced through the efforts of four individuals. The jealousy of Rome, excited to its highest pitch by the eloquence of the elder Cato, resulted, 146 B.C., in the annihilation of Carthage, an industrial centre whence for five centuries had radiated toward the interior of Africa peaceful and commercial influences. Eight centuries later the hordes of the Arabian Caliph Omar in turn overwhelmed the Roman colony at Alexandria, destroying forever its literary influence by the burning of its great library.

Conversely the missionary labors of David Livingstone, from 1849 to 1873, inculcated peaceful methods and cultivated moral tendencies destined to introduce Christianity and develop civilization. Not only did Livingstone, in the eloquent words of Stanley, " weave by his journeys the figure of his Redeemer's cross on the

map of Africa, but, scattering ever his Master's
words and patterning his life after the Master
stamped the story of the cross on the hearts of
every African tribe he visited."

Initiating routes of travel, suggesting new
commercial fields, and organizing stable forms
of government, came a man of harder metal, of
indomitable will and courage, Henry M. Stanley,
who merits the title of Stanley Africanus.

A Welshman by nativity, born near Denbigh,
in 1840, he came to the United States at the age
of sixteen and thenceforth cast his lot with
America, and as a citizen of this country made
his explorations under its flag. It is reputed
that he exchanged his natal name of Rowlands
for that of Henry M. Stanley, for a merchant
of New Orleans who adopted him; but in any
event his early life was passed without the loving and modifying influences of a home, his
youth almost equally destitute of those adventi-
tious surroundings that properly mould the character and insure opportunities for success to
young men. Thus he stands forth a self-made
man to whom strength has been accorded to
develop the manhood that God implanted in his
soul.

Stern experiences in the American civil war,
brief life in the far West, and special service in
Turkey had shaped Stanley into a reliant, self-
contained man when his first African journey
came to him, in 1868, through assignment as
newspaper correspondent to accompany the
British army in its invasion of Abyssinia. He

participated in this wonderful campaign, which led him four hundred miles through a country of indescribable wildness and grandeur, across rugged mountains, along deep valleys, up to the fortress-crowned crest of Magdala, ten thousand feet above the sea.

Difficult as were the mountains of Abyssinia, they were less dangerous than the African region later to be traversed by him; a journey unsought, but which came to him as the fittest man for the time and service.

A telegram and five hours' preparation carried Stanley from the blood-red fields of revolutionary Spain into the famous search journey that gave to an anxious world news of the long-lost Livingstone. For twenty years this great Scotch missionary had carried the gospel of Christ and its civilizing influences from one end of Africa to the other; once he had crossed the continent in its greatest breadth, and now, vanished from the sight of the civilized world in his renewed missionary labors, for two years his very existence had been problematical.

The search expedition owed its inception and maintenance to James Gordon Bennett, Jr., whose brief orders to Stanley were: "Find Livingstone and bring news of his discoveries or proofs of his death, regardless of expense." The personnel, methods, and arrangements devolved entirely on Stanley, but his preliminary route was to lie through certain countries. It thus occurred that between Madrid, his starting point, and Ujiji, on Lake Tanganyika, the camp of Living-

stone, he saw the gayties of Paris; was present at
the eventful opening of the Suez Canal that revo-
lutionized Eastern commerce; ascended the Lower Nile to scrutinize with interested eye Baker's
prospective expedition to the Soudan; divined
under the mosques of the Bosphorus the political

The Hut where Livingstone Died.

riddles of Sultan and Khédive; examined the
uncovered foundations of Solomon's Temple in
the Holy City; meditated over the historic
battle-grounds of the Crimea; penetrated the
Caucasus to Tiflis for news of the Russian expedition to Khiva; and, traversing Persia through
the Euphratan cradle of the human race, entered
India, whence his route lay to Zanzibar and the

dark beyond. What a contrast those preliminary journeys afforded, across effete countries whose varying and recorded phases of civilization are contemporaneous with the history of the human race, to the threshold of a vast region whose barbaric freshness is such that its entire history lies within the memory of living man.

Stanley landed at Zanzibar, January 10, 1871, and, fortunately, was at once impressed with his ignorance of outfitting, which he thought he had learned from books. Resorting to the Arab traders he proved such an apt pupil and skilful organizer that he enlisted twenty-seven soldiers, gathered one hundred and fifty-seven carriers and five special employees, which, with two white assistants, Farquhar and Shaw, made his aggregate force one hundred and ninety-two. He had his African money—beads as copper coins, cloth as silver, and brass rods as gold; canvas-covered boats for navigation; asses and horses for special work; fine cloth for tribute to local chiefs, which, with tentage, medicine, etc., made some six tons of freight.

March 21, 1871, the rear guard marched out of Bagamoyo, the town on the mainland opposite Zanzibar, and taking a route never before travelled by a white man, Stanley reached Simbamwenni in fourteen marches, the journey of one hundred and nineteen miles having occupied twenty-nine days, during which the commander came to fully realize the difficulty of his undertaking, the inefficiency of unpractised subordinates, and the uncertain loyalty of carriers.

The onward march resembled all in Africa: thorns and jungle to wound the naked carriers, rivers to be forded or crossed on almost impracticable bridges, swamps many miles in length and so miry as to tax the utmost strength and energy of man and ass, insolence and exactions of local potentates, thefts by natives, desertions of carriers, the oft-recurring fever, and occasionally a death.

The 20th of May, Stanley was at Mpwapwa (Mbambwa), delighted physically at its fair aspect and upland picturesqueness, but mentally anxious over Farquhar, whom he left here sick, and the loss of his asses, which he fortunately was able to replace by twelve carriers. He reached, on June 22d, Unyanyembe, after a devious journey of five hundred and twenty miles to cover an air-line distance of one hundred and fifty. Here had just arrived a relief caravan for Livingstone, which had left Zanzibar four months prior to Stanley's. Near by, at Tabora, the chief Arabian town of central Africa, Stanley was surprised to find the Arabs at war with a savage chief, Mirambo, thus barring the usually travelled road to Ujiji.

Here Stanley lost three months, and participated in an unsuccessful campaign with the Arabs against Mirambo, vainly hoping that thus his road would be opened. Five of his men were killed in the war, others deserted, so that only eleven carriers remained, and altogether his prospects of success steadily diminished.

Despairing of the old route, Stanley, having

with great difficulty recruited his force of carriers, decided to try a circuitous trail to the south in order to reach Ujiji, which lay to the northwest. Failure and destruction were predicted, but with confidence in himself Stanley, on September 20th, marched on with Shaw and

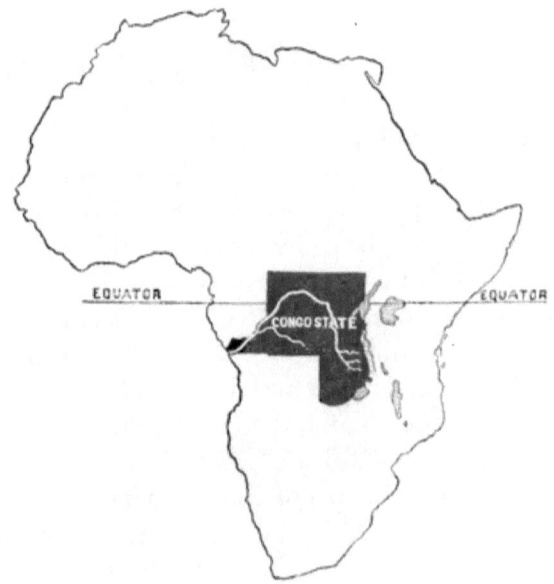

Map showing Position and Boundaries of the Congo State.

fifty-six others. Illness caused him to soon send back Shaw, his only white companion; frequent desertions weakened his force; an incipient mutiny of his panic-stricken men on the Gombe River threatened complete destruction to the party; insolent chiefs exacted extortionate tribute; desert marches without water and scant food discouraged and weakened the men; but the leader pushed on with unflagging energy despite every obstacle. His route lay through Igonda, Itende, the beautiful country of Uvinsa, across rocky Uhha to the Malagarazi River, where his heart was gladdened by rumors from the natives that a white man had lately arrived at Ujiji from Manyuema.

Pushing on with feverish haste, on November 9, 1871, he had the indescribable joy of looking down on magnificent Lake Tanganyika, and on the following day, with his gigantic guide, Asmani, proudly striding in advance with the Stars and Stripes as his standard, Stanley marched into Ujiji, and there accomplished his mission by meeting Livingstone and ascertaining the results of his late labors. Livingstone's primary mission —the suppression of the slave trade by means of civilizing influences—had not materially progressed, but he had strong hopes of the future. Geographically, however, he had been most successful, having made important discoveries in the water-sheds of Lakes Tanganyika and the Nyanzas, and found an unknown river, the Lualaba, which in a later exploration Stanley proved to be the Upper Congo.

Stanley found Livingstone with only five carriers and without means of trade. Supplying all deficiencies from his own stores, he assisted Livingstone in his exploration of Lake Tanganyika, and the twain returned together to Unyanyembe. In the meantime both Farquhar and Shaw died, and Stanley, turning over his surplus stores to

Livingstone, bade him farewell and God-speed, and started for Zanzibar. On March 14, 1872, eight weeks later, Stanley was again enjoying civilization at Bagamoyo, while Livingstone was awaiting means of returning to his life-task, soon to be ended by his death among the tribes he loved, for "Greater love hath no man than this, that a man lay down his life for his friends."

Over four months of intercourse with Livingstone steadily increased Stanley's admiration for this great man. He describes him as a high-spirited, brave, impetuous, and enthusiastic man, with these qualities so tempered by his deep, abiding spirit of religion as to make him a most extraordinary character. In all his relations with his servants, with the natives, and with Mohammedans, Christianity appeared in its loveliest and most potent forms, constant, sincere, charitable, loving, modest, and always practical. It was this abiding faith in God which made Livingstone a man of unfailing devotion to his sense of present duty, of wondrous patience, unvarying gentleness, constant hopefulness, and unwearied fidelity—qualities which made his missionary work in Africa unprecedentedly successful.

Abuse, misrepresentation, and incredulity from geographic societies, critics, and press greeted Stanley's account of his discovery of Livingstone, and only gradually did his traducers yield to the convincing evidences of his astonishing success.

Turning to his old work, Stanley, in the winter of 1873-74, again entered Africa, accompanying as newspaper correspondent the British army, which invaded to a distance of one hundred and forty miles the deadly marshes of the Ashantee Kingdom, and destroyed its capital city, Coomassie.

When the death of Livingstone brought Africa into prominence again, Stanley, believing he could complete so much of the missionary's work as concerned exploration, turned thither at the head of an expedition under the auspices of the London *Telegraph* and the New York *Herald*, the object being the survey of the lacustrine system at the head of the White Nile and a journey thence westward across the continent.

Leaving Bagamoyo, November 17, 1874, Stanley reached Lake Victoria Nyanza in March, 1875, his journey of seven hundred and twenty miles being marked by pestilential fevers, struggles through thorny jungles, and scant food and water. Circumnavigating the lake, he found it to be over four thousand feet above the ocean, while its proportions—nearly twenty-two thousand miles in area and in places over five hundred feet deep—assumed those of an inland sea. Here Mtesa, a powerful and able negro king, of Mohammedan faith, proved most friendly and greatly aided him, furnishing an escort, which enabled Stanley to explore a part of the adjacent mountain region. From Ujiji he then explored Lake Tanganyika, finding it to be about half the size of Victoria, with an elevation of about twenty-seven hundred feet.

Important as were these discoveries they paled

before others, made in following the Lualaba
River of Livingstone, which changed the map
of Central Africa and altered the destiny of

Tippu Tib.

that vast and untraversed region. The journey
to Nyangwe, Livingstone's "farthest," entailed
horrible hardships on the carriers. This Arab
village was reached via the Luama, which, of

hitherto unknown course, was found by Stanley
to be an affluent of the Lualaba. At Nyangwe
Stanley felt that his accomplished journey of
over eight hundred miles from the east coast
promised well for his coming voyage to a known
point on the other coast, nine hundred miles
due west. He made an agreement with an Arab,
Tippu-Tib, trader in human flesh or ivory as
chance offered, to escort the expedition about
six hundred miles west through the unknown
regions. The country proved to be primeval
forest, almost trackless, its tropical undergrowth
a veritable jungle of thorns and vines. Game
was scanty and other food equally so. Finally,
progress was so slow and the path so devious
that Stanley, yielding to his appeals, discharged
Tippu-Tib and decided to descend the river
by canoes and his frame boat. He embarked
at Vinya Njara, with one hundred and fifty
in his party, on December 28, 1876, intrusting himself with sublime audacity to a river
flowing no one knew whither, save it was away
from civilization, and with the knowledge that
the country they were entering was peopled by
tribes entirely hostile and intractable, as the
slave-traders said. Day after day they drifted
steadily to the north. Was it or was it not the
Nile of Livingstone's prediction? Then day by
day the course trended to the east. Yes, it could
only be the Nile. After two hundred and forty
miles the trend was to the northwest, whither,
week after week, for about three hundred miles it
kept its puzzling flow toward a point of the com-

pass where it could join no river known to man. It had, too, assumed proportions and volume truly Amazonic, filled with islands and swollen from one to seven miles in width. All efforts to gain a knowledge of its final course were then fruitless, for the few barbarous natives they could win to speech answered in uncouth jargon, scarcely intelligible to the interpreters: "It is the river — the river!" The terrors of the silent stream in its majestic solitude were almost preferable to the presence of populous villages, which here and there lined its banks, for the inhabitants, ferociously hostile for the greater part, refused trade and boldly assaulted them. Skilful canoemen and good archers, the savages slaughtered unwary stragglers, harassed the rear and attacked the front, while their horrible threats that the bodies of the slain should serve as food at their cannibalistic repasts instilled terror in the minds of many of Stanley's followers. Skirmishes were frequent, and now and then a severe fight which taxed Stanley's forces to the utmost. Again the river had here and there series of cataracts which caused no end of trouble; delay, and danger to the party, nine men being drowned in one day.

Fortunately the river had turned to the south, and then to southwest, where, after another thousand miles, it flowed through a narrow gorge, one hundred and fifty miles from the sea, so that no doubt longer obtained as to it being the Congo. The terrible falls near the gorge entailed enormous labor to pass them, and barely

failed of destroying the party. In all twenty-
eight cataracts were passed, and finally the river
became so precipitous, the falls so high, that they
had to abandon their boats and march overland
to Boma, an English trading-post, five days'
journey distant. Fatigue, famine, and exposure
further enfeebled them and now made daily inroads among the ranks of those who had so far
survived, and the entire party would have perished on the very threshold of civilization and
plenty had not Stanley's messengers, sent on
with urgent appeals, obtained help at Boma,
where the expeditionary force arrived August
12, 1877. They had made a river journey of
seven thousand miles, proved the Congo to be
second only to the Nile, and crossed Africa.

When Stanley, in 1877, intrusting his life and
fortunes to a mighty and unknown stream, voyaged toward the very heart of the Dark Continent, even his wildest dreams could not have
foreshadowed results equal to the reality of a
near future. His voyage in its potentiality was
second only to that of Columbus, as the outcome
of the succeeding five years plainly indicates.
All Europe, alive to the commercial importance
of the Congo Basin, hastened to reach its borders
or encroach on its limits by means of enlarged
dependent colonies; commerce and religion,
hand in hand, traversed its rivers by steam and
lined its banks with beneficent settlements, while
the merciless Arab devastated its villages and
dragged its decimated natives into slavery.
Then came a political wonder — the peaceful

creation of a vast tropical empire more than a
million square miles in area, the Congo Free

Emin Pasha.

State, erected and admitted into the community
of nations by act of an international conference,
in which participated fourteen European powers
and the United States, our own country being

fittingly the first to officially acknowledge the existence of the new state its adventurous citizen had given to the world.

The voyage through the Dark Continent was obviously potent of future results, and Gambetta, in 1878, clearly forecast the effects of Stanley's journey. The great French statesman said: "Not only have you opened up a new continent to our view, but you have given influence to scientific and philanthropic enterprises which will have its effect on the progress of the world. What you have done has interested governments —proverbially so difficult to move—and the impulse you have imparted, I am convinced, will go on year after year."

Slowly recovering from the effects of famine and fatigue incident to this arduous journey, Stanley returned to Europe in January, 1878, and was met, as he stepped out of the express train at Marseilles, by two commissioners of King Leopold of Belgium, who informed him that his Majesty contemplated a new enterprise in Africa and desired his assistance. While heartily indorsing the proposed work of Leopold his physical condition was such that active co-operation was impossible, and he was even unable to visit his Majesty. Five months later, with physical energies renewed, after a visit to Leopold, Stanley eventually agreed to the proposition which contemplated the establishment of a grand commercial enterprise for controlling the trade of the valley of the Congo. It involved the erection of commercial and military stations along the overland route and the establishment of steam communication wherever available. In short, a colony of Europeans was to be founded in the Congo Basin, whose great fertility, healthy climate, and enormous population seemed to especially favor the development of African civilization. The action of Leopold evidently grew out of Stanley's declarations that "the question of this mighty waterway (the Congo) will become a political one in time," and his conviction that any power possessing the Congo would absorb the whole enormous trade behind, as this river was and must continue to be, the grand commercial highway of West and Central Africa.

Stanley accepted the mission, visited Zanzibar, where he enlisted sixty-eight Zanzibari, mostly his old soldiers, and by sea reached Banana Point, on the west coast, August 14, 1879. Two years previous he had reached this place after descending the newly discovered Congo; now he was re-entering its fertile basin in order to establish civilized settlements, with the intention of subduing Central Africa by peaceful ways and to remould it into harmony with modern ideas, so that justice and order should ever obtain, violence and the slave trade forever cease.

He returned to Europe in 1882, his success far exceeding the expectations of the committee. In this time, with the aid of sixty-eight Zanzibari and a few Europeans, he had constructed three trading-stations, launched a steamer on the Up-

Finding Nelson in Distress at Starvation Camp.

per Congo, established steam communication between Leopoldville and Stanley Pool, and also constructed wagon-roads between Vivi and Isangila, Manyanga and Stanley Pool. He pointed out to the committee the imperative necessity of a railroad between the Lower and Upper Congo in order to preserve uninterrupted communication, which scheme was approved by the committee provided Stanley would take charge of the work. Although his health was impaired, he agreed to return to the Congo and complete the establishment of stations as far as Stanley Falls, which he duly accomplished, not leaving Africa until there were five promising trading-posts — Vivi, Leopoldville, Kinshassa (Stanley Pool), Equator, and Stanley Falls, the last about two thousand miles inland from the west coast.

On Stanley's return to Europe the question of organizing the basin of the Congo into an independent state was agitated. As a result fourteen of the European powers and the United States united in a conference at Berlin and formally agreed, on February 26, 1885, that the entire Congo Basin should be erected into a nation to be known as the Congo Free State. Thus less than eight years after Stanley's famous journey he beheld the country that his genius had rescued from oblivious darkness erected into a new state and admitted into the community of nations.

The last journey of Stanley into Africa was for the rescue of the Egyptian governor of Equatoria, Edward Schnitzer, a German by birth, better known as Emin Pasha. On the death of General Gordon, by whom he was appointed governor, Emin had been left to his fate at Wadelai by the Egyptian authorities, from which point he wrote on December 31, 1885, saying that for nineteen months he had been forgotten and abandoned. On July 6, 1886, he wrote beseeching help. In this contingency the sum of £21,500 was raised—£10,000 from the Egyptian Government, the rest subscribed in England—for the expenses of a relief party, and all eyes turned to Stanley as the natural leader. He was engaged in a very profitable lecturing tour in the United States when the expedition was finally decided on. Three days after the receipt of a cablegram that his plans were accepted, Stanley sailed for Africa *via* England, using such despatch that he had his expedition of 680 men, 61 being Soudanese soldiers, ready to leave Zanzibar on February 25, 1887.

Stanley decided to make the journey by vessel around the Cape of Good Hope to the Congo, by which river he expected to get within 200 miles of Lake Albert. The co-operation of the infamous Arab trader, Tippu Tib, the most powerful trader in Africa, was obtained by making him governor of Stanley Falls, in the Congo Free State.

Following the Congo to the Aruwimi, Stanley turned up that stream and camped at Yambuya, about sixty miles above the mouth and over one thousand three hundred miles from the sea. To this point he had lost 57 men, and now divided his forces as follows: Advance guard, under himself, 389; Yambuya garrison, 129, under Major Barttelot; other supporting guards in rear, 131; original force, 706.

On January 28, 1887, Stanley started for Lake Albert, 330 miles distant in an air line, through an entirely unknown country. It proved to be a virgin forest, the greatest of the world, through which a path had to be cut almost the entire distance. For one hundred and sixty days they marched through an almost unbroken forest-bush, jungle, marsh, and creek. The scattered villages, filled with barbarous and hostile tribes, were abandoned at their approach; poisoned skewers, covered with green leaves, were planted in the paths, and twice the party was attacked.

On October 6th affairs came to a crisis, as provisions had failed, save scanty wild plants; many, stricken with disease, including Stairs, one of the officers, could go no farther. No less than one hundred and twenty-six men had been lost by death and desertion, about half from each cause, and all must perish unless the party divided. Stanley left Nelson and 52 men in camp on Ituri River, about 1° 5′ N., 28° 30′ E., and started ahead for relief. After terrible privation, and nearly perishing of starvation on the way, they reached Ipoto, October 17th, where food was purchased from the natives. As soon as possible Jephson, Stanley's able and loyal assistant, returned to Nelson's relief and brought him and three men to Ipoto, nine carriers having died and forty deserted. December 4th, Stanley with 175 men emerged from the forest and nine days later reached Lake Albert, whence Wadelai, Emin's station, was distant four days' journey by water, or twenty-five by land.

Finding no boats on Lake Albert, Stanley was obliged to retreat from its desolate shores westward to a fertile region, where he built Fort

Bodo and planted crops, while a detachment brought up his steel boat, in which Jephson reached M'swa and was met, on April 26, 1888, by Emin, who had been notified by Stanley's native courier. Two days later Emin and Stanley met at Lake Albert, when propositions and plans

A Stockaded Camp.
(From a photograph.)

as to Emin's movements were made and discussed with no definite results.

The equation of Emin's character seems to have been best stated by Vita Hassan, his friendly subordinate for twenty years, who considers Emin's many virtues as those of a missionary rather than of a governor or commander, and attributes his infirmity of indecision to innate goodness of heart. It was nine months before Emin, his army mutinous, himself and Jephson imprisoned, with death as an alternative, decided to return with Stanley to Zanzibar.

In the meanwhile Stanley, anxious as to his rear guard, returned through the dreaded forest hoping from day to day to meet it, but saw no signs until he reached Banalya, on the Aruwimi, a few miles from where he had left it. Here he found it in a state of inactivity and disorganization, its chief, Major Barttelot, murdered by a native, Jameson and one hundred and two out of the original two hundred and seventy-six dead, and twenty-six deserted. Again the journey through the forest and its hostile tribes to Lake Albert, where Stanley with the hesitating Emin Pasha and his followers started for Zanzibar on April 1, 1889.

The return journey, made as far as Lake Victoria Nyanza over unknown ground, resulted in the discovery of Mount Ruwenzori, a snow-clad peak under the Equator, estimated to be seventeen thousand feet high. Moreover, of vastly more importance, Stanley ascertained that Lake Albert Nyanza through the Semliki River, drained a large lake, named Albert Edward, thus determining the secret of the long-sought and ever retreating source of the White Nile. Small streams feed Lake Albert Edward from the south, whose extreme limit is placed by Stanley in 1° 10′ S. latitude.

December 4, 1889, found the party arrived at

Ruwenzori (The Snowy Mountain) identified by Stanley with "the Mountains of the Moon."
Ascended 10,677 feet above sea-level by Lieutenant Stairs. Total height about 16,600 feet.
(From a drawing by Mr. Stanley, made at the time of the discovery.)

Bagamoyo, the coast town opposite Zanzibar. The work which Stanley was sent to do, as all other tasks assumed by this great explorer, was ended, and Emin Pasha once more looked on the faces of his countrymen.

Crowned with highest honors from all the powers of Europe, no tribute, as Stanley has said, gave such gratification as that from the United States, which, proud of the achievements of its great citizen, extended to him the unprecedented honors of its official, well-considered, and merited commendation, wherein, under date of February 7, 1878, it was "*Resolved*, by the Senate and House of Representatives in Congress assembled, That, regarding with just pride the achievements of their countryman, Henry M. Stanley, the distinguished explorer of Central Africa, the thanks of the people of the United States are eminently due and are hereby tendered him as a tribute to his extraordinary patience, prudence, fortitude, enterprise, courage, and capacity in solving by his researches many of the most important geographical problems of our age and globe, problems of a continental scope, involving the progress of our kind in commerce, science, and civilization."

THE END.

www.ingramcontent.com/pod-product-compliance
Lightning Source LLC
Chambersburg PA
CBHW032031220426
43664CB00006B/438